How To Start And Run
Your Own Corporation

S-Corporations For Small Business Owners
Second Edition

by Peter I. Hupalo

This publication is designed to provide information in regard to the subject matter covered. It is sold with the understanding that the publisher and the author are not engaged to render legal, accounting, tax, or other professional services. If legal advice or other expert assistance is required, the services of a competent professional should be sought.

ISBN 978-0-9671624-5-4
Library of Congress Control Number: 2013916693

Printed in the United States of America

HCM Publishing
P.O. Box 18093
West Saint Paul, MN 55118

Other Books By Peter Hupalo:

Thinking Like An Entrepreneur: How To Make Intelligent Business Decisions That Will Lead To Success In Building And Growing Your Own Company

Becoming An Investor: Building Wealth By Investing In Stocks, Bonds, And Mutual Funds

How To Start And Run A Small Book Publishing Company: A Small Business Guide To Self-Publishing And Independent Publishing

Table Of Contents

Introduction

Welcome! I'm glad you purchased *How To Start And Run Your Own Corporation: S-Corporations For Small Business Owners.* I hope this book provides you with useful information about forming and operating your corporation.

Like you, I'm an entrepreneur. I'm not a tax professional. I'm not an accountant. And, I'm not a lawyer. However, as an entrepreneur, I've acquired some understanding of corporations over the years. It's this personal understanding and knowledge I hope to share with you throughout this book. After reading this book, I highly recommend acquiring a knowledgeable business attorney and a knowledgeable business accountant to help you with your corporation. After reading this book, you'll be better acquainted with important topics, which should make your time with lawyers and accountants much more productive.

All new S-corporation owners will eventually encounter topics such as stock basis and the S-corporation Accumulated Adjustments Account. To help new corporation founders, I've tried to summarize what I've learned and come to understand over the years about these corporate concepts that might at first confuse you. I hope I've made understanding these topics easier.

Don't be intimidated by corporate business structure. Once you've formed a corporation and operated it for a year or two, much of the formality of corporate business structure, such as holding annual meetings and documenting corporate actions via meeting minutes or consent resolutions, will become second nature to you.

I highly recommend that you seek further information about corporate business structure from your state government. Many states hold free classes in conjunction with the IRS to help new C-corporation or S-corporation owners. See if your state has classes. I highly recommend them.

Different entrepreneurs will have different goals for their corporations. For example, some entrepreneurs will seek angel financing for their companies or have multiple shareholders. Other entrepreneurs will just want to form a one-person corporation and fund the corporation themselves. Some entrepreneurs will want to loan money to their corporations (to get it back quickly with no tax consequences) while others will just contribute capital to the corporation in exchange for shares of stock. Some entrepreneurs will want to start retirement plans to sock away tax-deferred money. More advanced topics, which are important but not absolutely essential to get up and running, are marked as "Optional." Those sections can be read when, and if, needed.

Tax Rates

To help you decide between various business structures, it's often useful to examine personal and corporate tax rates. These rates are given in Appendix A.

Chapter 1
Choose Your Business Structure (Wisely!)

Entrepreneurs and angel investors should study and learn about basic business structure. As the old financial saying goes, "It's not how much you earn, but how much you keep that matters." The wrong business structure can cost you extra tax dollars, hinder financing availability, and subject you to unanticipated risk exposure.

Anyone starting a new business needs to choose a business structure. Do you incorporate your business? If so, do you choose a C-corporation or an S-corporation tax structure? How about remaining a sole proprietorship? Or, if there are multiple business owners, what about becoming a partnership? And, what about the Limited Liability Company (LLC) structure?

Issues of liability, taxation, ease of transfer of ownership, ease of business administration, and access to capital will help determine your optimal business structure. The decision is important. The best decision depends upon your personal goals and the inherent nature of the business you wish to start, so you might want to consult your business and tax attorneys to help you choose your business structure. This book will help entrepreneurs understand business structure, with a focus upon corporations, and, in particular, S-corporations.

Sole Proprietorships

Sole proprietors file Schedule C (or the easy version C-EZ) with their 1040 Individual Income Tax Return to report their earnings or loss from operating a business. Schedule C is just like any other schedule attached to the 1040. You follow your nose. When the IRS says "subtract," you do. When the IRS says, "Enter the amount here and also on Line 12 of Form 1040," you do. In the end, all of your hard work is summarized by one line on your 1040 Tax Return showing your net profit or loss from running a business. Profits are taxed as ordinary income. Losses reduce your taxable income.

Sometimes, consistent losses may be deemed ineligible for a tax deduction due to "hobby loss rules." Hobby loss rules prevent a camera buff from claiming $5,000 worth of camera accessories as tax-deductible "business expenses," while the hobbyist generates no revenue and doesn't plan to run a business. He only wants to get a big tax deduction for his toys.

Some entrepreneurs consider the tax-deductible fringe benefits each business structure is allowed to provide and under what conditions the tax-deduction can be lost. Corporate fringe benefits are often better than sole proprietor fringe benefits. I personally feel fringe benefits shouldn't be a major factor in choosing a business structure.

If your sole proprietor business earnings are above $400, you also need to file Schedule SE (SE for Self-Employment) with your personal tax return. Many employees don't realize that half of their Social Security tax is paid by their employer, while only half is taken directly from their paycheck. New sole proprietors are sometimes chagrined when they discover that about 15% of their earnings are consumed in self-employment taxes.

As a business owner, you'll learn about many taxes of which the average employee has little knowledge. Your self-employment tax is the equivalent of employee/employer Social Security and Medicare Benefits tax, better known to employees as FICA (Federal Insurance Contributions Act). On the positive side, these contributions give you future Medicare and Social Security benefits. On the negative side, these taxes reduce the amount of money you take home today. That money could have been reinvested in your business or invested elsewhere.

Social Security taxes can play an important role in your decision whether to choose S-corporation status or remain a sole proprietor. For a moderately profitable, single-owner business earning $70,000 per year, and paying the full amount to the owner, choosing an S-corporation business structure and paying half the amount in wages and half in dividends could "save" about $5,000 per year in Social Security taxes. I put "save" in quotes, because you would receive less Social Security during retirement. We will discuss this in more detail later. Incidentally, over a forty-year period, due to the power of compounding, at a 10% rate of return, $5,000 invested annually represents over $2 million. So, for many entrepreneurs, the decision between deciding to pay more into the Social Security system or deciding to minimize your Social Security taxation with an S-corporation represents a multimillion dollar decision affecting your wealth upon retirement.

Becoming aware of the taxes and tax rates you face under the different business structures is crucial to minimizing your overall taxation.

The advantage to sole proprietorships is simplicity. You simply start your business, and if you're the single owner of the company, and if you form no other business structure, your company is automatically classified as a sole proprietorship.

The disadvantage of being a sole proprietor is that you and your business are considered the same legal entity. If someone falls in your retail store and wins a big judgment against your retail company, structured as a sole proprietorship, that judgment is also against you as an individual. Your personal assets are at risk. For some businesses, that is acceptable. For other businesses, it is not.

The inherent liability exposure of your business should be a key factor in helping you decide whether or not you should incorporate or else choose a limited liability company (LLC) business structure. For example, a writer working from home has far less liability exposure than a retail store owner. The writer could remain a sole proprietor with far less fear of being sued or losing a substantial legal judgment.

Further, as I explain in *How To Start And Run A Small Book Publishing Company*, a self-published author operating as a corporation only gains minimal protection in the event of a libel or copyright infringement lawsuit. This is because such a lawsuit will probably list the writer, as an individual, as one of the defendants, even if the writer operates as a corporation or LLC.

One disadvantage of operating a sole proprietorship is that your business's tax reporting number is often the same as your Social Security number if you don't have employees. Corporations use "Employer Identification Numbers" or EINs. To apply for an EIN, fill out IRS form SS-4.

For certain businesses that receive royalties or commissions, the royalty payer will request your taxpayer number, because by law this information must be reported to the IRS. This usually isn't a problem, but in this age, identity theft is a concern. Rather than trust that other companies will adequately protect your SSN, you can supply your business's EIN, keeping your personal SSN more secure and private. The other option is to not provide your tax reporting number and allow a portion of the payment to be sent to the IRS. Then, when you compute your taxes, don't forget this amount should be added to your tax payments. Let the IRS know the name and the EIN of the payer.

Unless you form some other business structure for your company, you're a sole proprietor if you're the sole owner of your company.

Partnerships

If you start a business with business partners, unless you form a corporation or some other business structure, you will be deemed a partnership. Partnerships offer little liability protection for entrepreneurs. Your personal assets are at risk.

I personally dislike the partnership business structure, because you are personally liable for the debts of your company, even if the liability is incurred by your business partner against your wishes. This is a case of the actions of another person exposing you to personal liability. If you have business partners, I strongly recommend you consult an attorney and consider the benefits of incorporation or the LLC alternative. At the very least, you'll want your attorney to evaluate any partnership agreements.

Limited Liability Company

Many entrepreneurs today use the limited liability company. A limited liability company is much like a partnership, but with the liability protection of incorporation.

One disadvantage of the LLC is that money paid to members of the LLC who are active in running the business is usually subject to Social Security tax. The S-corporation structure allows you to pay part of this money as wages and part as dividends, which can result in substantial tax savings.

Some people feel that limited liability companies are easier to administer than corporations, i.e., the paperwork is less cumbersome. We'll discuss corporate administration, such as keeping minutes of shareholder meetings and documenting corporate decision-making through resolutions. Such compliance with formality is important in the event your corporate structure is ever challenged, e.g., someone tries to "pierce the corporate veil" and argues that you should be personally liable for the debts of the corporation.

One limitation of an S-corporation is that an S-corporation can only have one class of stock. An S-corporation cannot issue preferred stock. Preferred stock can provide dividend or liquidation preferences to the investor. A large part of successfully financing a mid-sized business venture is structuring the deal in such a way that it's appealing to potential angel investors, who might desire preferred stock.

While investors can divide their investment in a corporation into an equity portion and a debt portion and while you can create voting and non-voting shares for both C-corporations and S-corporations, the fullest variety of financial structuring can be achieved through the Limited Liability Company structure or the older Limited Partnership structure. (Old joke: "Why do they call them limited partnerships?" Answer: "Because you'll only get a limited part of your capital back!")

Suppose you decide to produce a movie. You raise $15 million. Your film manages to breakeven and earns your company $15 million. Suppose you and your investors each own 50% of the corporate shares. You produced the film, while the investors contributed the capital. While you might like earning $7.5 million, your investors wouldn't be too happy about losing $7.5 million of their investment!

Yet, you might not like giving up 99% of the return and ownership and control of the corporate common shares as a just compensation for the large risk the investors are taking. That tremendously limits your financial potential from the endeavor in the event it's a smashing success. It also eliminates your control.

So, you could imagine the investors asking for a deal like this: Until the investors receive their initial investment back, 100% of the earnings from the endeavor go to the investors. Once the investors have recovered their initial investment, profits will be split 50-50 between the investors and the production company. For this deal and for more complex financing terms, a Limited Liability Company (LLC) might be your best structure.

If you contemplate a limited liability company structure, I recommend consulting an attorney. Corporate law tends to be better established. Otherwise, LLCs are very much like S-corporations in that earnings can be taxed on a "pass through" basis, while limited liability is also provided.

To Form an LLC, all you need to do is file "Articles of Organization" with your Secretary of State. Most states provide template articles of organization that you can fill out and submit.

Many entrepreneurs who recognize the tax benefits of S-corporations form LLCs and then have them taxed as S-corporations! If you do this, much of this book will apply and help you understand the taxation of your company. Once you understand corporations, though, there really isn't much more difficulty to a corporation than an LLC.

If you wish to have your LLC taxed as an S-corporation, all you need to do is file IRS Form 2553. This election achieves two things: 1) It elects to have your LLC taxed as a corporation; and 2) It elects to have that corporation taxed as an S-corporation. If you go this route, you do not need to file IRS Form 8832, which is used to tax a LLC as a C-corporation.

Corporations

To get liability protection, many entrepreneurs incorporate their businesses. A corporation is considered a separate legal and taxable entity from the owners of the corporation. Most corporations are C-corporations, taxable under Subchapter C of the IRS Code. (Note: C-corporations are totally unrelated to Schedule C which attaches to a personal 1040 tax return and which applies to sole proprietors.) Just as you, as an individual, file a Form 1040 personal income tax return and pay taxes on your earnings, a C-corporation files Form 1120 and pays taxes on its earnings.

C-corporations have employees and shareholders. Shareholders own the corporation. Employees render services for the corporation. You will likely be both a shareholder and an employee of your corporation. If you're an angel investor in a company, you might be a shareholder without being an employee. But, angel investors are often on the board of directors. It's common for a founder to be a shareholder, the Chief Executive Officer (CEO), which is a corporate officer and an employee of the corporation, and a member of the board of directors.

There are two primary ways to withdraw money from your corporation. As an employee of the corporation, you're entitled to just compensation for services you render the corporation. As the president of your corporation, you're entitled to a salary. So, you may have the corporation pay you a salary. This is the first way most entrepreneurs remove money from an incorporated business.

The disadvantage to paying yourself a wage is that wages are subject to various employment taxes, for example, Social Security and Medicare taxes, in addition to income tax. While corporations don't pay self-employment taxes (you're an employee of the corporation and not self-employed), paying yourself a wage lops off about 15% of the wage in employment taxes.

The second primary way that a corporation passes money to its shareholders is with dividend payments. (For S-corporations, "dividends" should technically be called "distributions." We will interchange those terms freely within this book.) Because you're a shareholder of your corporation, you can receive corporate dividends, if they're approved by the board of directors. (And, of course, dividends can only be paid if the dividends aren't prohibited by law. For example, a company cannot pay dividends if doing so will leave the company insolvent and there are bondholders and other creditors who are owed money who will not be paid.)

A C-corporation is a separate taxable entity. So, if the corporation earns $1,000, it pays taxes on the $1,000. Suppose $850 remains after paying corporate income tax. Suppose this $850 is paid to you as a corporate dividend. Then, you, as an individual taxpayer, must also pay income tax on the dividend received.

Historically, dividends were taxed as ordinary income, at rates up to 39.6%. From 2003 to 2012 the maximum dividend tax rate was set at 15%. The American Taxpayer Relief Act of 2012 compromised at a maximum tax rate on dividends of 20%.

After paying income tax at your personal marginal dividend tax rate, you may have $680 of the original $1,000 in your pocket after all taxation. So, you effectively paid 32% of your earnings in federal income tax.

This is what's meant by "double taxation" of C-corporations. Double taxation usually means that a corporation has earnings which were taxed as income to the corporation. Then, those earnings were paid as dividends to the shareholders. The shareholders need to pay personal income tax on the dividends received. You usually don't want to pay double income taxation on money withdrawn from your company.

Because of the heavy tax hit, smaller C-corporations hesitate to pay dividends or never pay them at all. Often, the goal is to retain the profits within the company to fund further growth and profitability.

Sometimes the long-term goal is to create a company of sufficient value so that it can be sold to another company or taken public. This provides a very profitable and tax-efficient exit strategy for entrepreneurs and angel investors alike. In situations like this, lower capital gain tax rates apply to the sale of the corporation. Large, publicly-traded corporations operate as C-corporations.

Incidentally, we should notice that in most situations double taxation of corporate dividends is more punishing than paying added employment taxes on money withdrawn as salary or wages. So, some C-corporation entrepreneurs try to increase their wages to very high levels. The IRS frowns upon "excessive wages" paid from a C-corporation, which it feels are dividends in disguise. The IRS can reclassify ultra-high salaries as dividends. However, today, corporate officer salaries can be quite high. We'll discuss officer compensation in more detail later. If you form a C-corporation, download IRS Publication 542: *Corporations*.

S-Corporations

To relieve small businesses from the burden of double taxation of dividends, while at the same time offering small business owners the liability protection of incorporation, the IRS adopted the S-corporation status. By filing IRS Form 2553, you can elect to have your corporation taxed as an S-corporation. This means the corporation is taxed under Subchapter S of the IRS code. *Unless you elect to become an S-corporation, a corporation is automatically a C-corporation.* Be sure to decide early on whether you wish to form a C-corporation or an S-corporation, and if you decide the latter, file Form 2553 in a timely fashion.

The majority of knowledge an entrepreneur needs about corporations applies to both C-corporations and S-corporations. For example, keeping corporate minutes applies to both C-corporations and S-corporations. And, forming a C-corporation is similar to forming an S-corporation. The difference amounts to Form 2553 which determines how the corporation is taxed.

By electing S-corporation status, you're effectively choosing to have your corporation treated as a partnership from a taxation standpoint. The S-corporation is treated as a "pass through" tax entity, where the profits aren't taxed to the corporation. Rather, the profits pass through to the shareholder, who pays personal income taxes on them. S-corporation status is merely an election to have a corporation taxed differently than the usual C-corporation.

Because S-corporation status is intended for small businesses, the corporation must meet certain IRS requirements to be eligible. For example, your corporation can only have one class of stock, can have at most 100 shareholders, and can have no non-individual-non-people shareholders, with only a few exceptions. (Remember, corporations are separate legal entities and can own shares in other corporations. With only a few exceptions, an S-corporation *cannot* have another corporation as a shareholder.)

The primary difference between C-corporations and S-corporations is how they are taxed. *While C-corporations are taxed as separate taxable entities, S-corporations are treated as "pass-through" entities. In other words, S-corporations typically pay no income tax. Rather, S-corporation taxable income flows through to the individual shareholders.*

If an S-corporation pays dividends (also known as "distributions"), those dividends will be taxed to the individual shareholder at his or her personal income tax rate. Such dividends are only taxed once. In this way, S-corporations are taxed like partnerships. Double taxation doesn't apply to S-corporations. In another chapter, we'll show exactly how S-corporation earnings are taxed at the shareholder level.

S-corporation status is conveyed by the IRS. If conditions change to make a corporation ineligible for S-status (e.g., inappropriate or too many shareholders) the corporation reverts to C-corporation status. This is why it's crucial for S-corporations to be careful not to allow too many shareholders or not to inadvertently create more than one class of stock. And, it's important not to have shareholders the IRS doesn't allow to own shares in an S-corporation. For example, a non-resident alien cannot own shares in an S-corporation. Because of this, many S-corporations have buy-back shareholder agreements to prevent shares from transferring to ineligible parties. We'll discuss this in detail later.

If S-corporation status is inadvertently lost, it can usually be quickly recovered by taking the appropriate corrective actions. For example, a corporation that discovers its shares have been transferred to a non-resident alien could redeem the shares.

While C-corporations file Form 1120, S-corporations file Form 1120S (S for S-corporation). Form 1120S is usually only informational in nature. There usually isn't any tax due with the filing. We'll go over a sample 1120S tax return in detail in another chapter. I highly recommend consulting a knowledgeable business accountant to help you understand your corporation's tax forms.

To record the flow of income to the S-corporation shareholders, the corporation files two other schedules. Schedule K (part of the 1120S) and Schedule K-1, *Shareholder's Share of Income, Credits, Deductions, etc.* (a separate form).

Schedule K-1 is shareholder specific, taking into consideration each shareholder's percentage ownership of the S-corporation. Schedule K-1 is given to each shareholder and helps the shareholder prepare his or her individual income tax return. A shareholder does not file Schedule K-1 with the IRS. Instead, the shareholder uses the information provided from the K-1 to complete 1040 Schedule E. For any business structure, it's important to familiarize yourself with the tax forms and other forms the business must file to remain in compliance with the law.

Because of the "pass through" nature, S-corporations are a good structure for profitable businesses when you wish to remove most of the earnings. A highly-profitable personal consulting business would be a good example. In this case, there is little need to reinvest substantial earnings in the business, and there is little likelihood of taking the company public or selling shares to investors, so an S-corporation is usually superior to a C-corporation.

Many start-up companies aren't profitable right away. Just as income from an S-corporation flows through to the individual shareholders, so do any business losses. Such losses can offset other sources of income to reduce the shareholder's personal income taxes.

This is one reason investors with other sources of income often favor the S-corporation structure for a newer business which anticipates losing money until the business becomes established.

For example, suppose a rich angel investor purchases 40% of a new S-corporation's stock for $25,000 and the corporation loses $10,000 in its first year. The angel investor would usually report a tax-deductible loss of $4,000, which might reduce his personal taxes by $2,000 (we assume the investor effectively pays half of his gross income in income taxes). Such investors will also need to understand the concept of passive income, if they aren't active in the businesses they finance.

A 2007 IRS income study showed the average S-corporation had profits of about $100,000 on income of about $1.5 million. The average S-corporation was about ten times bigger than the average sole proprietorship. The S-corporation is a popular choice among tax-savvy entrepreneurs.

Do I Need More Than One Corporation?

Some people will say you need to form multiple corporations to better protect your assets and maximize your tax savings. The most extreme case I've heard involved a taxi-cab company which incorporated each taxi-cab separately. When a judgment went against the cab company, it was deemed the companies weren't independent, and the assets of all the "companies" were subject to the judgment.

If you operate widely-different businesses, then consider incorporating each business separately. One could be an S-corporation, and the other could be a C-corporation, if desired. Otherwise, most business owners probably only need to operate one corporation for their business.

Some people will tell you by forming multiple corporations, you can split your income so more of it falls into the lower C-corporation income tax brackets. Income splitting is discussed in more detail later. I'm not a big fan of starting multiple C-corporations solely for the purposes of income splitting. If your goal is to grow a business, a single C-corporation or S-corporation will work nicely. If you wish to remove a large amount of profit for personal use from your company, an S-corporation or LLC will probably work best.

Most people promoting "income splitting" among multiple C-corporations fail to consider how the money within the C-corporations will flow through and benefit the entrepreneur or investor.

More complex business structures can also be created. For example, you might own a limited liability company (LLC), and your LLC might become a partner in a partnership. Limited partnerships provide liability protection to the limited partners, i.e., the investors who aren't active in the business, but limited partnerships don't provide liability protection to those who operate the business, who are known as the general partners. While general partners of a limited partnership and partners in a partnership don't have limited liability, in this case, limited liability *is* provided to the active partner, because the partner is operating through a LLC, which provides liability protection.

Tax Shelters

Recall the joke about Limited Partnerships—They're limited because you'll only get a limited part of your investment back! In the past, the IRS allowed certain losses to be passed through to investors, even if the loss was far in excess of the investor's investment in the company.

For example, maybe an investor invested $5,000 but received $20,000 in tax losses that were passed through to the investor. Such losses could save the investor more than $5,000 in taxes. Such structures were called "tax shelters." The IRS frowns on such tax shelters and seeks to prevent individuals from "buying" tax losses. Partially because of this, many tax-related concepts, such as "passive income" and "basis" exist. Entrepreneurs will need to have a basic understanding of these tax-related concepts.

The Truth About "Asset Protection" & Small Business

Years ago, there was a big sign at a metal recycling yard that said the recycling company was not responsible for damages to the vehicles of people who entered the yard. Sure enough, a forklift backed into somebody's truck, doing substantial damage. The man said, "Yeah, I saw the sign. I know you're not responsible" and left the yard. The truth is the company was legally responsible for damages it caused others through its own negligence. You can't simply post a sign saying you're not responsible for your actions and expect it to have validity!

Had the truck driver consulted a knowledgeable attorney, he would certainly have been compensated for the value of his damaged truck. When substantial amounts of money are involved and litigation seems appropriate or likely, consult an attorney.

Other businesses suffer "death by litigation," even if they do everything properly. Many promoting "asset protection" strategies fail to mention that you must not only set up and run your business properly, but you need to be prepared to defend your business in a court of law. In America, anybody can sue anybody for anything. Larger companies know they can entangle smaller businesses in legal fights that cost millions of dollars and last for a decade. Such conflicts often revolve around patents or trademarks. The smaller party loses the suit, not because they were in the wrong, but because they ran out of money defending their position.

The same thing can happen with protecting corporate business structure or personal assets. Some attorneys might back off, like the truck driver with the damaged vehicle, while some attorneys might find a way to keep hammering at your personal assets, driving up your legal costs.

The lesson: The same "asset protection" strategies used by the super wealthy, i.e., those worth hundreds of millions of dollars, aren't always employable by the average small business owner. The super wealthy can spend $2 million a year or more in attorney fees, often in litigation against the IRS, while the small business owner would be destroyed by the legal costs.

Chapter 2
A Step-By-Step Guide To Incorporating

1) If you haven't done so already, decide what your business will do. Will you manufacture custom T-shirts? Sell computer consulting services? Become a professional pet sitter? Do you plan to hire employees? Grow your business to sell it? Do you plan to generate a lot of income for distribution to yourself?

2) Write a marketing plan for your product or service. Write a business plan. Neither of these steps is formally required to form a corporation, but many corporations are started and immediately closed when the incorporators realize their idea isn't viable. Knowing what you plan to do and making some estimates about your future income will help you decide if an S-corporation or a C-corporation is more desirable.

3) Decide if the corporate business structure is for you. Some bad corporation books give people the impression that they should form a corporation even if they don't own a business or plan to run one. Only if you're running a company do you need a corporation. And, some low-risk endeavors can be operated as a sole proprietorship.

4) Decide upon a corporate name. You can reserve a corporate name with your secretary of state or the equivalent office in your state. Some experts recommend having two names in case your first choice

is already taken. If you plan to do business in many locations, you should check the name's availability in all of those locations.

You might also want to consider applying for a trademark to prevent other people from using your business name. Trademarks are an example of intellectual capital, and they can obtain considerable worth. If you want to operate your business under a name different than the formal corporate name, your corporation (like any business or individual) can file a DBA ("Doing Business As"), also known as a certificate of assumed name, with your state.

5) Decide if you're going to incorporate by yourself or use the services of an incorporation service or an attorney. If you're forming a corporation with other entrepreneurs or investors, I'd recommend consulting a knowledgeable business attorney to be sure your articles of incorporation and bylaws achieve what you desire with regard to voting and corporate governance. It's also good to establish dispute resolution mechanisms when everyone's happy. You may also want to draft shareholders' agreements at this stage.

6) Decide how you're going to finance your corporation. If you'll need to raise capital for your business, write a financing plan. This will help you decide how many and what kind of shares to authorize. For example, do you plan to offer preferred stock in addition to common stock? An S-corporation can only *issue* one class of stock. But, any corporation can authorize multiple classes of stock, if it anticipates a use for them down the road. Decide if you wish to issue Section 1244 stock. Decide if your S-corporation should have both voting and non-voting common shares, etc.

The simplest financing involves self-financing your business: You contribute capital to the corporation in exchange for some number of corporate shares. You own 100% of the corporation.

7) Choose a state in which you want to incorporate. Usually, this will be the state in which your business is located. For companies planing to go public, it might be Delaware.

8) File articles of incorporation with the state in which you're incorporating. They can be very simple. Many states provide a basic template you can use. Many states also allow online filing

at your secretary of state's website. Appendix B contains sample articles of incorporation for Minnesota and Texas.

As a general rule, don't put any more information in the articles of incorporation than is required by the secretary of state. There are two reasons for this. First, articles of incorporation are public documents available for inspection by anyone. So, there is little reason to outline your business in detail. Most corporations can be started to engage in any legal business endeavor. Secondly, because articles are filed with the secretary of state, any change to the articles of incorporation involves extra filing fees and submitting amendments to the secretary of state.

When filling out your articles of incorporation, you'll need to list a registered agent for the corporation. The registered agent is a resident of the state where official communications to the corporation can be sent. If you incorporate in your own state, you can be your own registered agent. If you decide to incorporate in a state in which you don't reside, there are companies that will serve as registered agents for an annual fee, typically about $100.

After your secretary of state approves your articles of incorporation, it will send you a certificate to show that you've incorporated properly. Your corporation will receive its own charter number, which is seldom used. Congratulations, you're now a corporation! Be sure to see if there are any other state requirements for a new corporation, such as publishing a public notice of the new corporation in a qualified newspaper.

9) Purchase a corporate start-up kit, which contains sample bylaws, resolutions, and election options for your corporation. It also contains a corporate seal, stock certificates, and a stock transfer ledger to record who receives shares of stock. You don't need a corporate start-up kit, but they're handy.

10) Hold an organizational meeting of the shareholders.

11) Issue stock to each new shareholder in exchange for appropriate consideration from the shareholder. Often, the percentage ownership in the corporation of each founder will be determined in advance. Enter the shareholder's name and contact information in the stock transfer ledger. Typically, paper stock certificates are given to the

shareholders stating that they're owners of so many fully-paid-for shares in corporation ABC, Inc., or whatever.

12) Elect members to the board of directors and have the board elect officers of the corporation. If you deem it desirable, previous to incorporation, you could have a shareholders' agreement or incorporators' agreement which states how everyone will vote and how directors will be chosen.

It's important to understand the difference between shareholders, directors, and corporate officers, like the CEO. The shareholders are the owners of the corporation. Their ownership is represented by shares of stock. To oversee the corporation, shareholders elect a board of directors, who make major high-level strategic decisions for the company. One decision made by the directors is selecting a president, who is a corporate officer. The president or CEO manages day-to-day business operations.

If you're a one-person corporation with no investors, you'll be the only shareholder, the only director of the corporation, and its only officer. Still, follow the corporate formality: Issue yourself stock. As shareholder, elect yourself as the sole member of the board of directors. Appoint yourself as the corporate president.

13) Get the new corporate secretary to quit playing with the corporate seal! Get him or her to record minutes of the meeting. In short, any major action should be documented in resolutions and/or in the corporate minutes. For example, if a director objects, claiming that some action is inappropriate, this should be recorded in the minutes.

Minutes of a meeting can be as simple or complex as you want. At a minimum, the date of the meeting, the shareholders or directors present at the meeting, a call to start the meeting, the important issues decided at the meeting, and a call to end the meeting should be included.

14) Adopt bylaws for the corporation. These are the outline for how your corporation will operate. For example, the bylaws will set the date for the annual shareholder's meeting. Often, in small corporations, bylaws are created and set aside and almost never examined again. Yet, if a lawsuit against the corporation arises, the

bylaws may be requested. Further, if there's a dispute between shareholders, shareholders may turn to the bylaws to decide what's proper.

If there's a conflict between the articles of incorporation and the bylaws, the articles of incorporation take precedence. Unless you have a particular need to deviate from them, you can use the bylaws from your corporate startup kit. On ThinkingLike.com, I link to a template of corporate bylaws provided by SCORE.

15) Have the board of directors adopt any resolutions that are deemed appropriate. These usually just state: "Resolved that ..." and fill in whatever your corporation has approved. Then, the resolution is signed by the directors and/or the shareholders. You don't need fancy legal language. (We should note that fancy legal language is designed to tersely cover many legal aspects that general language sometimes overlooks. Such legal language can often provide extra levels of protection when drafting legal documents, such as contracts.)

For example, if you deem it appropriate to open a bank account in the corporation's name at Money Bank, you could write something like: "Resolved, the treasurer is authorized to open a checking account at Money Bank in the name of the corporation." Other resolutions, such as qualified retirement plans, will require more detail to be sure these resolutions are valid. Possibly, some resolutions will have a copy of a contract attached to the resolution. Then, the resolution can refer to the attached document.

Document any shareholder loans to the corporation with a resolution. You must be certain to include the party lending money to the corporation and the payment terms of the loan, including a timetable for repayment and an interest rate. A separate loan agreement should be drafted, and a copy should be kept with the resolution. "Resolved, the corporation will enter into the loan agreement (agreement attached) in which John Doe agrees to lend the corporation $10,000 at 10% interest to be paid annually. The principal will be due in two years on... ." And, give the maturity date of the loan.

To prevent loans from being reclassified as equity by the IRS, a reasonable interest rate and repayment schedule must be set.

Further, loans from shareholders shouldn't be in proportion to their equity. If shareholder loans greatly exceed equity, the corporation could be labeled "thinly capitalized."

Of course, your corporation can borrow money form any willing lender. Loans, unlike the sale of stock do not dilute equity in your company.

16) Apply for an employee identification number (EIN) with IRS Form SS-4. This number uniquely identifies your corporation to the IRS for all tax purposes, not just employer taxation. Appendix C contains IRS Form SS-4. You'll also need to apply for a state tax ID number. Check with your state.

17) Make any special elections, such as filing Form 2553, if you wish to be taxed as an S-corporation. Be sure to meet the deadlines for filing. If you know you wish to operate an S-corporation, it's best to file Form 2553 immediately after forming your corporation. Companies that operate for years as a C-corporation and then elect S-corporation status involve more complexity, because some of the earnings are classified one way and some of the earnings are classified another. Appendix D shows Form 2553.

18) Register for all forms/registrations that the corporation must submit to various agencies. For example, if you have employees (and officers are employees), the IRS will demand Forms 940, 941, etc., and you'll need to familiarize yourself with the basics of employment taxes. *Make a calendar listing the dates that all tax forms or informational returns are due.* The IRS has its own calendar, which you could use as a base. Be sure to add all state filing dates to your calendar. Appendix E shows a simple tax calendar.

Many states have free classes, held in conjunction with the IRS, to help new company owners understand corporate taxation, sales tax, employment tax, and business taxes. See if your state offers such classes and, if it does, register for them. (You might want to do this even before you incorporate.) At the very least, most states provide free information about starting a business in the state.

If your S-corporation earns a lot of money, from a tax standpoint, that money passes through to you. Because income taxes are a "pay as you go" tax, you'll need to register to pay estimated quarterly tax payments, using form 1040-ES.

19) Begin operating your corporation. If decisions arise that are beyond the day-to-day authorization of the president and CEO, hold a special meeting or use a consent resolution to approve the action.

For example, if Microsoft offers to purchase your new corporation for $10 million, you'd need to call a special shareholders' meeting to discuss and vote upon the sale. Business that doesn't demand special, immediate action can be taken care of at the annual shareholders' meeting, whose date was set in the bylaws. Midsized corporations might schedule regular meetings of the board of directors in the bylaws. If you're an officer, director, or shareholder, be sure you attend the meetings. If you're the corporate secretary, be sure you properly notify everyone who needs to know about the meetings.

20) At the end of your corporation's first year, file your annual corporate tax return. If you're operating as an S-corporation, you'd file IRS Form 1120S. If you go with a regular C-corporation, you'd file Form 1120. File the appropriate state informational or income tax return. Also, many states require annual registration of corporations. This usually amounts to filling out a form and sending it to the secretary of state. The due date should be on the tax and filing calendar you made. If not, add it.

21) Pat yourself on the back! You filed your articles of incorporation, you applied for your EIN, you've gone through your first shareholder meeting, and now have some familiarity with resolutions and corporate bylaws. Once you go through the process, you'll see corporate formalities really aren't that difficult. Using your tax calendar made in Step 18, much of your tax reporting and required governmental filings will be easy going forward.

Conclusion

Starting a corporate business might seem overwhelming at first. However, once you've set up your business, you'll find running a corporate business doesn't differ that much from operating a business as a sole proprietorship or as a partnership. In each case, you invent products or sell products or services. Major changes in business decisions, loans, mergers, or anything out of the ordinary should trigger a special meeting of the board of directors or of the shareholders to consider the out-of-the-ordinary day-to-day business transaction. The documentation of important decisions is crucial to show you're following proper corporate procedure. Lack of corporate decision-making is one factor that can be used to "pierce the corporate veil" and claim you aren't running the business as a corporation. Day-to-day business decisions should be handled by the president.

You might want to pass a resolution giving the president the authority to transact any day-to-day business. But, that's usually assumed.

Chapter 3
Choose A State

In which state should you incorporate your business? This depends upon several factors. If you plan to "do business" in all fifty states, you might want to choose Delaware as your state of incorporation. We will discuss the concept of "doing business in a state" in more detail later. Another popular choice is Nevada.

Reasons For Incorporating In Delaware

1) Delaware has relatively low-cost fees to incorporate.

2) Delaware has no corporate income tax for corporations doing business exclusively in other states.

3) Delaware law tends to be favorable toward corporations.

If you reside and do business in Delaware, there probably is little reason to incorporate in any state other than Delaware. If your business plans to go public or operate in many states, you might want to consider Delaware. Nevada has similar advantages.

Reasons For Incorporating In Your Own State

A better option for a business might be to incorporate in the state in which the business plans to operate. Many states now have favorable corporate laws, comparable to Delaware, which encourage more business in those states. Delaware was one of the first states to adopt business-favorable laws, and that's partly why so many corporations were formed in Delaware.

For example, in the past, some states didn't allow a one-person corporation, where one person was the only shareholder, the only officer, and the only member of the board of directors. So, in the past, if you planned to operate a one-person corporation, you might have been forced to choose a state other than the state where your business was located. Delaware was as good a choice as any. I believe all states allow one-person corporations today.

Foreign And Domestic Corporations And The Concept Of "Doing Business"

There is much bad advice floating around about where to incorporate. Many people will tell you that you won't pay corporate state income tax if you incorporate in Delaware. This isn't fully true.

There are two kinds of corporations: domestic corporations and foreign corporations. Domestic corporations are corporations operating (a.k.a. "doing business") in the state in which they're incorporated. Foreign corporations are corporations doing business in any state other than the state of incorporation.

So, suppose you incorporate in Delaware, but you "do business" in Texas. Relative to Delaware, you'd be considered a domestic corporation. But, in Texas, you'd be considered a foreign corporation. If you incorporate in Texas and do business in Texas, your corporation is a domestic corporation relative to Texas. But, it's a foreign corporation with respect to Alaska, Alabama, and the other non-Texas states.

Regardless of your state of incorporation, your corporation is required to qualify to do business in any state in which you wish to "do business." Qualifying to do business in a state is much like filing articles of incorporation in that state. You must formally register in that state.

"Doing business" typically means that you have offices in the state, or employees in the state, or you generate revenue within the state. You'll want to check with each state's requirements of "doing business" in states in which you intend to operate.

For example, if you own gas stations in Nevada, Texas, Oregon, and Wyoming, you clearly are doing business in all of those states. You generate revenue within each of those states. You have business locations in each of those states. And, you have employees in each of those states.

You could choose to incorporate in any of the fifty states, but you'd need to qualify to do business in Nevada, Texas, Oregon, and Wyoming. You're considered qualified to "do business" in the state in which you incorporate. That's the purpose of the articles of incorporation. (In addition to being qualified to do corporate business in a state, you'll face other regulatory issues. For example, many industries require state-specific licensing requirements. Your business must also meet all federal, state, and local requirements relative to your type of business.)

Suppose you incorporate in Texas. Relative to Texas, you're a domestic corporation. But, you still need to register to do business in Nevada, Oregon, and Wyoming. In Nevada, Oregon, and Wyoming, you'd be considered a foreign corporation. (Note: The concept of "foreign" has nothing to do with foreign countries. Each state is considered "foreign" to every other state.)

Because you're doing business in Nevada, Texas, Oregon, and Wyoming, your corporation is subject to the laws of each of those states. *In particular, your corporation is subject to income taxation in each of those states.* This doesn't mean that your net earnings from business in all states will be taxed by each state. Usually, your portion of business activity in each state will determine the level of taxation in that state. Business activity will often be measured by some combination of revenue, property owned in the state, and employment payroll in the state. You'll need to check with the specific states to see how corporate income taxation works in each state in which you plan to do business. And, yes, you'll need to complete state income tax returns for each of those four states.

If you had incorporated in Delaware, you'd still be subject to state tax in Nevada, Texas, Oregon, and Wyoming. It is incorrect to say that incorporating in Delaware will prevent income taxation at the state level in those states. (Note: Nevada also doesn't have a corporate state income tax.)

Fortunately, for many small businesses, you'll only need to qualify to "do business" in one state. For example, if you own a mail-order company, probably all of your buildings and employees are within one state. That is the only state in which you'll need to qualify to do business.

Suppose all your buildings and employees are located in Texas. Even though you might sell to customers in every other state via mail order, you won't need to qualify to do business in each of those states. (But, if you have business locations and employees in each state, you need to qualify to do business in each state and you need to pay the appropriate fees. Plus, you'd probably need to register annually in each of those states and keep up-to-date on each state's corporate law, because it affects your business.)

Given the need to qualify to do business in each state in which you plan to operate and that your corporation is subject to taxation in each of those states, you might want to consider incorporating in the state in which you plan to do business. If you reside and do business in Texas, you might want to incorporate in Texas. If you do business in Minnesota, you might want to incorporate in Minnesota. If you do business in Texas and incorporate in Delaware, you'll have more paperwork to do.

In addition to state income tax, many states impose a state franchise tax on corporations doing business in the state. This is an extra tax for the privilege of doing business in the state. In many states, this tax isn't very large. It's more like an extra little fee. Incorporating in a different state usually won't reduce your corporate franchise tax.

You might want to examine the corporate franchise fees and conditions for your state before you incorporate. California, in particular, really punishes smaller corporations and LLCs by soaking them for a minimum annual franchise fee of $800. No doubt, such a high fee discourages some start-up entrepreneurs from getting adequate liability protection.

Some states calculate a corporation's franchise tax based upon the level of activity in the state. So, if you generate $1 million dollars or less in revenue, you might pay $30. If you generate $5 million or less, but more than $1 million, you might pay $100, etc.

Other states charge a franchise fee based upon the number of authorized or issued corporate shares. The idea is probably that a corporation with a large number of shares is a larger business and should, therefore, pay more tax. The danger here is that you authorize one million shares for a one-person business and wind up doing business in a state which has a franchise tax based upon the number of authorized shares. This is one reason you should examine the corporate franchise taxes in each state in which you plan to do business before incorporating.

Incidentally, you should be careful not to issue too few shares just to avoid franchise taxes based upon the number of shares. The more shares authorized, the easier it is to divide equity in your company and to have shares available to sell to potential investors and business partners. It's crucial to mention that selling shares involves security laws. You'll probably need to consult with your business attorney if you plan to sell shares to investors. But, if you only authorize one share, that share represents 100% of your company. If you authorize 10 shares, each share represents 10% of your company. If you authorize 100 shares, each share represents 1% of your business. So, if you plan to sell or give someone 5% of your company, it's easier to achieve with more shares. You can also authorize more shares in your corporation in the future by amending the articles of incorporation, if necessary. But, if your state of incorporation charges a franchise tax based upon the number of authorized shares, you might want a smaller number of shares.

You may also want to examine a sample set of articles of incorporation and bylaws for the specific state in which you wish to incorporate. Many states base corporate law upon the Revised Model

Business Corporation Act (RMBCA). But, each state might differ in certain areas.

Ask each secretary of state about qualifying to do business in each state in which you anticipate doing business. And, consider forming your corporation in the primary state in which you intend to do business. You may also wish to consult your business attorney to help you understand the advantages/disadvantages of incorporating in various states.

Why is there so much misinformation about the supposed advantages of incorporating in Delaware? Partially, Delaware was an early pioneer in adopting laws favorable to corporations, and much of the advantage to incorporating in Delaware was true in the distant past. Delaware might still hold some advantages for your business today, but unless you plan to go public or do business in many states, you might find that incorporating in your home state is best.

Chapter 4
Basis

Basis In C-corporations

Basis is a tax concept which measures your investment in a company or other wealth-producing asset. Knowing your initial investment in a company is necessary to calculate the net taxable profit or loss you'll have when you sell corporate stock or when the stock becomes worthless due to total company failure.

For example, suppose you purchase stock in a C-corporation for $10,000. This could be a company you're starting or a large publicly-traded company. The $10,000 represents your initial investment in the stock and is the "basis" when you calculate taxable gains or losses upon future sale of the stock.

If you sell the stock three years later for $30,000, you have a profit of

Sales Price - Basis = $30,000 - $10,000 = $20,000

That $20,000 is taxable to you at some rate. The tax rate will depend upon the current capital gains tax rate and other factors determined by the IRS. (For example, if the C-corporation stock has been held more than five years and it qualifies as a small business stock under Section 1202 of the IRS Code, 50% of the gain would be excluded from taxation. Thus, the effective tax rate would be cut in half.)

If we assume a capital gains tax rate of 20% and because the stock doesn't qualify for Section 1202 exclusion, you owe $4,000 in taxes in our example.

Notice that you didn't pay tax on the full amount ($30,000) you received. *Part of that money was not gain. It was your initial investment which is returned to you untaxed. It was a return of your capital. The basis amount measures this initial investment.*

Suppose, rather than a gain, your stock became worthless. All of the corporation's money was lost, and the corporation decided to go out of business. In this case, you have a loss of $10,000.

Sales Price - Basis = $0 - $10,000 = -$10,000

Again, we see that the basis measures your investment in the company and is your net tax-deductible loss in this case. How much money is saved on taxes due to a capital loss of $10,000? It depends.

For example, if the stock is subject to Section 1244 of the IRS Code (decide if you want Section 1244 stock when you incorporate), the IRS allows the loss, within limitations, to be deducted as an ordinary loss, rather than a capital gains loss.

If the $10,000 loss is treated as a capital loss and if the capital gains tax rate is 20%, you'll reduce your taxes by $2,000. This assumes, of course, that you can deduct the full capital loss in the current year. If the loss is subject to Section 1244 and if your tax rate is 39.6%, you'll reduce your taxes by $3,960 by using the loss to offset ordinary income, rather than capital gains.

For an income-rich investor, having stock subject to Section 1244 of the IRS Code is desirable because it substantially increases the tax deduction for the complete loss of an investment. So, if the company fails, it's essentially like getting another $1,960 back in this case. Reducing ordinary income is better than reducing capital gains because ordinary income is taxed at a higher rate than capital gains.

More About Basis And Section 1244 Stock (Optional)

The IRS sets limitations upon stock qualified under IRC Section 1244. For example, the company must be a small corporation with a total capital contribution of one million dollars or less. Other limitations also affect taxation.

For example, Section 1244 allows a loss to offset ordinary income only up to $50,000 on an individual income tax return (the limit is $100,000 if filing jointly). If you invested $100,000 and the company goes bankrupt, Section 1244 allows you to use $50,000 of that loss to offset ordinary income. The other $50,000 must be treated as a capital loss.

If your initial investment in the company was $100,000, your basis in the stock was $100,000. However, notice that part of that basis was treated differently in terms of exactly how much it saved you in taxes due to IRS rules ($50,000 of the basis was used to offset ordinary income, while $50,000 of the basis was used to offset capital gains).

An important restriction of Section 1244 stock is that the stock must have originally been issued by the corporation in exchange for founding capital. The stock cannot be purchased from another individual who had previously been issued stock.

So, if your corporation authorized 1,000 shares of stock and you instantly issued all 1,000 shares to yourself and you later decided to seek an investor, selling him 200 of your personal shares, the investor couldn't benefit from Section 1244. The stock wasn't original issue.

If, however, you had issued yourself 800 shares initially and decided to seek an investor, who purchased the remaining 200 shares from the corporation, the investor's stock would be eligible for Section 1244.

The purpose in requiring Section 1244 stock to be originally-issued stock is to encourage investment in new, small companies by giving those investors who contribute money to a small business an extra tax advantage. Its purpose is not to reward individuals buying and selling shares of stock among themselves. In this case, the capital isn't going to the corporation. It's going to individuals. Notice this is also an example of retaining enough authorized but unissued shares for future capital purposes. It also demonstrates the value of planning ahead and thinking about your capital structure before you form your corporation.

The limitation that Section 1244 stock be original capital contribution also applies to those who participated in the initial financing of the company. Suppose you originally contributed $10,000 to your corporation in exchange for stock. Your basis is $10,000. This is original issue stock and can participate in Section 1244. But, suppose you then contribute another $5,000 to the company when the company requires more capital and no more stock is issued. You still hold the same number of shares, but your basis is now $15,000.

Because of IRS limitations, contributions beyond an investor's initial contribution are not eligible for Section 1244 treatment. Only $10,000 of your investment can benefit from Section 1244. The other $5,000 would need to be treated as a capital loss if the company fails.

Sometimes, people speak about a "Section 1244 basis." "Section 1244 basis" measures the proportion of basis that is subject to Section 1244. In the above case, your "Section 1244 basis" would be $10,000. The equation is:

(Total Loss)(Original Stock Basis/Total Basis) =
$$\text{Section 1244 Loss Basis}$$

($15,000)($10,000/$15,000) = $10,000

Your Section 1244 basis in a stock is limited to your initial cash or property contribution for that stock. Further increases in your stock's basis do not benefit from Section 1244 treatment.

I think the most appropriate way to view this is that your total basis is $15,000, but only $10,000 of that is subject to special treatment under Section 1244. The other $5,000 in basis is treated differently because of the Section 1244 limitations.

Hopefully, your company will be greatly successful, and this discussion of Section 1244 stock will never apply to you! However, by being aware of such issues, you can enhance the desirability of your company's shares to investors and demonstrate that you're aware of important issues affecting their investment.

Net Operating Losses And Tax Loss Carryforwards (Optional)

You might want to consult a knowledgeable business and tax attorney when you form your corporation, because he/she can inform you about tax-saving strategies, such as getting the benefit of Section 1244 stock. Angel investors will probably be more willing to invest in your company if they can treat a capital loss as a deduction from ordinary income.

The above examples assume a sale of corporate stock. Now, what about operating losses *within* the company for a C-corporation? After you contribute $10,000 to the corporation, suppose the corporation spends $3,000 to create and market a product. Assume the product is unprofitable and the company loses the full $3,000 within the year, but the corporation remains in business.

Let's assume the company has $7,000 in cash and no other assets at the end of the year. No income has been generated. The company lost $3,000. How are your personal taxes and basis affected? They aren't. You do not receive a personal deduction for the corporation's loss. The $3,000 loss is a loss to the C-corporation, which is a separate taxable entity. If this is the company's first year, the loss will need to be carried forward and can reduce corporate taxes in future years (tax losses carried forward to future years are sometimes called tax loss carryforwards). Remember, C-corporations are separate taxable entities. The $7,000 within the corporation and the $3,000 tax loss belong to the corporation, not to you.

If the company continues to do poorly and eventually fails, or if your stock is sold, then, the basis of your stock becomes important, as previously discussed. If the shares are declared worthless, you have a $10,000 loss—the basis of your initial investment. The loss of money invested into the corporation and the loss of money by the corporation are two different things.

If the company remains in business, earning money some years and losing money other years, your basis is unaffected, and you do not receive tax deductions. Nor are you forced to pay personal income taxes on any of the corporate earnings. (If money is paid to you as a C-corporation dividend, the dividend is taxable as income to you, but it doesn't affect your basis). The C-corporation receives all of the tax deductions and pays all the incurred income taxes on its earnings.

What happens if the company never earns money before being shut down? It can never use its tax loss carryforwards. But, it's still fair if you think about it. You invested $10,000, and you were eventually able to deduct the loss of the $10,000 personally.

Incidentally, suppose a company loses $10 million dollars and has no other assets. Do you see any potential value or asset worth for this corporation? Ask yourself: If the corporation were sold to another company or merged with it, what would happen to the corporation's tax loss carryforwards?

At a 34% corporate tax rate, $10 million in tax loss carryforwards is worth about $3.4 million to a company earning profits. So, in the past, many profitable companies purchased companies that offered "rich" tax losses that they could use to offset income from their profitable operations. ("Investments" that return more than the initial investment through savings in tax deductions are sometimes known as "tax shelters." Because basis measures an investor's investment in a company, you can see how the concept of basis helps prevent investors from getting tax deductions in excess of their investment in a company. The IRS can simply disallow deductions in excess of the basis.)

Today, the IRS will disallow the transfer of tax loss carryforwards to an acquiring corporation if the primary reason for acquiring the corporation is to acquire the tax loss carryforwards. So, the company with only tax loss carryforwards has no value. The IRS doesn't like the idea of people selling tax deductions! But, if the acquiring company has another primary business reason for buying the business, it will be allowed to utilize the tax loss carrryforwards and treat them as the original company would have.

So, operational losses and profits within a C-corporation are taxed to the corporation. Not to shareholders. Can the basis of your stock change in some other way? Suppose you invested $10,000 in your C-corporation and feel the company still has potential, but the company needs more money. You could contribute another $5,000 to the corporation, and your basis would be increased to $15,000. Your investment in the corporation is now $15,000.

Basis Per Share

You could also calculate your average basis per share by dividing your total stock basis by the number of shares. If shares are acquired for different amounts at different times, each share for the different offerings of the same company can have a different basis. Sometimes, by specifying which shares are sold, you can choose to sell shares with a higher basis.

For example, if you purchase 100 shares on January 2, 2012, for a total capital contribution of $10,000, each share has a basis of $100. If you later purchase 100 shares on February 21, 2013, for a total of $20,000, each share has a basis of $200. When selling 50 shares, you could specify that you're selling the February 21, 2013 shares to achieve a slightly higher tax basis. For more about the taxation of capital gains, I recommend *Capital Gains, Minimal Taxes* by Kaye Thomas.

If you contribute more money to a one-person corporation, you can issue more shares, if you like, or not. If you have multiple shareholders and more money is contributed, you probably want to issue more shares in proportion to the money contributed or according to some other criteria agreed upon by the shareholders.

For example, if an angel investor has already invested $500,000 in your company and owns 20% of your company, and your company now needs $100,000 more, it's not really fair to expect the investor to kick in more money without increasing his percentage of ownership in the company.

Remember, money exchanged for equity is at risk of loss. There is no obligation on the part of the corporation to repay this money to the shareholder. While the angel investor obviously wants to see the company succeed, he probably doesn't want to give it $100,000 more for no other benefit. So, maybe, the angel investor will get another 5% ownership of the company or whatever. We discuss the advantages of successive rounds of financing in another chapter. In any case, the angel investor's total basis is now $600,000. Capital paid in by shareholders is called "paid in" capital.

Suppose, however, it's deemed the corporation doesn't need the full $500,000 initially raised. If part of an investor's initial investment is returned, his basis is decreased by that amount. It's important to take care to show that it's a return *of* capital and not a return *on* invested capital. While returns *on* invested capital are taxable, a return *of* capital isn't taxable. (This is a key reason why many entrepreneurs loan their C-corporation money. After the company is doing well, they want this money back and don't want to be taxed on the return of their initial investment amount.)

If you have major investors and confront issues like this, you'll probably want to consult your business and tax attorney.

In any case, remember, profits and losses within a C-corporation do not usually affect the shareholder's basis. Nor do the payment of dividends affect basis for C-corporations. It's only when money is transferred to the C-corporation or from the C-corporation, as an investment, that basis should be affected, because basis measures the investor's investment in the corporation.

Basis In S-Corporations

Because of the pass through nature of taxation of S-corporations, basis is calculated differently for S-corporations. Profits and losses typically affect the shareholder's basis in S-corporation stock. *Profits increase basis regardless of whether or not the profits are actually distributed to the shareholder. (When a person is taxed on income he/she didn't receive, it's called phantom income.) Losses reduce basis. Losses may only be deducted from personal taxes up to a shareholder's basis.*

Suppose an entrepreneur invests $10,000 into a new S-corporation (assume only one shareholder). Suppose the corporation loses $2,500 in its first year. That loss flows through to the shareholder and is used to reduce the shareholder's taxable income. Because the entrepreneur has received a tax benefit due to his initial investment, his basis is reduced by $2,500. The new basis is $7,500. In a sense, reduced basis shows that the shareholder is entitled to a smaller future tax benefit. Some tax benefit has already been consumed.

If, over the next three years, the S-corporation loses $2,500 each year, basis is reduced by $2,500 for each of those years. Each of those years, the $2,500 loss is also used to offset personal income.

At the end of four years, the company has passed though losses totaling $10,000, reducing the shareholder's basis to zero. The shareholder is typically no longer entitled to tax deductions for this investment.

Assume the company ceases to exist. If calculating basis had *not* reduced the shareholder's basis for each of those loss years, the entrepreneur would have another $10,000 loss to offset personal income upon closing the company. This would mean that for a $10,000 investment (and total loss of that investment), the shareholder would be able to deduct $20,000 in tax-deductible losses. Obviously, the IRS will not allow that! Reducing basis for losses passed through is a way of adjusting and calculating the shareholder's net investment in the company to determine future tax loss deductions.

Suppose the S-corporation is successful and earns $3,000 its first year. Profits are not taxed at the corporate level for S-corporations. This $3,000 profit passes through to the shareholder and is taxable to the shareholder at the shareholder's personal income tax rate. How does this $3,000 profit affect the shareholder's basis?

The S-corporation's shareholder's basis is increased by $3,000 *due to the profits earned*. This is true whether the profit is actually distributed to the shareholder or whether the company retains the money to fuel future growth. *Due to the profits*, the shareholder's new basis is $13,000. (However, *distributions* reduce S-corporation basis. So, if the $3,000 is paid to the shareholder, there is also a

$3,000 reduction in the shareholder's basis *due to the distribution*, bringing the shareholder's net basis back to $10,000.)

What if the company reports a loss of $13,000 in the next year? In most cases, the shareholder can deduct the full $13,000 from his or her personal income taxes, reducing taxes by the loss multiplied by the incremental ordinary income tax rate. So, if the shareholder is in the 39.6% income tax bracket, the shareholder essentially saves $5,148 in taxes.

(Again, it's important to distinguish between internal losses of the S-corporation passed through, which reduce personal income taxes by offsetting *ordinary income*, and a total failure and dissolution of the corporation, which may have limits on how the losses may be used. In particular, upon complete corporate failure, you'll need to investigate whether losses may only offset capital gains or may be fully deductible against ordinary income. See the discussion of IRS Section 1244 stock. However, in practice, a failed S-corporation will probably have passed through losses on its road to failure, as did our example company, losing $2,500 per year, so Section 1244 stock will usually have less significance than with a C-corporation. The amount lost will have already been passed through and will have already offset ordinary income.)

In any case, upon total company failure, the shareholder eventually is able to deduct a total of $13,000 for the full loss. Depending upon the situation, that loss offsets ordinary income or else must offset capital gains. If the corporation continues operationally, the offset is to ordinary income.

Why do S-corporation profits increase shareholder basis? In particular, suppose that a company started with only $10,000 grows into a company that has earned total profits of $10 million. Why should the shareholder have a basis measured in the millions of dollars when the only investment was $10,000?

With C-corporations, losses in the current tax year can be carried back to offset income from previous years (or, they can be carried forward, reducing the taxable income of future years). With an S-corporation, such losses can also be utilized, but by the shareholder. So, if in its next year, our corporation suffers a loss of $500,000, this

$500,000 loss is deductible to the shareholder. That's why basis increases with profits. If you've contributed $10,000 to the company, and the company earned $1,000,000, you've been taxed on that $1,000,000. So, from a tax standpoint, it "looks" as if your current investment in the company is $1,010,000. (And, because those earnings have already been taxed, when they are distributed, it looks as if the distribution is a return of capital, not a return on capital.)

In the above cases, we assumed one shareholder to simplify matters. If a company has multiple shareholders, basis changes, due to profits and losses, work just like profits and losses, which flow through to the shareholders in proportion to their percentage ownership of the S-corporation shares.

So, if a company has two shareholders, one holding 60% of the shares and another owning 40% of the shares, and the S-corporation loses $3,000, $1,800 of the loss flows through to the 60% shareholder, and $1,200 of the loss flows through to the 40% shareholder. The 60% shareholder's basis is reduced by $1,800 and the 40% shareholder's basis is reduced by $1,200 if they utilize the deductions. Similarly for profits and the resulting basis increases.

Each shareholder should calculate his or her own basis annually. For example, on the IRS K-1 Form that will be provided to the 60% shareholder, his pro rated portion of the loss is reported as $1,800, and he uses that information to adjust his basis.

S-Corporation Distributions And Basis

Distributions to a shareholder decrease the shareholder's basis. This is true because distributions reduce an investor's effective investment in the S-corporation (the amount of money at risk of loss is reduced).

Consider an extreme case. Wealthy investor Frank invests $50 million into Juicy Start-Up Company. Juicy Start-Up Company immediately distributes $49,900,00 to Frank. The $49,900,000 returned is called a return of basis. It reduces Frank's basis by $49,900,000. Thus, his true investment in the company stands at $100,000. Not $50 million. And, if you think about it, it's fair. Frank didn't really invest $50 million in the company. He invested $100,000.

Basis And Wages (Optional)

Sometimes, people wonder if wages affect basis. No. Not directly. Wages, salaries, and bonuses are paid to officers, directors, and other employees of the corporation. They are a tax-deductible expense to the corporation, much like any other tax-deductible expense, such as cost of goods sold (cogs). Wages aren't paid to shareholders acting in a shareholder sense. Wages go to employees. So, if, as an officer, you receive $40,000 in salary, that doesn't relate to your shareholder status and doesn't affect your basis in the stock.

Wages paid obviously reduce *profit* reportable to the corporation. Suppose you're a one-person owner of an S-corporation. After all other expenses, but before any salary to yourself, assume that your corporation earns $80,000. If you pay yourself a wage of $30,000, this leaves $50,000 in profit. That profit flows through to you, increasing your basis by $50,000. If you had paid yourself a wage of $50,000, $30,000 would remain as profit, and your basis would increase by $30,000.

A whole host of other issues determine how much you wish to pay yourself as an employee of an S-corporation. Generally, you must pay yourself a wage comparable to what other employees doing similar roles earn, before you can pay employment-tax-free dividends. Wages are subject to employment tax, but you do receive increased Social Security benefits upon retirement. Wages also can be reduced by contributions to tax-deferred or tax-advantaged retirement vehicles, such as IRA's, 401(k)'s, SEP-IRA's, etc. How much you can contribute to these tax-deferred retirement vehicles depends upon your wages. *Basis concerns will probably not enter into your decision about the level of wages to pay yourself.*

S-Corporation Basis Worksheets

To help you calculate your stock basis in your S-corporation, you can use the following simple worksheet:

Stock Basis At Beginning Of Tax Year (Not Less Than Zero)	_____
+ Additional Capital Contributions To Corporation	+_____
+ Income Items	+_____
- Distributions	-_____
- Non-Deductible Expenses (Line 16c of Schedule K-1)	-_____
- Losses	-_____
Stock Basis At Year End	_____

We have already discussed the role of additional capital contributions, income, distributions, and losses. Notice that non-deductible expenses, as reported on Line 16c of Schedule K-1, also reduce shareholder basis. If a shareholder's basis were not reduced for his/her share of non-deductible losses, upon sale of corporate stock, non-deductible expenses could be converted into tax-deductible expenses. The IRS doesn't allow this.

Similarly, a simple worksheet can be used for most shareholder loans:

Loan Basis At Beginning Of Tax Year	_____
+ New Loans To Corporation	+_____
- Loan Repayments (Schedule K-1, Line 16e)	-_____
Loan Basis At End Of Tax Year	_____

Loan Restoration (Optional)

We're neglecting something called "Loan Restoration" in these worksheets, because it won't apply to many S-corporations. In particular, suppose a shareholder contributes $5,000 in stock and

$10,000 in loans to his corporation. If the corporation suffers a loss of $8,000, all $8,000 is deductible from the shareholder's income taxes.

First, the $5,000 in stock basis is used to reduce the shareholder's income taxes by the loss deduction of $5,000. This reduces the shareholder's stock basis to zero. Then, the remaining $3,000 is attributed to a decrease in the *loan basis*. This $3,000 is also usually tax deductible. The shareholder's loan basis is reduced by $3,000.

It's important to understand that loans should be repaid according to a set loan repayment schedule. If the corporation is losing borrowed money, this becomes difficult. If a loan is reclassified as a preferred class of stock, S-corporation status can be lost. S-corporation owners want to avoid that.

In the above case, suppose the company reestablishes profitability and is able to repay the loan in full. The $3,000 in loan basis must be "restored." In particular, suppose the corporation earns $30,000. Of this $30,000 in income, $3,000 is used to "restore" the basis in the loan. So, that $3,000 of earnings cannot also add to the shareholder's stock basis. So, amounts of loan restoration must be *subtracted* on the shareholder's stock basis worksheet.

Incidentally, those familiar with partnerships might incorrectly think that if the S-corporation shareholder guarantees a loan, then, the amount of the guaranteed loan is also "at risk" of loss and should add to the shareholder's loan basis. This isn't correct. The IRS doesn't allow guaranteed loans to affect S-corporation shareholder basis. This differs from the rules for partnerships.

So, if the shareholder must guarantee a loan to the corporation, many advisors suggest the shareholder borrow this money directly from the lender and, then, lend it to the corporation. This makes the loan a shareholder loan, which increases the shareholder's loan basis. Either way, the shareholder is at risk for repayment of this particular loan. I'm a fan of using equity financing to fund high-risk ventures and using debt financing to fund low-risk ventures and short-term cash demands.

Chapter 5
Shares—Authorized, Issued, Outstanding

Shares divide up the interests in the corporation. For example, in most corporations, common stock is authorized and issued which gives the stockholder certain rights. Among those rights are typically the right to vote for the board of directors and to participate proportionately in any dividends the board of directors declare. Further, upon dissolution of the corporation, common-stock shareholders are entitled to receive a portion of the residual wealth that remains after bondholders and preferred stockholders have been paid.

Authorized shares are shares that the articles of incorporation have authorized the corporation to issue. Not all authorized shares are necessarily issued. Some are held in reserve for future use, such as successive rounds of financing.

Preferred Stock (C-Corporations)

In addition to common stock, corporations can authorize preferred stock, which has some preference over the common shares. For example, before common stockholders can receive dividends, preferred stock shareholders will first receive the dividends to which they are entitled. The preferences of preferred stock should be clearly stated in the articles of incorporation.

Liquidation preference means that if a company dissolves, the preferred stock with a liquidation preference receives preferential treatment in the dissolution. So, preferred stockholders are paid before common stockholders.

Classes Of Stock (C-Corporations)

Corporations can also issue different classes of stock. For example Class A stock might be entitled to certain rights, while Class B stock might have other rights. In addition to rights, preferred stock and certain classes of stock might have restrictions which don't apply to the average common-stock shares. For example, possibly, preferred stock has no voting rights and the common stockholders elect the entire board of directors, who set policy for the corporation.

Similarly, different classes of stock can restrict rights. For example, possibly, Class A shares and Class B shares exist. Each class of shares participates equally in dividends and the distribution of assets upon liquidation of the corporation. But, maybe, Class B shares have no voting rights. This structure can be used to give control of a corporation to a minority shareholder, while a majority shareholder receives a larger share of any financial benefit the corporation generates.

Because S-corporations can only have one class of stock (which will be the common stock), S-corporations won't have preferred stock. However, the IRS has ruled that one class of stock can differ in voting rights. So, an S-corporation can have voting and non-voting shares. They just can't be called different *classes* of stock. No dividend or liquidation preferences can be given, however.

Issuing Shares And Percentage Ownership

Suppose Tom's Trombones, Inc., authorizes 1,000 shares of common stock. This means Tom's Trombones can potentially be divided into 1,000 pieces, each representing equal voting rights and rights to participate in dividends and a share of the money remaining upon liquidation. The articles of incorporation can always be amended to authorize more shares, preferred stock, or different classes of stock, if need be.

If Tom is the only shareholder, he doesn't need to issue himself 1,000 shares. He can issue himself only one share. Then, only one share is issued and outstanding. Only issued and outstanding shares participate in voting and dividend distributions. Tom owns 100% of the company, regardless of whether he issues one, ten, a hundred, or a thousand shares.

If Tom's Trombones receives an investment from Tom's uncle Henry of $50,000 and it is determined that Henry should own 30% of the company, you'll need to do just a bit of math to figure out how many shares each should receive.

For example, if Tom receives seven shares and Henry receives three shares, Henry now owns 30% of the company, while Tom owns 70% of the company. Of course, Tom could also have received fourteen shares, while Henry received six.

If we do some basic math, we can calculate how many shares should be issued to determine a certain percentage ownership:

Percentage Ownership = Number of shares held by person divided by the total number of shares issued

Equivalently: Number of shares held by the person = Percentage ownership times total number of shares issued

So, assume we plan to issue 200 total shares and Henry is to receive 30% of the company. We calculate $(0.30)(200) = 60$. So, Henry receives 60 shares, while Tom receives 200 minus 60 or 140 shares. Even though ownership in a company is expressed in shares, when a company is formed, people usually think in terms of percentage of ownership of the company. What percentage ownership should each person receive relative to their contributions to the corporation?

Typically, those who contribute more time or money to a company receive a higher percentage of ownership.

The same basic math works for determining percentage ownership among several people. For example, if Betty, June, and Allison form a company and it's decided that Betty should own 51%, June 20%, and Allison 29%, we could calculate as previously. Assume the corporation plans to issue 700 shares.

Betty receives (0.51)(700) = 357 shares
June receives (0.20)(700) = 140 shares
Allison receives (0.29)(700) = 203 shares

Computation is simpler if the total number of shares is 10, 100, 1000, or ten to some other power.

Shareholder Agreements, Buy-Back Agreements, And Treasury Stock (Optional)

When forming a company and issuing shares, it might be a good idea to also consider shareholders' agreements which set forth the rights and responsibilities of shareholders. For example, if a shareholder also works as an employee and is terminated, that shareholder might no longer wish to hold shares in a small, illiquid company (an illiquid company is one whose shares aren't easily valued and sold). And, the company may no longer want that person as a shareholder.

If shares are subject to transfer restrictions, buy-back restrictions, or other limitations imposed by shareholders' agreements, it's important for the stock certificates to state that the shares are subject to a shareholders' agreement. If the certificates fail to do this, a party who purchases the stock may not be bound by the conditions of the agreement.

Suppose June decides she no longer wants to be involved with the company. The other shareholders or the corporation can buy June's shares. If a corporation buys back stock, the stock is called treasury stock. Treasury stock is much like authorized, but unissued, stock. It doesn't vote, and it doesn't participate in dividend distributions.

If the corporation buys back June's 140 shares, the total number of outstanding shares is 560, which is the sum of Betty's and Allison's shares. Betty now owns 357/560 = 63.75 percent of the company, while Allison owns 203/560 = 36.25 percent of the company.

While Betty and Allison each own a higher percentage of the company when the corporation purchased June's shares, the relative ownership of Betty to Allison has remained the same: 51/29 =1.75 and 63.7/36.2 =1.75.

In this example, Betty always holds a controlling interest in the company. Sometimes, when a shareholder sells his/her shares back to a corporation or to other shareholders, controlling interests in a corporation change.

For example, if each person had owned one-third of the outstanding shares, each would have an equal say in voting. It would take two of the three to vote for a particular shareholder action. But, if June sold her one-third ownership to Allison, Allison would become the majority shareholder.

Because of the potential to change control and to prevent interests in the corporation from going to people to whom the other shareholders object, one restriction on stock can be buy-back agreements and preemptive rights. Buy-back agreements typically require that a shareholder wishing to sell his/her stock must first make the stock available to the corporation or to the other shareholders, as stated in the agreement.

If the corporation doesn't buy the shares, each shareholder might have the right to buy the departing shareholder's shares in proportion to his/her current shareholdings relative to the other remaining shareholders or according to some other pre-agreed-upon formula. Unlike with preemptive rights, discussed later, the proportion isn't trivially calculated as the current percentage ownership of the shareholder.

Let's work a slightly wrong calculation to demonstrate a point. Suppose the shareholders' agreement allows Betty to purchase 51%

of June's 140 shares (71.4 shares), while Allison would have the right to buy 29% of June's shares (40.6 shares).

Because June owns 51% of the shares, while Allison owns 29%, this might seem to make sense. Because fractional shares don't exist (actually, fractional shares do exist and are called script, but we'll assume we don't want fractional shares), those numbers would need to be rounded. Round-off effects should be considered, if deemed important, if a departing shareholder sells to other shareholders (ten times the current number of shares can be issued appropriately to each shareholder, if authorized, to pick up an extra decimal place). The big problem is that only 112 of June's 140 shares have been purchased! What happens to the other shares?

So, to simply say that each shareholder has the right to buy a departing shareholder's shares in proportion to each shareholder's percentage ownership of the company doesn't achieve the desired result.

A way around this is to "renormalize" the number of shares for calculation purposes. Betty and Allison will now own 100% of the company, but, previously, they only held 80% of the company.

So, rather than 51% ownership, upon losing June, Betty's ownership in the company will actually be 51% divided by 0.8 which is 63.75%. The agreement might want to allow Betty to purchase 89.25 shares, while Allison purchases 50.75 shares, which could similarly be calculated as $(140)(29\%)/0.80 = 50.75$ shares. Again, what happens to fractional shares might be an issue. Possibly, the corporation could buy-back any fractional shares. Betty would be allowed to purchase 89 shares, Allison 50 shares, and the corporation one share. Or, if absolutely needed, fractional shares could be allowed.

Things can be made exact simply by authorizing and issuing enough shares so that fractions don't become a problem. In this case, Betty should own 63.75% of the shares, while Allison should own 36.25% of the shares. If we multiple those percentages by a large enough number, 10, 100, 1,000, etc., we'll eventually wind up with a non-fractional number of shares. For example, 63.75% times 10,000 is 6,375 while 36.25% times 10,000 is 3,625. So, we could authorize and issue more shares to solve this problem also.

This example points out several things. First, things that started off relatively simple can get more complex. Initially, three shareholders owned a small number of shares and everyone was happy, but, upon one shareholder leaving the company, many topics arose. Who had the right to buy the departing shareholder's shares and how many? What did the shareholder's agreement specify? After working out the math, did the basic buy-back agreement even make sense?

While a fractional share issue might seem like a big deal in shareholder-shareholder sales, it probably isn't. A larger problem of allowing shareholders to buy a departing shareholder's stock is the reality that some shareholders might not have the money to purchase shares while others do.

For example, suppose Betty is the entrepreneur who started the company, while Allison is a wealthy investor. If June's shares are valued at $1,000 each, does Betty have $89,000 to buy 89 shares? What happens if Betty can't afford to purchase the shares while Allison can? In this case, the percentage ownership changes. Betty is still the majority stockholder, because she initially held 51% of the corporation. (If you own 51% of the initial shares, it doesn't matter who acquires the other shares—you still hold the controlling interest.)

But, if all three entrepreneurs had held one-third of the company, upon June's leaving, if Allison had the right to buy shares and did so, while Betty had the right, but lacked the cash, Allison could become the majority shareholder.

You probably can see a slight advantage of simplicity in allowing the corporation, itself, to buy back a departing shareholder's shares. However, like many individuals, small corporations are often strapped for cash. What if the corporation doesn't have $140,000 in cash to pay June? Are payment terms acceptable, where June is paid over a few years?

Details like this should be spelled out in a shareholder repurchase agreement. One advantage to consulting an attorney experienced in corporate matters is that he/she should be able to point out the stumbling blocks in a potential shareholders' agreement. And, many lawyers will have template agreements that might serve your needs at low cost. You shouldn't have to pay for intensive drafting of a new agreement if the attorney simply pops one off his computer that has been used a hundred times before.

Buy-back agreements, if adopted, should consider the common cases where the corporation may want to purchase a shareholder's shares. Death of a shareholder is a possibility. Without a buy-back agreement, the entrepreneur's stock becomes part of his/her estate and could go to an heir.

Suppose Betty dies. She was an ambitious, hard-working, and knowledgeable businesswoman. But, Betty's only heir is her twenty-year-old son, Bill, who's a slacker. Allison probably doesn't want Bill as a shareholder and business partner. Part of what Betty contributed to the company was her talent and work. Bill probably should receive financial compensation for Betty's shares, not an interest in the business. Shareholder agreements help anticipate situations like this.

Bankruptcy of a shareholder is another issue. If a shareholder goes bankrupt, that person's interest in the small corporation could go to a creditor. That might or might not be a problem for the other business owners. As a general rule, small corporations often place many restrictions upon the transfer of shares.

In addition to agreeing to buy back a departing shareholder's stock and the payment terms, valuation is a huge topic. No doubt, June will argue the shares are worth $5,000 each. Betty and Allison will agree they're worth about $500. The truth is probably somewhere in between.

Formulas, based upon profitability, cash flow, company revenue or other criteria, can be used to value the company. If valuation isn't addressed in the shareholders' agreement, rest assured it could become a hot issue when a shareholder leaves.

Often, absolute shareholder transfer restrictions have not been upheld by the courts. For example, if June can get a serious buyer to offer $2,000 per share, and Betty and Allison are only offering $1 per share, while a buy-back agreement will give Betty and Allison the right to acquire the shares, they'll need to do so at a reasonable valuation. They may need to match any serious offer. Of course, if June sends in her aunt August as a ringer to offer $2,000 for the shares, that's not a valid offer. Some people get very sneaky when large amounts of money are involved!

While a simple formula of valuation has simplicity and certainty, it can pose other problems in certain cases. For example, valuation of a business changes dramatically if a company goes public. Possibly, a company for which a knowledgeable business buyer would pay only $3 million might sell for $30 million or more on a publicly-traded stock market (there are entrepreneurs who hunt around for private businesses to purchase with the intent of taking them public to greatly raise the valuation). What if Betty planned to take the company public and wanted June to leave at a lower valuation?

Suppose June worked for the corporation and was doing a good job, but was then fired. Termination of an employee is often a condition to buy-back that employee's ownership interest in a company. Clearly, June would not be happy, and this could lead to a lawsuit. In addition to shareholders' agreements, shareholders working within the company as employees sometimes have employment agreements that outline the criteria for termination.

As Harvey Mackay says, the most valuable clause in a contract isn't a clause. It's knowing and trusting the people you deal with. It's not a good idea to acquire an untrustworthy shareholder.

For many small corporations, transfer of shares is restricted and isn't a common event. The same shareholders may hold their interest in the corporation for their entire lives. Compare this to large publicly-traded corporations which might sell the same share of stock five times in a day among frenzied day traders.

Corporations are allowed to repurchase their outstanding shares. Such shares are called treasury stock, as you recall. Corporations can also sell this treasury stock, subject to security laws, of course. Perhaps, surprisingly, perhaps not, a company isn't allowed to profit by trading in its own stock. Obviously, a company has inside knowledge of itself.

Repurchase of stock or sale of treasury stock often leads to what most people would call "gains" or "losses." However, the IRS doesn't allow a company to profit by trading stock in itself, so this "profit" isn't taxed or even called a "profit." Rather, it's added to an equity account called "Paid-In Capital from Treasury Stock Transactions."

Assume company officers knew their company had a major drug that might be approved by the FDA. Suppose the company remained quiet, arguing that disclosure of the approval wasn't deemed necessary to the public, because the approval hadn't truly happened yet and wasn't assured. Suppose also that the company repurchased many shares for $10. Then, upon FDA approval, the stock zooms to $40 per share. It would appear the company "made" $30 per share by buying and selling the same shares.

Here's another way to understand why profits/losses aren't recorded for treasury stock transactions. Suppose a company repurchases a share of stock for $10. Company cash is reduced and the company has one fewer outstanding share. So, it appears as if capital were returned to some investors and the total contribution to corporate capital is less. Then, if the company later sells the same share for $30, that's a separate transaction. Cash is increased by $30, but there is one more share outstanding. So, it appears that the total contribution to capital is greater and that investors have contributed more money to the company. Thus, treasury stock transactions are financing operations.

In many cases, a company does nothing illegal or unethical, but the company still has increases or decreases in equity that occur due to treasury stock transactions.

The possibility of self-dealing and self-serving stock trades by a corporation, its officers, or directors is less an issue for small non-public companies. In the above example, investors who sold shares back to the corporation for $10 might argue the company didn't disclose the drug approval properly. Such regulation is under the SEC.

Home-care maven Martha Stewart was accused of getting insider information telling her that the FDA would not consider the approval of a drug of a corporation in which she was a shareholder. Apparently, before disclosing this factual information to the public shareholders, many company insiders told friends and family to dump their shares. This is an example of insider trading and an SEC no-no.

Officers and directors of a corporation have a responsibility toward the shareholders and the corporation. When that responsibility is misused, it invites shareholder lawsuits, criminal investigations, etc. Directors and officers must be sure to treat all their shareholders fairly. Failure to do so can result in loss of liability protection and even criminal penalties.

Occasionally, with a small corporation, a "freeze out" of a minority shareholder's position becomes an issue. Let's consider June's case, again. Suppose, when she became a shareholder, it was also agreed that she'd be an employee of the corporation and would be compensated at $30,000 per year for her work. She paid $100 per share for her shares for a total of $14,000. Now, if she's fired from her position or leaves, what happens in the absence of a buy-back agreement?

Suppose Betty and Allison continue to run the company successfully. They hold controlling interest and elect the board (in the absence of cumulative voting or voting by class of stock, etc.). Suppose Betty and Allison pay themselves $60,000 per year as officers. After that, little money remains in the corporation, but what money remains is retained by the corporation and used to grow the business. Maybe, next year, Betty and Allison, as members of the board of directors, vote themselves, as officers, raises. And, they use corporate cars. And, Betty's boyfriend, twenty years her junior, is hired at $30,000 per year. His duties don't seem that important to June.

Obviously, from June's perspective, this situation sucks. Betty and Allison are running the company and having fun. They are benefiting, because each is earning excellent income and getting other corporate perks. But, June is left out in the cold. She has no way to recover her initial investment in the company or gain any financial benefit from her initial investment. When this happens to a minority shareholder, it's called being frozen out. Minority shareholders need to be alert to the unpleasant possibility of being frozen out of their interest in a corporation. Buy-out agreements help give shareholders an exit strategy, if they are "frozen out."

Angel investors sometimes call companies where money is invested into the company but no adequate way exists to achieve a financial return on the investment the living dead. A minority shareholder can always petition to have a corporation dissolved if fraud or a deadlock occurs.

Preemptive Rights And Successive Rounds Of Financing (Optional)

Preemptive rights refer to the case where newly-authorized shares are issued. The purpose of preemptive rights is similar to the purpose of stock buy-back agreements. Preemptive rights help protect the initial founders and investors in a corporation. Preemptive rights give existing shareholders the right to purchase newly-authorized shares in proportion to their current stock holdings.

For example, suppose John owns 15% of Toy Industries, Inc. Assume he holds 150 of 1,000 authorized and outstanding shares. Because Toy Industries, Inc., needs to raise more capital, it decides to create a new issue of another 1,000 shares. John has the right to purchase 150 of the newly-issued shares so that his percentage ownership in the company remains at 15%. Preemptive rights allow the individual to maintain the same percentage of ownership in the company when new shares are issued. When a shareholder's proportional interest in a corporation drops, due to the issuing of new shares, we see that the original shareholder's equity has been diluted. Preemptive rights help prevent equity dilution.

Notice the added confusion of "renormalization," discussed previously, doesn't apply to newly-issued shares and preemptive rights. This is because if a shareholder holds x% of the currently outstanding shares and y new shares are authorized and issued, and the individual is given the opportunity to purchase x% of the new shares (x% times y), the individual retains the same percentage ownership in the corporation.

It might seem that preemptive rights help an entrepreneur retain control of a corporation and they can. For example, suppose an entrepreneur owns 55% of a corporation's stock. If a new issue is made and the entrepreneur holds preemptive rights, he/she can still retain a majority of the shares.

To illustrate, suppose 1,000 shares are currently outstanding and our entrepreneur owns 550 shares. The new issue is of 1,000 shares. If one other person purchased all 1,000 shares, our entrepreneur would now hold 27.5% of the shares. The new shareholder would own 50% of the shares and now holds more voting power than the entrepreneur.

But, suppose the investors are collectively paying $10 million for 45% of the newly-issued shares. What does our entrepreneur need to pay for his or her 55% of the shares? Many people starting businesses need to raise capital and don't have the money to pay for more shares purchased under preemptive rights.

If preemptive rights involve a purchase of shares with cash, some people may lack the cash to utilize their preemptive rights. This isn't to say preemptive rights aren't something to consider. However, the right to purchase shares for cash holds little value to those without cash or the means to personally raise the cash to purchase the shares.

Sometimes, with respect to issuing shares, you'll hear the term "consideration," which refers to the benefit that the corporation receives for newly-issued shares. Consideration means that a corporation must sell its shares for no less than the value of the shares, as determined by the board of directors. Cash, property, or services already rendered are acceptable consideration for the issuance of shares.

By thinking less in terms of number of shares and more in terms of percentage ownership, you'll probably be able to more easily achieve what everyone wants. Then, calculate the number of shares to achieve the percentage ownership expected.

For example, suppose our $10 million investor expects to own 40% of the corporation and that is agreed to be a fair percentage for the $10 million. While the number of shares is quite arbitrary—the same company can be divided up into 100, 1,000, 10,000, or a million shares—percentage ownership is more absolute. Forty percent of the company is forty percent of the company.

Suppose our entrepreneur owns 55% of the previous 1,000 shares authorized and outstanding. The other 450 shares are also outstanding to previous investors. There is only a total ownership of 100% of the company, so if the corporation gives the new investor 40% ownership, the previous owners will only be able to collectively hold 60% of the company, while previously they owned 100%. Their ownership interest is diluted.

While the entrepreneur might argue it's fair for him to receive 550 of the 1,000 newly-issued shares as a performance bonus, this is something that might not appeal to the original investors. They could argue that the entrepreneur isn't paying a fair value for the shares. This means the brunt of dilution is suffered by the original investors. Situations like this are likely to lead to problems.

Suppose that, of the total 2,000 shares, the entrepreneur does wrangle to get 1,100 total shares, 55% of the company. The new investors must own 40% of the company. Without this, they won't make the deal. With only 2,000 shares, we see that they'd need 800 shares. We can see there will be a problem, because it doesn't add up. The entrepreneur holds 1,100 shares. The original investors already hold 450 shares, and the new investors require 800 shares. The total number of shares is 2,350!

Working backwards, we see that if the entrepreneur were to force the full effects of dilution upon the original investors (I'm not saying to do this! Not only is it wrong, but the entrepreneur could wind up with serious legal problems), those investors already hold 450 shares. With the entrepreneur owning 55% and the new investors demanding 40% of the total shares, this would imply that the other investors can only hold 5% of the company.

Calculating 5% of x is 450, we see that x is 9,000 shares. In other words, if the original entrepreneur receives 4,950 total shares (he'd argue that he "deserves" a bonus of 4,400 shares), the $10 million investor receives 3,600 shares. Then, the entrepreneur owns 55% and the $10 million investor owns 40%. However, look at what happened to the hapless original investors. They used to own 45% of the company. Now, they only own 5%.

The original investors would almost certainly never approve of this, and a situation like this often leads to nasty lawsuits against the entrepreneur. Always treat minority shareholders fairly. It's not only right, but failure to do so can lead to problems.

It's probably not so much the dilution to which the shareholders would object, but rather the unfair way in which their equity was diluted relative to the entrepreneur's equity. In fact, if the company were to raise $10 million and the equity were diluted fairly, the shareholders might be quite happy. Sometimes, a smaller slice of a bigger pie is more tasty than a big slice of much less.

Working from a fair standpoint, we might see something like this: The original investors' equity plus the entrepreneur's equity should represent 60% of the company after the new investment of $10 million. Of this, the entrepreneur holds his proportion. Fifty-five percent of 60% is 33%. And, the original investors hold 45% of the 60% which is 27%. Notice the ratio of the entrepreneur's equity to the original investors' equity hasn't changed. Previously, the ratio of the entrepreneur's equity to the original investors' equity was 1.22, which also corresponds to their ratio under the new financing.

Entrepreneurs and investors should be alert to the danger of equity being undesirably diluted. When selling equity for a fair value, money is brought into the corporation which benefits all original shareholders by giving the company capital to grow the business. That dilution isn't necessarily bad. However, if equity is given away at too low a valuation or at too high a valuation of personal services rendered the corporation, then, some or all original shareholders suffer.

One lesson you should see from this example is the value of having plenty of authorized, but unissued, shares to allow for future funding. Those shares can be issued by the corporation. The second lesson is the danger of equity dilution.

Incidentally, if 2,000 shares had originally been authorized, but only 1,000 issued, some preemptive rights agreements wouldn't apply to selling the second 1,000 shares, unless, of course, the preemptive rights agreement specifically mentioned the currently authorized shares as being subject to such an agreement. In other words, when forming your contracts, be sure to distinguish between newly-authorized shares and issuing more of already authorized shares, so that you achieve the preemptive rights agreement you desire. If you hold 1,000 issued shares and there are 1 million authorized shares and if the preemptive agreement only applies to new *authorizations*, you already face considerable dilution.

Many successful entrepreneurs who take companies public wind up with 5% to 10% equity in their businesses by the time their companies go public. Many entrepreneurs try to raise as much money as they can as early as they can. This can be undesirable. When a company is less established, to attract investors requires giving up a larger portion of the equity. Successive rounds of financing can be more desirable, because more money is raised when the company valuation is higher. Thus, the entrepreneurs need to give up a smaller percentage of ownership of the company.

As Steven Covey, author of *The Seven Habits Of Highly Effective People*, says, "Begin With The End In Mind." The same is true of planning financing and the share structure of your corporation. Be sure to allow for future rounds of financing and the resulting dilution in equity.

Par Value And No Par Value Stock

Some stock, called par value stock, is given an arbitrary par value. For example, you can have $0.01 par value stock, $1 par value stock, or whatever. Corporations that issue par value stock usually set the par value very low, such as $0.01.

Par is arbitrary and meaningless with the exception that a corporation can't issue par stock for amounts less than par. So, if you have $10 par value stock, an original issue of the shares cannot sell them for less than $10 per share in received value. Par value stock can always be sold for more than par.

Once shares have been sold to investors, however, those investors can sell the stock for less than par value. Similarly, treasury shares can be sold for less than par value, because that treasury stock had originally been issued for par value or greater.

No par value stock doesn't set this arbitrary number. There really is no advantage to creating high-par stock. Suppose you set par at $100. The value of your stock to potential investors will be determined by their evaluation of the worth of your company, not some arbitrary value. If they feel your company is worth at most $50 per share, but you can't sell shares for less than $100, investors won't buy.

Typically, before issuing shares in a corporation, the board of directors will determine what value represents fair value for the shares. Thus, if you can sell shares for $200, based upon the value of the company, no par shares (or par shares with par less than $200) can sell for $200.

Because of the arbitrary nature of par, it serves little real purpose, and many corporations prefer to issue no par stock. Some states charge annual fees based upon such things as the number of authorized shares or the total par value of all authorized shares. Thus, issuing high par value stock can lead to a corporation paying higher annual fees.

The par value of stock is set in the articles of incorporation, which always describe the shares a company is authorized to issue. Or, the articles describe the stock as being no par value.

Paid-In Capital And Retained Earnings

When capital is paid in to a company, the basic accounting equation, Assets = Liabilities + Equity, must always be in balance. This basic equation says that a company's assets must either be financed via some form of debt (liabilities) or some form of investment in the company (equity). Equity represents the owners' interest in the company. Equity is often called common stock, or the capital account, or sometimes just capital.

Another way to write the accounting equation is Equity = Assets - Liabilities. This says that if we add up all the assets of the corporation and then subtract all the money the corporation owes to other parties, the remaining amount is the net worth of the shareholders. (This net worth would be called the "book value," which may or may not correspond to the true market value of the company.)

For example, suppose Bubble Gum Industries, Inc., issues 1,000 shares of no par value stock for $100 each. The total paid into the company is $100,000. Immediately after issuing the shares, the basic balance sheet and accounting equation looks like this:

Assets
$100,000 Cash

Liabilities
$0

Equity (Or Common Stock)
$100,000

So assets = cash. Notice that only issued shares bring assets into a company. Authorized, but unissued, stock doesn't affect the accounting equation.

If Bubble Gum Industries, Inc., purchases a bubble gum maker for $10,000, the balance sheet changes into:

Assets
$90,000 Cash
$10,000 Bubble Gum Machine
_____

$100,000 Total Assets

Liabilities
$0

Common Stock (Equity)
$100,000

Again, the equation is in balance. With no par value stock, all paid-in capital is usually entered into one account, called the common stock account. With par value stock, two accounts are usually used. The capital account records the amount paid in up to the par value of the stock, and a second account, called "paid-in capital," or "paid-in capital in excess of par," contains the rest.

These are just accounting conventions and don't affect real money. Either way, the same amount of money is in the corporation. These accounts do not affect where real money is kept. Many people hear the word "account" and think bank account or brokerage account— a specific place where money is kept. To an accountant, an "account" can be used to intellectually divide things up in some logical fashion. The real money is probably in a bank account, a real asset account. But, the money is also considered capital and "kept" in a capital account on the other side of the accounting equation.

If Great Golf Balls, LTD, issues 1,000 shares of $1 par value stock for $50 per share, by convention the equity portion of the balance sheet is divided into two accounts, a capital account with $1,000 which represents the number of shares issued times the par value and a second account called "paid-in capital in excess of par," which has $49,000 allocated to it. Again, the accounting equation balances:

Assets
$50,000 Cash

Liabilities
$0

Equity
$1,000 Common Stock Issued
$49,000 Paid-In Capital In Excess Of Par

$50,000

It's a shame that "paid-in capital in excess of par" is often shortened to just "paid-in capital," because "paid-in capital" clearly indicates that the money has been paid-in by shareholders. Properly speaking, common stock and "paid-in capital in excess of par" are both paid-in capital. Purchasing shares or giving money to a corporation is one way to increase the shareholder's equity in a corporation. Either way, that money is paid-in.

Equity in a company can also be increased as the company earns profits. Profits increase equity through an account called "retained earnings." Each year, as a company earns profits, those profits add to retained earnings, increasing the balance of equity. Years of losses decrease equity as the losses are subtracted from the retained earnings account. Retained earnings can be negative.

Suppose, in its first year of operations, Bubble Gum Industries, Inc., earns a profit of $30,000. The end-of-the-year balance sheet might look like this:

Assets
$110,000 Cash
$10,000 Bubble Gum Machine
$10,000 Accounts Receivable
_____

$130,000 Total Assets

Liabilities
$0

Common Stock (Equity)
$100,000 Common Stock Purchased (Paid-In Capital)
$30,000   Retained Earnings
_____

$130,000 (Total Shareholders' Equity)

Notice that the profits of $30,000 have been added to an equity account called "retained earnings." The total equity or owners' interest in the corporation is the sum of capital invested in the corporation ("Paid-In" Capital) and profits earned (Total Equity = Total Paid-In Capital + Retained Earnings). Due to the profits, shareholders now have more equity in the corporation. Because equity is the owners' interest in the corporation, retained earnings ultimately belong to the shareholder. The worth of the corporation has increased and more capital is within the corporation.

Of course, dividends could be paid, reducing the retained earnings, and, thus, reducing the total equity of the shareholders, but giving them dividend cash instead. Those dividends are probably paid with cash, which reduces the amount of cash. Thus, the basic accounting equation remains in balance. For example, if a $5,000 dividend were paid, cash would be reduced by $5,000, while retained earnings would also be reduced by $5,000.

We should note that a corporation is usually expected to maintain a minimum level of capitalization, equivalent to the total outstanding par value of its stock. So, corporations don't typically pay dividends if doing so would reduce the total owners' equity below the total par value of all outstanding stock.

It's important to note that retained earnings are not an actual physical account, such as a bank account, where cash actually sits. In the above case, some of the retained earnings is cash. Another portion is in accounts receivable. Accounts receivable is money owed to the corporation. Retained earnings do not mean that an actual amount of cash sits within the corporation in some special, ear-marked bank account. The retained earnings could be cash, but they could also be any other asset, such as land, buildings, accounts receivable, etc.

Incidentally, for more advanced accountants out there, we neglected depreciation of the bubble gum machine. Depreciation means that we expense part of a long-lived asset each year. All entrepreneurs who are not familiar with basic accounting should take an accounting class at a local community college or university or devote some time to self-study of accounting and bookkeeping.

Studies have shown that even taking one basic accounting class can greatly reduce the chances of business failure. Two books I highly recommend are: *Keeping The Books: Basic Record-Keeping and Accounting For The Small Business, Plus Up-to-Date Tax Information* by Linda Pinson and Jerry Jinnett and *The McGraw-Hill 36-Hour Accounting Course* by Robert L. Dixon and Harold E. Arnett.

Chapter 6
Debt And Equity Financing

Loans

Debt financing involves the corporation borrowing money. A loan is made to the corporation with the understanding that a fixed rate of interest will be paid at regular prearranged intervals. At the end of the term of the loan, the full amount of the loan will be repaid.

If a corporation fails, before shareholders can recover any of their investment in the corporation, all loans first need to be paid in full. If a corporation liquidates and lacks the capital to repay all debts, the shareholders will receive nothing, and the lenders will receive whatever portion of their loan the corporation is capable of paying.

While people borrowing money to a corporation expect the full return of their money according to a prearranged schedule, the loan to the corporation doesn't involve any ownership of the corporation. If the company does exceptionally well, the lender isn't entitled to any more than full repayment of the loan and the appropriate interest.

In most cases, interest paid on borrowed money is a tax-deductible expense to the corporation. Interest expense reduces profitability, which reduces taxable income.

Suppose ABC Corporation borrows $100,000 and agrees to pay 10% interest annually. Suppose ABC Corporation earns $25,000 before interest expense. ABC will pay $10,000 in interest, which reduces net taxable income to $15,000.

Equity

Equity involves ownership. Equity is represented by shares of stock. There is no obligation for a corporation to repay equity investments to shareholders. For example, a successful corporation might retain capital for growth and pay no dividends. There's no timetable for the repayment of equity.

If a corporation fails, a shareholder is usually only liable up to the amount of his/her investment in the corporation. So, if John invests $1,000 in a corporation, the most John will typically lose is $1,000.

However, if a corporation does well, equity, representing ownership, can allow the shareholder to profit. For example, if John owns 10% of the corporation and the corporation is later acquired by another company for $100,000, John is entitled to receive $10,000 upon liquidation.

The corporation can pay dividends to John. Dividends paid to shareholders are not tax-deductible to the corporation (unlike loan interest) or to the shareholder. They're usually considered a return on investment. ("Dividends" from S-corporations are called "distributions" and are usually not taxable at the corporate level. The income was taxed when it was earned, not when it is distributed. Distributions are not tax-deductible expenses to the corporation.)

Loans From Shareholders To The Corporation

Loans from shareholders to a corporation are usually treated the same as any other loans, as long as certain formalities are maintained. First, the loan must be made at "arm's length" which means that the terms and conditions of the loan are comparable to terms that would be available through similar loans made by non-shareholders.

Loans must be made at arm's length to prevent the IRS from reclassifying the loan as an equity investment and the interest received as dividends.

Consider an extreme case (which would NOT be allowed by the IRS as a valid loan). Suppose each shareholder loans the corporation an amount of money that is proportional to the shareholder's equity investment. So, if the corporation borrows a total of $10,000 and John owns 10% of the corporation and Tim owns the other 90%, John loans the corporation $1,000 and Tim loans the corporation $9,000.

Further, suppose the loan agreement doesn't specify a fixed repayment date and the interest payable is determined solely at the discretion of the board of directors of the corporation. Clearly, no non-shareholder lender would make such a loan. We can see this "loan" is really a lot like equity. It's not an "arm's length transaction."

Suppose the company struggles for two years, and no "loan" repayments are made. But, in the third year, the company does very well and earns $20,000 before any interest expense. The board decides it will pay "interest" of $5,000 on the loan, with John receiving $500 and Tim receiving $4,500. Upon examination, what John and Tim are doing is treating the loan as an equity investment and treating the interest payments like dividend payments. This will almost certainly be reclassified as a non-loan equity investment by the IRS.

Why would Tim and John want to do this? *Because interest is a tax deductible expense for the corporation, while dividend payments are not tax deductible.* What Tim and John want to do is to remove money from the corporation subject to as little taxation as possible. This aspect of loans by shareholders primarily applies to C-corporations, not to S-corporations, because C-corporation entrepreneurs often seek ways to withdraw money from their C-corporations without paying doubly-taxed dividends.

Suppose Tim is in the 28% personal income tax bracket (implying a 15% dividend tax rate. See Appendix A). Assume the C-corporation earns $20,000 and pays out a dividend of $5,000. The C-corporation pays income taxes of 15% on that $20,000 which includes a tax of

$750 on the $5,000 to be paid out as a dividend. Then, Tim pays $675 on his portion ($4,500) of the dividend (recall Tim owns 90% of the corporation, so he's entitled to 90% of any declared dividends).

If, however, the $5,000 distributed to John and Tim were in the form of interest on a loan, then, the loan would be fully tax deductible to the C-corporation saving $750 in corporate income taxes.

Interest received by shareholders is fully taxable to the shareholder, just as a dividend paid is taxable to the shareholder. (We observe that for C-corporations the dividend becomes taxable to the shareholder when the dividend is *paid*. With S-corporations, actual distributions are usually not taxable, but the individual shareholders pay income tax when the profits are *earned*. So, in both S-corporations and C-corporations, money received by the shareholder is taxable to the shareholder.) However, interest is deductible to the corporation, while dividend payments aren't. This is why shareholder loans to S-corporations are somewhat less desirable than shareholder loans to C-corporations.

Suppose John and Tim operate as an S-corporation. As before, they earn $20,000. Assume no shareholder loans are made to the corporation. The S-corporation pays out $5,000 in distributions. Recall, when a C-corporation pays out cash to shareholders, it's called a dividend. When an S-corporation pays out cash to shareholders, it's properly called a "distribution."

John is taxed on his portion of the S-corporation income, which is ten percent of $20,000 or $2,000. He is taxed at his personal tax rate of 28%. Tim is taxed on his portion of the S-corporation's income, or ninety percent of $20,000, which is $18,000. He is also taxed at his personal tax rate. Whether or not any of this money is paid out as "dividends" (i.e., distributed) is immaterial. If the corporation pays out $5,000 in distributions, no other tax is due. This income has already been taxed to John and Tim. So, the payment of an S-corporation distribution doesn't trigger any taxation.

Suppose, rather than paying a distribution, this $5,000 had been an interest payment from the corporation to John and Tim. In that case, the S-corporation's income is reduced by $5,000 to $15,000. That

$15,000 passes through to John and Tim. John is taxed on $1,500 at his personal income tax rate, while Tim is taxed on $13,500 at his personal income tax rate. However, John receives $500 in interest from the corporation bringing his total personal taxable income to $2,000. Similarly, Tim receives $4,500 in taxable interest income. So, Tim is taxed on a total of $18,000.

Thus, Tim and John are taxed on the same amount of net income regardless of whether this income comes in the form of S-corporation dividends or interest paid on loans.

There are two important points. First, interest paid on loans isn't subject to employment tax, even if the loan is from an employee-shareholder. Corporate employees including officers can receive salaries. But, this salary is subject to an extra 15.3% employment tax. And, in the S-corporation situation, before distributions can be paid to shareholders, employee-shareholders will need to receive a fair wage for their services. Otherwise, the IRS might reclassify distributions as wages subject to employment taxation.

Lending money to an S-corporation at arm's length allows some money to be withdrawn from an S-corporation, even if wages aren't being paid and the company is only marginally profitable. For most profitable corporations, reasonable salaries will be paid to the officer-shareholders. Once this happens, it doesn't matter if the extra money being removed from the S-corporation is classified as distributions or interest. Taxation is the same. For C-corporations, the classification is important, because interest is deductible from corporate income and C-corporations pay income tax.

Secondly, money lent to the corporation can be repaid tax free. So, if Tim lends his corporation $9,000 and the corporation becomes profitable and no longer requires this capital, the loan can be repaid and no taxes are due on the $9,000 Tim receives. That loan principal isn't income to Tim. It's a repayment of his own money.

Thus, loans are especially suited to non-employee investors who hold an equity stake in a C-corporation, but who wish to see a cash return of their investment. Possibly, an investor will desire an equity position and will also make a loan to the corporation. The loan gives the investor a way to recover a portion of his capital from the company when the company no longer needs the capital. A loan repayment is better than a doubly-taxed C-corporation dividend.

Angel investors are often concerned with an "exit strategy" that involves how they will see an actual cash return on their investment. Balancing a loan with equity gives them a way to recover their initial cash outlay. Many investors will then reinvest this money in another company.

Accrual Accounting And Shareholder Loans

The IRS has special rules about when the interest on a shareholder loan can be deducted as an expense of the S-corporation. In particular, the IRS requires that the loan interest expense not be deducted until the interest payment is actually made to the shareholder. Essentially, because the shareholder loaning money to the corporation will be on a cash-based accounting for his/her personal income taxes, the loan to the S-corporation will also be treated on a cash-basis accounting. This prevents clever entrepreneurs from gaining a tax-advantage by holding money for excess time periods before income tax is paid, but after an interest expense deduction is claimed.

Suppose John loans $10,000 to his S-corporation and 10% interest is charged for the use of the money. If interest is paid yearly, $1,000 in interest expense is deductible to the corporation, and John receives $1,000 in interest that is taxable to him as personal income.

However, suppose the interest owed to John isn't payable for five years. We can calculate that John will be owed (1.10) to the fifth power times $10,000 in five years. That amount is $16,105. Compounding explains why John is owed more than just $15,000. (For those who want to know more about compounding, I cover the topic in both *Thinking Like An Entrepreneur* and *Becoming An Investor*). In five years, John receives his $10,000 principal back and $6,105 in taxable interest.

On an accrual basis accounting, a company would usually report the appropriate interest expense annually. For the first year, the deductible interest expense would be $1,000. For the second year, it would be $1,100. The extra $100 in interest comes from the fact that the corporation is holding $1,000 more of John's money during the second year. The third year, corporate interest expense is $1,210, etc.

Now, suppose that because John didn't receive the interest income, he didn't need to pay income tax on his accrued interest. (This *isn't* true. There are special rules for the taxation of zero-coupon bonds, which will be discussed later.) In this *hypothetical* case, you could see that, each year, the corporation would be receiving an interest tax-deduction, while John is not paying income tax on that interest until the fifth year. This would have the effect of sheltering the interest income from taxation.

Thus, even if the first year's accrued interest expense were $1,000, the S-corporation *couldn't* report that $1,000 in interest expense as tax-deductible *until* it's actually paid to the shareholder. The interest expense would become tax-deductible to the corporation in the same year the $1,000 in interest income was reported as taxable income by the shareholder.

The IRS has a second mechanism to prevent such an occurrence of tax-sheltering. A bond which returns both its full principal and its full interest at maturity is called a "zero coupon" bond, because the interest paid annually is often called a "coupon." So, a bond paying no interest until maturity has no coupon. The IRS taxes zero coupon bond interest *as if* it were received annually, even though it isn't actually received annually. This is another example of the taxation of phantom income.

So, even though John didn't receive the $1,000 in first-year interest, he reports it as taxable interest income, due to the nature of the taxation of zero-coupon bonds. But, other IRS rules say the $1,000 *isn't* deductible to the corporation *until* it is actually paid (The S-corporation must treat the interest expense on cash-basis accounting). Thus, the IRS seems to squeeze something for itself out of this deal. You can see shareholder zero-coupon type bonds are probably not particularly desirable.

Further, there is more danger that a bond that doesn't pay interest regularly will be reclassified as equity in disguise. This need for S-corporations to treat the deductions for loan interest paid to shareholders on a cash basis can also come into play if the corporation is in default on a loan, i.e., it has accrued interest that should have been paid, but hasn't actually been paid yet. The interest expense isn't deductible until the interest is actually paid to the shareholder.

Whenever a shareholder loan is made to an S-corporation, it's important the loan meets any "safe harbor" conditions to assure the loan won't be reclassified as equity. Regular payment of interest on a preset schedule is one of those safe harbor conditions. The interest rate should also be reasonable. And, the loan should be documented properly in the minutes and in a shareholder loan agreement.

Shareholder Leasing To The Corporation (Optional)

When the corporation rents or leases assets, the amounts paid for leases/rent are tax-deductible business expenses. This assumes the item rented is necessary or useful to the business and the lease is made at "arm's length," which means that rental fees and terms aren't too far away from what is considered usual.

Suppose a new corporation is formed. The founder decides to purchase a building for $300,000 for the new business. One possibility would be for the entrepreneur to contribute $300,000 to the corporation in exchange for stock and have the corporation purchase the building. However, this means the building is a corporate asset and is subject to the liabilities of the corporation. So, if the corporation is sued for $1 million and loses the lawsuit, the building is at risk in the judgment. This is true even if the lawsuit arises from use of a corporate product far away from the building. The building is a corporate asset. It can be lost.

Many businesses rent office and manufacturing space. They don't own property. So, it would be entirely acceptable for the entrepreneur to purchase this building personally and lease its use to the corporation. In this case, the building is property personally owned by the entrepreneur and not by the corporation. As long as the corporate veil wasn't pierced, a liability against the company couldn't lay claim to the building. Even if the company failed and wound up owing much money, the entrepreneur would still own the building.

The rent payments would give the entrepreneur one way of removing money from the corporation, and his/her taxable rate probably wouldn't be affected by the choice of leasing the property to an S-corporation or having the S-corporation own the property.

For example, suppose the S-corporation pays $1,000 per month in rent. We assume that is a fair rate, based upon the current rental market, to keep the loan at arm's length. Over the year, the entrepreneur receives $12,000 in rental income. The S-corporation's income is also reduced by $12,000—the expense of renting the offices. Thus, the entrepreneur and sole corporate owner pays the same amount in income tax. Rent and leasing expense on rented or leased assets paid to shareholders is similar to interest expense paid to shareholders who lend the corporation funds.

For C-corporation owners, renting personal assets to the corporation represents another way for shareholders to receive money from the corporation without the income being subject to double taxation. Care must be taken to be sure the rental agreement is properly structured and at arm's length.

For example, if $1,000 per month were considered an appropriate rental rate for the property, based upon what other local businesses paid for rent, and if the C-corporation were very successful and agreed to pay $50,000 per month for the rent, this wouldn't be acceptable to the IRS. In this case, the rent is clearly excessive and is being used solely to avoid C-corporation double taxation. It's being used to reward the shareholder without paying doubly-taxed dividends. The corporation would not enter into such an agreement with a stranger, i.e., it wouldn't be an arm's length transaction. A leasing arrangement like this is likely to get the IRS's attention and cause problems for the entrepreneur.

Of course, if the corporation owns the building, all expenses of the building become tax-deductible to the corporation. For example, utilities, maintenance, etc. Also, depreciation is allowed on the property. So, if a building costs $300,000 and has a useful life of 20 years, annual straight-line depreciation of $15,000 per year is allowed.

(Check with the IRS publications to determine your depreciation options for property).

Depreciation for real estate buildings is a unique expense. While depreciation allowance for machines roughly corresponds to a real decrease in value of the machine, because it wears out, buildings tend to *appreciate* in value. This means that while a depreciation expense is allowed which reduces taxable income, the value of the building is probably actually growing. From a tax standpoint, this is very desirable.

Most of the deductions will also be allowed if the individual owns the building, including depreciation. The individual will fill out Schedule E which attaches to his/her personal 1040 income tax return to report his/her rental income and related expenses. Because the property is increasing in value, a build-up of wealth occurs either within or outside the corporation. Often, the entrepreneur will prefer that the growth in wealth happens outside the corporation. This favors leasing. This is especially true for a C-corporation, where upon liquidation any growth in value within the corporation could become subject to double taxation.

While some business owners enjoy investing in real estate, it isn't for everybody. Owning real estate is a great deal of work. You're likely to be one of your better tenants! Some small businesses that acquire buildings find they don't need all of the space, so they rent space to other businesses. Sometimes, in addition to renting space, other services, such as Internet access, administrative assistance, etc., are provided to these other businesses. The entrepreneur's building becomes a mini-business incubator.

How About Renting Office Space In Your Home To Your Corporation? (Optional)

The building example is the sort of lease that occurs regularly within the business world. A business needs a location, but doesn't wish to invest a large sum of money to purchase real estate, so the business leases the property from some other party who owns it. These transactions can clearly be at arm's length. They offer the entrepreneur the opportunity to protect some property from possible bankruptcy of the corporation, to remove some income from the corporation, and to acquire an appreciating asset, which is depreciated from a tax standpoint, which reduces the property owner's personal taxable income.

What about a corporation that consists of a single owner where the owner works from home? Some tax "experts" and incorporation books suggest the sole entrepreneur should consider leasing space within his/her home to the corporation.

This would allow the owner to remove income from the corporation. For example, if a corporation rents one room of office space for $400 per month, that becomes $4,800 per year which the corporation reports as an expense. It reduces the corporation's income by $4,800. It also becomes $4,800 per year that the owner personally reports as rental income. However, because you're personally renting property for profit and will report this profit on Schedule E, it can be argued that you're personally entitled to deduct expenses associated with renting the office space. So, for example, you might be able to deduct a portion of your utility bills. Plus, you might be able to deduct an allowance for depreciation. Thus, your taxable rental income might be reduced by several thousand dollars.

So, some argue, if your home is worth $200,000 and you rent one-quarter of the space to your corporation and you depreciate over twenty years, you can report a depreciation expense of $2,500 per year calculated as 25% of $200,000 divided by twenty years. Plus, you can deduct one-quarter of your utility bills. Suppose that's $200. This implies your net rental income is only $2,100 and not $4,800. Thus, you personally report only $2,100 as taxable rental income, but you actually receive $4,800 in rent from the corporation. That $4,800 is fully deductible from the corporation's profits.

If you think about it for a moment, what's really happening here is that you're writing off a portion of your home and the expenses of homeownership as a business-rental expense.

However, there are some real complications to this. First, if you ever sell your home, you'll need to recover this depreciation when it turns out that the property has actually appreciated in value. Be sure local zoning or other factors don't interfere with your rental plan. Also, the classification of your home as a residence might be affected. This can have negative financial consequences upon the sale of your home. Further, this sort of transaction is likely to draw IRS scrutiny.

How can it be argued that this truly is an arm's length transaction? For example, in the absence of your corporation, would you rent 25% of your home to Happy Jack's Mail Order Emporium? Probably not.

One danger of any loan or lease to a corporation if it isn't treated as a proper arm's length transaction is that it could be declared a dividend in disguise by the IRS. If you operate an S-corporation and receive a dividend camouflaged as an interest payment or as rent, it's likely to be considered a *preferred* dividend distribution, which implies a second class of stock. Preferred distributions of dividends and second classes of stock aren't allowed to S-corporations, and your S-corporation status could be revoked by the IRS. Further, it might be argued that such favorable arrangements between you and your corporation compromise limited liability.

Personally, I'm not a fan of renting your corporation space in your home. While a few thousand in extra tax deductions is appealing, I see too many potential disadvantages. If, however, you decide to rent your corporation office space in your home, be sure to properly document the transaction. Have a corporate resolution approving the decision to rent the space. Draw up a formal leasing contract (you can find templates easily) between you, as the owner of the home, and your corporation. Be sure the transaction is as much "arm's length" as possible. For example, find out what rental space goes for on a per foot basis and charge your corporation no more than that. Read the IRS instructions for Schedule E carefully and be sure that certain deductions aren't *forbidden*. Finally, you might want to consult a tax attorney and get his/her opinion about renting your corporation space from your home.

Incidentally, while some experts argue that renting office space to your corporation is allowed, others argue that it's entirely forbidden by the IRS. This brings up a good question: Suppose you consult two experts (say two business attorneys or two business accountants) and they give you contradictory advice. Surprisingly, this isn't as uncommon as you might expect! What do you do?

Being the conservative sort, *I'd follow the advice least likely to get you into trouble with the IRS*. Other more aggressive entrepreneurs tend to follow the advice most likely to save them tax dollars. Occasionally, they pay less in taxes, and there doesn't seem to be an issue. Other times, their decision leads to paying back taxes, penalties, and interest. In the worst case, their aggressive decisions will lead to a loss of S-corporation status and double taxation will be paid on past earnings.

While you will be subject to any taxes, penalties, and fees the IRS deems appropriate, your situation might be more favorable if a tax professional has examined your returns and approved of your decisions. You can always say: "I asked my tax preparer about that and he said it was OK." At the very least, that might get you some sympathy. And, if your actions are too far removed from arm's length, a good tax professional will probably point that out. Plus, tax professionals generally keep up-to-date about changing aspects of tax law that you, as an entrepreneur or an investor, might not know.

Also, ask the IRS directly. Ask the IRS for their opinion about what you anticipate doing to see if it's correct. However, the tax laws are complex and not even the IRS professionals will always give the correct advice and interpretation of the law. In the event you receive bad advice from the IRS, you may still be liable for unpaid taxes, i.e., incorrect advice from the IRS doesn't let you off the hook. You're still liable for whatever tax the tax laws say you owe.

However, I personally feel the IRS is less likely to be harsh on you if you have documentation from the IRS showing that you asked to have the issue reviewed by the IRS and they agreed with your decision, interpretations, and tax elections at the time.

If you don't understand some aspect of the IRS instructions about some point (about shareholder loans to a corporation or whatever), the IRS website (IRS.gov) has a link which allows you to send e-mail questions to the IRS.

IRS Letter Ruling (Optional)

If your corporation faces a thorny tax issue and you really need to know how the issue will be treated by the IRS, you can have the IRS make a "letter ruling" about the issue. Letter rulings are rare for smaller corporations which have straight-forward issues. Going beyond just asking the IRS for advice, a private letter ruling (PLR) involves asking the IRS to take a close look at the issue and then "ruling" on it. The ruling is binding contract between your company and the IRS on how the tax issue will be treated. Other businesses can't take somebody else's letter ruling as precedent, although, occasionally, the IRS will decide to generalize a letter ruling into tax law.

Chapter 7
Angel Investors (Optional)

Entrepreneurs who have businesses they plan to build to substantial size and who wish to raise money for their corporations should consider angel investors as a possible source of financing.

Angel investors are usually business people with a net worth between $5 million and $20 million. They tend to invest in companies they understand and in companies they feel have good potential for profitable growth. Typical investments range from $20,000 to $200,000.

Many angel investors will invest with a "syndicate" of other angel investors, increasing the potential capital base of the corporation. "Syndicate" just means that a group of angels invests together in a venture. In addition to giving the corporation access to more money, a syndicate usually gives the corporation access to more business knowledge, personal connections, and other resources.

Private Placements And SCOR

If you seek investment from an angel investor, you need to learn a bit about raising capital. If you're seeking an angel investment, you're seeking a private placement. Private placements are exempt from the full securities registration process.

The "safe harbors," which allow you to avoid full securities registration (a process that can cost hundreds of thousands of dollars), are sometimes referred to as Regulation D offerings. The Securities and Exchange Commission (SEC) regulates investments. Regulation D contains two particular "rules" of interest to entrepreneurs seeking private investment.

The first is Rule 504. Rule 504 allows a corporation to raise up to $1 million. Further, to simplify the process and keep the costs of raising capital low, many states allow what is known as a Small Corporate Offering Registration (SCOR, not to be confused with SCORE, Small Corps of Retired Executives, an organization that offers mentoring to entrepreneurs). Under SCOR, disclosure form U-7 must be filed. The North American Securities Administrators Association (nasaa.org) has information about SCOR.

States vary tremendously in their acceptance of SCOR. The value of SCOR is that it usually allows entrepreneurs to advertise for investment in their companies. A SCOR offering is almost a "baby" public company. You'll need to check with your state for more information about SCOR. Some states will approve most registrations, while other states reject many SCOR registrations. I've been told one doughnut company touted its SCOR offering at the state fair—buy a doughnut and, hey, do you want some stock to go with it?

Unlike SCOR, most private placements prohibit any form of advertising. Further, the investors you seek should usually be defined as "accredited investors," meaning they're deemed by the SEC to have sufficient wealth and business knowledge to evaluate the quality of an investment by themselves. Individuals with a net worth above $1 million are arbitrarily defined as "accredited."

Sometimes, selling shares to a non-accredited investor can lead to problems down the road for a corporation and the entrepreneur, because the investor will claim that he/she didn't have adequate knowledge to make an informed business decision about the investment. This investor might argue that you should repay the investment personally if the corporation fails. Further, certain disclosure documents are required when you sell shares to a non-accredited investor. Dealing only with accredited investors is easier.

Rule 506

For Rule 506 offerings, a private placement memorandum is usually given to each accredited investor. Any amount of capital may be raised by a Rule 506 offering. If you plan to seek investors, you'll probably want the help of a knowledgeable business attorney to prevent problems down the road.

Intrastate Offering Exemption

Section 3(a)(11) of the Securities Act (Intrastate Offering Exemption) helps local businesses avoid full securities registration. To qualify for the intrastate offering exemption, a corporation must be incorporated in the state in which it conducts business, and it may only sell securities to residents of that state. For more information about other exemptions from full securities regulation, visit SEC.gov.

Approaching Angel Investors

The best way to approach an angel investor is to have someone who knows the angel investor introduce you. Most angel investors are extremely private, and cold calling is seldom effective. Be sure you've written a solid business plan and are prepared to answer the "due diligence" questions that will be asked. Remember, the typical angel has considerable business knowledge. It's good to learn about the individual in advance. What are his/her tastes? Political views? Hobbies? What industries does the angel prefer and why? Personal chemistry is important.

There are several good books about angel investing to help you understand angel investors and to help you determine how to best position your company to make it attractive to angels. Two books I recommend are *Angel Investing: Matching Start-Up Funds With Start-Up Companies: The Guide for Entrepreneurs, Individual Investors, and Venture Capitalists* by Mark Van Osnabrugge and Robert J. Robinson and *Angel Financing: How To Find And Invest In Private Equity* by Gerald A. Benjamin and Joel B. Margulis.

SBA Loan Guaranty Programs

Angel investors look for large returns. *Angel Financing* tells us the angel investor who put $100,000 into Ciena Corporation saw the value of his investment grow into $285 million in three years, when the company went public. According to *Angel Investing*, the angel who invested in amazon.com turned a $100,000 investment into $26 million in a few years. Returns such as these are only achieved by taking an equity position in the company, not by making a loan to the company. Angel investors aren't usually interested in making loans to a company without taking an equity position.

However, there are groups whose mandate is to help small businesses. Some of these groups make loan guarantees.

The Small Business Administration (SBA.gov) often guarantees small business loans. This means if your company is unable to repay the bank, the SBA will repay a portion of the loan. Having a small business loan guaranteed by the SBA makes it more likely a small company will receive a bank loan. Of course, if you personally guarantee a loan to your corporation, you're personally responsible for repayment of that particular loan. The SBA will typically guarantee up to 85% of a loan under the 7(A) Loan Guaranty Program, which considerably reduces a bank's risk in lending a company money.

Crowd-funding

One major change in seeking equity funding that occurred since the first edition of this book was published is that smaller companies will soon be allowed to sell shares of stock online. This legislation (Jumpstart Our Business Startups Act, for 2013) was aimed at making it easier for companies to raise capital. This method is best if your venture doesn't appeal to wealthy investors. Seeking many small investments from individuals online is an emerging field. You'll need to research the current laws affecting such offerings.

Other online funding options are available today. One game console company Ouya raised $8.5 million in a month on the website Kickstarter. Currently, Kickstarter cannot be used to offer equity in a company or seek business loans. Its goal is to fund individual projects in the fields of art, comics, fashion, film, games, music, publishing, and technology. Money contributed to a project is considered a donation. Such funding has been derisively called "Buying The Beta" because contributors often get the product produced, which may not live up to expectations.

Other Financing Options

In addition to seeking angel investors and seeking to borrow money for your corporation, entrepreneurs should be aware of other financing options that exist. The financing methods you rely upon will depend upon the nature of your company.

One method of "financing" is to seek to acquire a needed resource without spending money on it. When the founder of GoPro created his first camera for recording action events from a first-person perspective, he merely sewed a camera onto an arm strap. The entrepreneur borrowed his mother's sewing machine. Having spectacular footage of their exploits gave surfers a better chance of "Going Pro" and earning money as professional surfers. Can you borrow or rent resources you need?

A small remodeling contractor can ask for a portion of his payment up-front, giving him money to purchase materials for the remodeling job. This is customer financing. With customer financing, it's important to know you now have an obligation to complete the job for the customer or you'll need to be able to refund the prepayment.

Supplier financing isn't as well-known as customer financing. Some suppliers are willing to provide inventory or materials on consignment or on other favorable terms. A few suppliers will take a small equity position in a successful business, making them an angel investor.

GoPro became a smashing success, as it grew from $350,000 in sales in 2005 to about $500 million in sales in 2012. During this time, the company evolved from a camera on the arm of a surfer to a more sophisticated camera. Rather than seeking investments from outside angel investors to grow his business, the entrepreneur turned to financing from his semiconductor supplier and manufacturer. A business's suppliers often have a unique insight into a company. The knowledge and experience suppliers and manufacturers can provide is often as valuable as cash.

Bootstrapping is another way to grow a business. Bootstrapping is financing a business from the profits of previous sales. Understanding cash flow and knowing how fast a business is paid for previous sales is important to successfully bootstrapping. Otherwise, a rapidly growing business can run out of money to produce a wildly successful product.

A rapidly-growing business which manufacturers a physical product and receives delayed payments will have a more difficult time bootstrapping than a company which provides software, for example.

Bootstrapping is related to the the mathematical nature of compounding in that a cash investment is made (to purchase or manufacture products) and after some period of time (a compounding cycle), the cash is returned to the business (accounts receivable are collected). In addition to the initial "investment," a "return" on the investment (profits from the sales) is earned.

Bootstrapping is discussed in detail in *Thinking Like An Entrepreneur: How To Make Intelligent Business Decisions That Will Lead To Success In Building And Growing Your Own Company.*

Chapter 8
Employee Stock Options
(C-Corporations) (Optional)

Employee stock options are complex, and you'll want the help of a good business attorney if your corporation decides it will offer employee stock options. Incentive stock option plans are used to reward valuable employees by giving them the opportunity to purchase shares in your company.

For example, if you're building a software development company to sell or take public, you'll have a slightly easier time recruiting quality programmers if they can participate in some form of equity compensation. A person with a 150 IQ might not want to work 75 hours per week so that only *you* can get rich. If he has the chance to earn a substantial amount through stock options, he might be much more diligent. If an employer demands that an employee work really hard and if the employee doesn't see any benefit for himself, he'll probably leave the company and take a position elsewhere. So, stock options are used to entice, retain, motivate, and reward valuable employees.

Stock options for private companies can become valuable if the company goes public (IPO) or if the company's stock is acquired by another company.

Stock options give the option holder the right to purchase a given number of shares at a stated price up until a particular date. For example, an employee, Janet, might have the right to purchase 1,000 shares of corporate stock for $15 per share. Typically, the price at which employees can purchase the stock (the so-called strike price) is just at or slightly above or below the current valuation of the stock. In this case, if the company has one million outstanding shares, the company might have a current worth of about $15 million.

Why is the right to purchase stock valuable? If the value of the stock were to remain constant and the company were to remain privately held by its original owner, the right to purchase stock might have little value. However, suppose the company's value grows substantially in the future. This could happen, for example, through an acquisition. If an offer is made to purchase the company for $45 million, Janet could realize a gain of $30 per share for her 1,000 share option. Her stock options essentially amount to a $30,000 bonus. If the company were to go public and trade for $100 per share, she'd stand to gain $85 per share or about $85,000.

Many long-term employees of public companies such as Microsoft have become rich via employee stock options. That's what gets some employees excited about stock option plans. They hope for huge increases in the value of their stock options. Stock options also have tax advantages for both the company and the employee. From the company's standpoint, a valuable employee is being rewarded without a direct cash outflow. Equity ownership is, however, potentially diluted. When the option is exercised, the employee will be taxed at the lower capital gains tax rates. Also, curiously enough, corporate tax accounting allows companies to expense exercised employee stock options from a tax standpoint.

You might be surprised to learn you probably paid more federal income tax than did Cisco Corporation in many years. The same is probably also true of Microsoft. And, these companies were profitable. These large companies were able to deduct substantial amounts for equity compensation, reducing their taxable income to next to nothing. In fact, many investors are pushing companies to treat employee stock options the same on the corporate books as they're treated on the company's tax returns. If employee stock options are treated as an expense on the corporate tax returns, they should also be treated as an expense on the financial statements investors receive.

While stock options sound appealing, they do have potential drawbacks. First, many employees don't appreciate stock options. They're most valuable for motivating financially-savvy workers. If you operate a home cleaning business, it's unlikely your employees will be interested in stock options. They'd probably rather receive a cash bonus.

You need to consider what happens when an employee leaves your company. Usually, you'll want to reacquire the person's stock or pay him a fair price for his stock options. Also, if you operate as an S-corporation, you might find stock options will be treated as a second class of stock, forcing the corporation to become a C-corporation. If many people have options and are exercising these options, you might even find you're subject to securities laws. The situation can become very complex. This is why professional legal assistance should be sought.

Finally, unless the company goes public or is acquired by another company, employee stock options might not be too highly desired by employees. Stock options are most appropriate to growth companies with plans for an IPO or sale to a larger company. Such companies usually operate as C-corporations.

In addition to stock options, another form of equity compensation is restricted stock or restricted stock units. Another way of rewarding employees, which won't dilute equity, is to pay bonuses based upon the corporation's profits.

If you wish to consider employee stock options, there are many sources to help you learn more. The Foundation for Enterprise Development (fed.org, which is in no way associated with the government) publishes several books, including *The Entrepreneur's Guide to Equity Compensation*. Another organization is The National Center for Employee Ownership (nceo.org) which publishes *The Stock Options Book*. Entrepreneur Terry Gold has some excellent information about employee stock options on his website terrygold.com.

If you have just one or two employees who demand an equity position in your company, you might avoid a formal employee stock option plan entirely and offer those individuals stock directly. Then, of course, the company can operate as an S-corporation without any fear that the stock options could be reclassified as a second class of stock.

The Angel Investor/Manager Employee

Perhaps, surprisingly, Gerald Benjamin and Joel Margulis, authors of *Angel Financing: How To Find And Invest In Private Equity* say one of the fastest growing areas of angel investing is the manager investor.

Typically, manager-investors are older business executives or displaced technical workers who have a relatively high level of wealth, but who aren't ready for retirement. They wish to invest between $100,000 and $200,000 and are, essentially, seeking to buy their next job, while also becoming partial owners of the endeavor they serve.

Of course, if you run a one-person corporation where you are the only corporate employee, employee stock options make no sense. If you own 100% of something, you can't give yourself any more of it! In any case, whenever you contemplate giving up ownership of your company, ask what is acquired in exchange for the stock. While money is nice, often the talents, contacts, and experience of a knowledgeable worker or angel investor is just as valuable.

It's also important for employees to understand their stock options. However, corporations offering stock options shouldn't give investment or tax advice regarding the options. The potential conflict of interest or even an appearance of a conflict of interest is too great. One book to help employees understand their stock options is *Consider Your Options* by Kaye A. Thomas (fairmark.com).

Chapter 9
Directors

Directors of a corporation are elected by the shareholders according to the articles of incorporation and/or the bylaws of the corporation. If the articles and bylaws are silent on some aspect of how directors are elected by the shareholders, then, the state's corporate law statutes determine that aspect of the election of directors. It's good to include in detail how the members of the board of directors are to be elected in the bylaws.

If a question about the election arises that isn't addressed in the bylaws or articles of incorporation, you'll need to dig through the corporate statutes to find the default legal answer. As always, corporate statutes take precedence over the articles of incorporation. The articles of incorporation take precedence over the bylaws. The bylaws are usually kept in a filing cabinet or drawer, while corporate statutes are kept in the law library. It's usually easier to go to the filing cabinet than to the law library to double check something! But, if the bylaws contradict the articles of incorporation, the articles rule. If the articles contradict corporate law, corporate law rules. This applies to the election of members of the board of directors, as well as everything else.

In small corporations, the directors are often also corporate officers and shareholders. In the smallest corporation, one person is the only member of the board of directors, the president, and the only shareholder. One person serves all roles. That person might also be the only employee of the corporation, or there might be other non-owner, non-director, non-officer employees. Sometimes, one person could serve as the only director and the only officer, but there could be multiple shareholders.

In the past, some states required more than one director. People who wanted to run a one-person corporation who lived in a state that demanded more than one member of the board of directors sometimes incorporated in another state, such as Delaware, which allowed a single director. Or, else, they found people to serve in the other required board roles.

Be very careful about creating corporate board roles where the board member is deemed to have little power and only serves due to some figurehead requirement. It's best to avoid this entirely.

For example, under certain circumstances, members of the board of directors can be personally sued for failure to act in the proper and best interest of the corporation. Board members have a responsibility to act *in the best interest of the corporation*. Board members are expected to use their personal judgment in deciding matters of corporate policy and in voting on corporate issues. This is one reason board members are not allowed to vote by proxy at board meetings. It's assumed board members should fully participate in board meetings.

If a board member fails to ask the appropriate questions or does inadequate research in addressing an issue before the board, and, then, votes on the issue, there is a higher likelihood that the board member could be successfully sued, either by shareholders or by other parties affected by the corporation's decision. So, putting your non-business parents, children, or friends into board roles can invite problems. (This doesn't seem to prevent public companies from putting politicians with little business knowledge on corporate boards. Often, these politicians "earn" hundreds of thousands of dollars from their board positions.)

If you contemplate creating a board position held by a "yes person," who merely rubber stamps your desires, you might want to consult a corporate attorney to help you decide if that's really the best course and to examine some other options.

Before 2002, many CEOs of larger publicly-traded corporations tried to stack the board of directors with friends and people who would invariably agree with the CEO and "rubber stamp" any corporate decision the CEO desired. When accounting irregularities or fraud were uncovered at some of these companies, not only did the CEOs get charged, but members of the board of directors were also held personally accountable for inappropriate oversight. They failed in their duty to the corporation. Shortly after, many business executives decided to resign from corporate board positions in other companies, because they didn't want to be subjected to lawsuits directed at members of the board and they didn't really desire to fully participate in the decision-making of the company.

It's good to be on the board of directors of your own company, because you want an active say in corporate decision making. It's less desirable to serve as a member of the board of directors in a company where you aren't an officer, a major shareholder, or intimately involved with the company. Being a member of a board of directors has some degree of prestige. And, many board members are highly-compensated for their participation on the board. Unfortunately, some people serving on boards don't take their roles too seriously and don't really know too much about the business or the corporate decisions. These people can be sued for breach of duty to the corporation. Well-known CEOs are often on the board of directors of multiple companies.

While shareholders are nearly always protected from lawsuits against a corporation, board members are not, if they did not use appropriate judgment in making board decisions. Further, directors have a responsibility to the corporation. For example, if a director has a conflict of interest on an issue, he must disclose that conflict or abstain from voting on that particular issue when it's before the board.

For example, suppose the CEO of Byte Computer is also a director of Crash Computer Systems. Assume the board of directors of Crash must vote to decide whether or not to acquire the assets of Smok'n Computers, which is going out-of-business. If Byte's CEO wants to purchase the assets for his own company, clearly he has a conflict of interest in voting against the purchase by Crash. He should disclose his conflict of interest and abstain from voting on the issue. If he fails to do this, it can be argued that he has misused his position on the board of directors of Crash.

Any business opportunities that result from an officer's or director's association with the company he serves must first be presented to that corporation. An officer or director cannot hear a business proposal in his role as officer or director and decide the opportunity is so desirable he wants to pursue the opportunity on his own through another company.

So, if Harry is on the board of directors of XYZ Corporation, a company that manufactures and develops games and someone approaches Harry about a new game for the company, Harry couldn't say: "Wow! I really like this idea! You know I've been thinking of starting my own game company, and I think this would be a great first product."

Harry would have a responsibility to first present the idea to the corporation he serves. Only if that corporation decided not to pursue the opportunity could Harry pursue it on his own. Further, Harry has a responsibility to disclose all material facts about the opportunity to the other members of the board so that they can make an informed decision about whether or not to pursue the opportunity.

For example, if the game is a golf game created and endorsed by Tiger Woods, Harry should not leave out the "Tiger Woods" information, which is significant to the corporation's decision.

Conflicts of this nature are probably more common in corporations where officers and directors are not major shareholders in the corporation and when they are associated with multiple, related businesses. If Harry owns 5% of the corporation's stock, pursuing the opportunity by himself and getting 100% of the reward is more tempting than if Harry owns 60% of the corporation's stock.

The purpose of the board of directors is to oversee and set policy for the corporation. All aspects of corporate behavior are subject to the board. Even though a corporation is a separate legal entity, a corporation has no mind of its own. The corporation can't just decide it wants to start a new division to sell used cars. It can't decide it wants to borrow money. It can't decide it wants to sell off its railroad division. Only real people can make decisions like that. So, all corporate actions and decisions are made by people acting as agents of the corporation.

Directors serve at the highest level of corporate oversight. Directors are elected by the shareholders to oversee the shareholders' interests, which, theoretically, should coincide with the best interests of the corporation. Directors usually elect corporate officers to carry out day-to-day business policy. But, directors usually want to participate in major corporate decisions, such as the sale of the business, the acquisition of another business, major contracts, etc. Often, on major issues, such as selling the business, the board should bring the matter before the shareholders for their vote. States provide certain shareholder rights that must be respected by the board.

It's usually recommended that boards of directors consist of an odd number of people. One, three, five, etc. Even numbers of people can lead to stalemates. For example, in a four-member board, two people vote for some issue, while two people vote against it. In business, a stalemate is seldom desirable. (The same is true of stock voting. Two 50% stockholders can lead to an undesirable stalemate.)

Concept Of Quorum

The concept of quorum applies to the number of directors who must be present to transact corporate business. (Quorum means the number of members of a body, usually a simple majority of the body, that, when duly assembled, is legally capable of transacting business.)

For example, assume a company has five members on its board of directors and three members have been deemed to comprise a quorum in the bylaws. Quorum equals three. Any three. This means that if proper notice of a meeting of the board of directors is given and any three or more directors show up, the directors present can vote on any topic appropriate to that meeting, and the vote will be binding to the corporation. If only two directors show up, then voting on that topic must be rescheduled. The two can vote on the issue before them, but it doesn't mean a whole lot! So, a vote would probably be pointless. No formal action can be taken.

As a general rule, all directors should try to participate in every board meeting and decision. However, you probably don't want to tie the hands of the corporation and prevent it from conducting business if a director is unable to attend the meeting. Thus, you usually don't want the quorum to be too high.

Suppose you have a five-member board of directors. And, you've set the quorum at five. This means all five directors must be present for the board to act. Suppose everyone is a diligent board member. Each member studies the issues and asks questions to understand the topics the board must address. Each member shows up promptly for board meetings. Each member, except one, that is. Freddy, your uncle, who's a wealthy film producer and who's invested in your company because he likes you, always tends to take off for a weekend in Hawaii, partying with the Swedish bikini team during your annual board meetings.

All four of you sit, prepared, ready to vote. You could all even agree on every issue and you form a majority. Freddy's vote wouldn't affect the decision. But, you can't take any binding action. Your quorum requirement demands that all the board must be present. You can't vote on the issue and have the vote be valid.

Your only solutions would be to: 1) move the board meeting to Hawaii to accommodate Freddy; 2) act through consent decrees, if allowed by the bylaws, articles, and corporate statutes. This is different than proxy voting, which isn't allowed for directors voting at board meetings; 3) conduct the meeting through electronic means, such as phone or Internet (if allowed by your state); 4) remove Freddy from the board; or 5) change the bylaws to change the quorum requirement that sets the number of board members who must be present for the board to make corporate decisions. Of course, your corporation must follow the proper procedures to achieve any of these options. You couldn't just pencil in four, rather than five, as the quorum number, for example. That wouldn't be following proper procedure for amending the bylaws.

You can see the disadvantage of having too high a quorum requirement for board decisions. There is a danger of never having enough members together at a meeting to take action. Consider setting a quorum which allows for a reasonable number of board absences at a meeting.

Some people argue a high quorum can help protect the interests of minority shareholders. Maybe, Freddy disagrees with everyone else on an important decision (he wants to fire the current president and elect himself president). By not showing up, he prevents the decision from being made.

Resolving conflicts by not showing up and not communicating is not a good thing for a small corporation. Once that happens, you're probably going to have trouble with your corporation. Nevertheless, you see the concept of getting enough people *to not* show up so that a quorum isn't reached and so that no vote can be made when a particular issue is involved. While this sounds strategic for larger corporate politics, for smaller corporations, you really want everyone to resolve conflicts though discussion, and you want all personal interactions to work cordially and without hostility. Having a team that works well together is crucial to success in business.

Consider the other extreme. You have five board members, and you set the quorum at one (technically, a quorum cannot usually be set below 1/3 of the total number of directors, but bear with me for this example). This means only one board member must show up to vote on appropriate issues. Suppose Fast Eddie is one member of your board. He calls a special board meeting. (Usually a director has the authority to call a special meeting according to the bylaws. The president also usually has the authority to call a special board meeting.) Fast Eddie holds the board meeting at 1:00 a.m. in the broom closet, is the only one to show up, and replaces the current president with his brother-in-law, Tommy, who desperately needs a job, because Tommy just lost his job as a janitor.

You don't want this to happen. A higher quorum helps protect the corporation from being bound by the vote of only a few directors who happen to show up. Corporate policies and procedures are often designed to help assure proper corporate operation and fairness to all parties.

Does Fast Eddie have the *authority* to call a board meeting by himself? Almost certainly. But, if too many people have the ability to call special board meetings, you might wind up with numerous meetings to determine such things as voting for a corporate mascot or the official corporate color.

Did Fast Eddie follow the proper procedures to assure that all other members of the board of directors were properly notified as to the time and place of the board meeting? Was the topic of the special board meeting clear? Was the meeting held in a place that is deemed to be appropriate?

You can see why corporate statutes, articles, and bylaws take care to define such things as what constitutes proper notice of a meeting, definition of a quorum for board of director meetings to be valid, etc. The intent is to assure that the interests of all shareholders and members of the board of directors are treated fairly.

Thanks to political corporate maneuvering and board of director meetings scheduled in such places as the middle of the Congo jungle, the North Pole, or Mount Everest, we have thousands of pages of corporate law that specifies exactly how board of director meetings are called, where the meeting is to be held, what notice of the meeting must be given, *how* this notice must be given to members of the board, and requirements for the meeting to be valid. For a smaller corporation, all the requirements might seem excessively complex, but, remember, corporate structure might involve six officers, thirteen members of the board of directors, and hundreds of shareholders. In cases like these, all those rules and formalities help assure fairness.

This is why many corporate formalities seem needlessly complex to a one-person corporation. Quorum, proper notice of meetings, cumulative voting, etc., are all concepts designed for larger corporations with multiple, conflicting interests of the shareholders and directors. Setting the quorum at 33% of the directors or 100% of the directors doesn't matter if there is only one director.

Minutes Of The Meeting

Have you ever seen a situation where two people were in total agreement one day? They shook hands and walked away. Two days later, they meet again and each seems to remember the agreement completely differently.

To document decisions made at a meeting, minutes of the meeting are recorded. You don't need to record everything said. But, important decisions should be documented in the minutes.

If a director feels the board is making an inappropriate decision, it is particularly important for the director to be sure his comments are recorded on the issue. This helps prevent lawsuits against the director. If the director states one thing and votes differently, his vote will probably carry the most weight in the eyes of anyone later examining his actions.

For example, if a director feels improper notice was given about a special meeting, he should state so at the start of the meeting and have his objections recorded in the minutes.

If your company is required to file with the SEC, sometimes, a director who resigns because he/she feels there are corporate improprieties will demand that his/her letter of resignation accompanies one of the formal corporate filings. This prevents minutes from being fraudulently rewritten to claim the director who departed agreed fully with some aspect of corporate policy. If you're ever in a situation such as this, consult with your attorney.

A Board Of One And Consent Resolutions

If you're a one-person corporation and the only member of the board of directors, you probably don't have any corporate political maneuvering or personality conflicts. The whole concept of a meeting with oneself is rather Zen. Many of your actions can be documented with consent resolutions. You merely write: "Be it resolved that...." and fill in whatever you, as a corporate director, are authorizing. Sign and date the resolution. More tersely, write: "Resolved ..." and fill in whatever has been resolved.

Consent resolutions are signed by all directors or by a majority of the directors, as determined by the bylaws and state statutes. You don't need to pass around one particular copy which has everyone's signature. You can send out multiple copies and have each director sign and return her copy.

Even a one-person corporation should be careful to document decisions authorized by the board, which consists of just you. Because the corporation can take no action on its own and must act through agents and because major actions should be approved by the board, documenting the board has approved the action is one factor in examining whether the corporate structure has been properly followed.

If you (as the board) have not approved a major action undertaken by you (as a corporate officer), it's possible it could be deemed that you have not been granted the proper authority to act on behalf of the corporation. You have not treated the corporation as a separate legal entity, and you have not performed as a proper agent of the corporation. This could subject you to personal liability. Many factors are examined to see if the corporate veil should be pierced. You want as many of those factors as possible in your favor. And, documenting corporate decisions properly isn't particularly difficult. But, it's a formality that must be done.

If your corporation is sued, it's likely that the bylaws and minutes of meetings will be requested to verify a particular action was approved. The plaintiff is looking for any evidence that proper corporate procedure hasn't been followed.

Directors' & Officers' Insurance & Indemnification (Optional)

Many larger corporations purchase directors' and officers' insurance to protect directors and officers from lawsuits targeted at them as agents of the corporation. You can get a quote on such insurance. It tends to be very expensive, and many small corporations do not have directors' and officers' insurance.

Many corporations also pass resolutions to indemnify actions of the directors and officers. Indemnification means the corporation will pay to defend officers and directors against lawsuits arising from their roles as officer or director. And, many resolutions grant broad powers to the president and/or other officers to act on behalf of the corporation. These actions help assure that corporate officers have the authority and confidence to act on behalf of the corporation.

Indemnification clauses sometimes also appear in shareholder's agreements to prevent shareholders from transferring their shares to parties that would invalidate S-corporation structure. The clause usually says the shareholder will take no action that will cause an inadvertent termination of S-corporation status. If the shareholder takes some action or transfers shares to an ineligible party that results in the termination of S-corporation status, the shareholder indemnifies the other shareholders with respect to any damages they suffer.

Indemnification clauses are always very serious, because they expose the person agreeing to them to potential liability. If the nature of your business requires frequent contracts, learning a bit about the terms that appear in contracts and about contract law is time well spent. As a rule, if you have the choice of drafting a contract or having the other party draft a contract, you should draft the contract. This helps prevent your exposure to needless risk through "indemnification" and other clauses.

I feel the same concept also applies to writing your own corporate resolutions. Some banks and other institutions are happy to give you "corporate resolutions" that you can merely fill out. They can contain extra language that doesn't benefit your corporation but seeks to protect the interests of the organization providing the resolution.

Cumulative Voting

Depending upon your state law, cumulative voting for directors by the shareholders may or may not be the default option of a corporation. It may or may not be allowed. Most states allow corporations to choose between regular voting and cumulative voting. Corporations determine whether or not to have cumulative voting in the bylaws.

Suppose you have five shareholders and three members of the board of directors to elect. Hank and Tom each hold 100 shares. Tina and Melody each have 200 shares. Bill has 700 shares. Typically, each share is allowed one vote in any election (we're assuming only one class of common stock).

With regular voting, Bill would essentially elect all members of the board of directors. Even if everyone else voted against Bill's selections, together, they only hold 600 shares, less than Bill's 700. So, Bill's three favorite candidates would be elected to the board of directors.

Cumulative voting is designed to protect the interests of minority shareholders (minority shareholders are those who own less than 50% of the corporation's outstanding shares) by helping them achieve representation on the board of directors. Cumulative voting is a mechanism to help assure proportional representation of the shareholders, based upon their percentage ownership of the company.

With cumulative voting, each shareholder is granted one vote for each share of stock held for each board position to be elected. *But, those votes can be allocated in any fashion desired when voting for members of the board of directors.* Effectively, each shareholder receives a total number of votes calculated as his/her number of shares times the number of seats to be elected. Those votes can be cast in any way the shareholder desires.

So, with 100 shares of stock and three board positions to be elected, Hank and Tom each have 300 votes. Tina and Melody are allocated 600 votes each. Bill gets 2,100 votes. Suppose Hank, Tom, Tina, and Melody each vote for Tom as a director. Tom receives 1,800 votes. No matter how Bill votes, Tom is elected to the board of directors.

Suppose Bill votes 1,900 votes for his friend Biff. Biff will have more votes than Tom. So, Biff is elected to the board of directors. But, Bill only has 200 more votes. And, Tom wins the second seat. The third seat will essentially be determined by Bill.

For example, if Bill casts 199 votes for Bob and one vote for Betty, then, Biff, Tom, and Bob are elected to the board of directors. Due to cumulative voting, the interests of the minority shareholders are represented. Tom has been elected to the board.

Notice, if Bill's thinking, he'll realize he doesn't need to cast 1,900 votes for Biff. He only needs to cast 1,801 for Biff to assure his election to the board of directors. In fact, unless Bill misallocates his votes, he'll elect two members of the board.

Assume Bill casts 901 votes each for Biff and Bob and 298 votes for Betty. Tom again receives 1,800 votes. Tom, Biff, and Bob are again elected as the three members of the board. Even if Tom had received 902 votes and the remaining 898 non-Bill votes had been cast for Earl, another candidate, the situation would look like this:

Tom: 902 votes
Biff: 901 votes
Bob: 901 votes
Earl: 898 votes

Again, the board consists of Tom, Biff, and Bob.

Mathematical formulas can be developed for optimal voting to determine exactly how many candidates you can elect to a board of directors, based upon your percentage of the total votes. It's possible to err in casting too many votes for a particular person and wind up getting fewer seats on the board than you could have achieved.

In many small corporations, where the number of shareholders is equal to the number of directors, each shareholder often casts his or her own votes for himself/herself. Then every shareholder is elected to the board. Sometimes, a minority shareholder will cast all his votes for his favorite candidate to help assure his/her election to the board.

Be sure when you form your corporation to decide if you want cumulative voting or not. It doesn't really matter for a one-person corporation—one shareholder, one officer, and one director, all the same person. As your company grows, you can amend the bylaws to change to or from cumulative voting, change quorum requirements, etc. So, don't worry too much trying to decide if the directors' quorum should be 33%, 100%, 51%, or whatever of the number of directors, or whether or not your one-person corporation needs cumulative voting.

If you're incorporating with others, you'll need to give these voting concepts some thought to decide what's best. Each shareholder might want to consult his/her personal business attorney to examine the proposed corporate voting mechanism, as well as other issues. I emphasize that you'll want to consult your *own personal business attorney*.

According to his ex-wife, when ex-GE-CEO Jack Welch and his wife divorced, Jack generously recommended several possible divorce attorneys to his wife. Of course, those attorneys were probably friends of Jack and had loyalty to him, not to his wife. His wife wisely found her own attorney and probably got a far better settlement. You don't want your advisors or legal counsel to have potential conflicts of interest. You want them to represent your, and only your, best interest.

C-corporations sometimes have more complex voting mechanisms. For example, maybe Class A shares of stock elect one director to the board (call him/her Class A Director), while other classes of stock vote among themselves to determine other directors. Thus, each class of stock, which can all be held by one shareholder, determines a given number of board members. S-corporations can only have one class of stock.

Close Corporations vs. Closely-Held Corporations

Some states recognize the full corporate structure requiring directors is a bit extreme for smaller companies. These states allow a corporation to register as a close corporation, governed by a special set of laws for smaller corporations. A small corporation can elect to be treated as a close corporation by stating so in its articles of incorporation. That the company is a close corporation subject to close corporation treatment by the state must also be clearly stated on the stock certificates.

One simplification of a close corporation is it usually does away with the board of directors. Instead, the shareholders can elect officers directly, and, effectively, the role of shareholder becomes the role of director. (Because directors are liable for many decisions made in a corporation and because all shareholders of a close corporation are effectively acting as directors, you can see why it's necessary for someone purchasing stock to know the corporation is subject to the close corporation laws.)

Because electing directors and following corporate formality are relatively simple, you might find there is little benefit to registering as a close corporation in your state. Consult with your business attorney if you're trying to decide if it's advantageous to incorporate as a close corporation.

Not to be confused with close corporations are "closely-held corporations." Closely-held corporations are just corporations which are owned by only a few shareholders. Closely-held corporations are subject to the regular corporate law of your state. If you and your sister form a corporation, you're automatically considered "closely-held." Most incorporated small businesses are closely-held, because there are usually only a few shareholders.

Chapter 10
Officers

Shareholders own the corporation and elect directors to oversee the affairs of the corporation. Once directors are elected, in theory, directors are supposed to look after the best interests of the corporate entity and not favor any specific shareholders' interests. In practice, directors often represent the interests of certain shareholders.

One of the first acts of directors is to elect officers. Officers manage the day-to-day affairs of the corporation. The actions officers are authorized to undertake or prohibited from taking are often stated in the bylaws or, sometimes, in the articles of incorporation. Generally, any event that is outside the realm of day-to-day operations should be brought to the board of directors or to the shareholders. For example, selling the corporation, merging it into another corporation, or making a major change in business direction are big issues that should be voted upon by directors or shareholders.

Day-to-day operations include buying inventory, hiring employees, entering into contracts for the corporation, etc. Such operations usually don't require any board approval.

Some transactions border between day-to-day operations and special, extraordinary decisions. For example, do you wish to give the CEO the authority to borrow money for the corporation and to enter into loan agreements? Or, should the corporation require board of director approval for loans to the corporation? If the loan is sufficiently large, it should probably be approved by the board of directors.

The President

The most powerful officer in the corporation is the president who is sometimes also known as the Chief Executive Officer (CEO). The CEO typically has full authority to enter into transactions for the corporation, unless the right is reserved to either the directors or to the shareholders. Often, the president is the lead entrepreneur of a venture. If, however, the lead entrepreneur who formed the corporation lacks key skills, such as management and negotiation ability, the entrepreneur or the board may choose to hire a more experienced or talented CEO.

Some entrepreneurs mistakenly assume they're the most natural choice as CEO. But, many talented entrepreneurs lack the management skills for day-to-day leadership. Worse, they sometimes lack the social skills necessary for building and growing a company. To help you understand the different personality types of successful entrepreneurs, I recommend *The Four Routes To Entrepreneurial Success* by John Miner.

Consider an engineer who invents a new product with the potential to be a blockbuster product in a huge market. Suppose this inventor is also a bit of a recluse, who isn't good at incorporating other peoples' ideas and insights into his plans. If the engineer tries to become the CEO, he might drive away his best employees and potential clients. Lacking the best people, the venture might fail. However, if the lead entrepreneur recognizes his own limitations and hires a talented CEO, who possesses people and management skills, the venture might be much more successful.

One of the most stressful and confrontational decisions directors must sometimes make is the decision to replace the lead entrepreneur as the CEO. Too often, the lead entrepreneur feels he's a naturally-talented leader and is blind to his own lack of managerial talent. Sometimes, the leader is a pacesetter or someone who causes tremendous stress for employees. What the CEO perceives to be motivating might actually demotivate employees. Many companies that fail might have survived if the CEO had been replaced earlier.

Because of the dangers of poor leadership, investors in a company must address the question of how to deal with an inadequate CEO. This can be addressed in the corporate bylaws and employment contracts between the CEO and the corporation.

Venture capitalists will often demand enough voting shares to replace the CEO if this should become necessary. Angel investors sometimes feel they're backing the lead entrepreneur and will stick with that person through success or bust. Thus, the talent and background of the lead entrepreneur who wants to become the CEO becomes a key factor in influencing the financing decision made by the angel investor.

Even if the idea for the company is great, if the lead entrepreneur insists upon being CEO, but clearly presents a management problem or lacks experience, the venture probably won't get funded. To receive investment capital from angel investors one of the most important things a new venture can do is establish a top-notch management team. This sometimes means the lead entrepreneur in the venture will need to find a quality CEO. It's also possible for the lead entrepreneur to remain as president and hire a manager, who effectively acts as the day-to-day CEO for the operation.

Apparent Authority

If an officer is formally denied the authority to enter into a business transaction, but does so anyway, the corporation can be held liable for the contracts the officer entered into.

Suppose the CEO enters into a loan agreement for the corporation that is beyond his authority stated in the bylaws. For example, the loan is for $1 million, and the bylaws state that the Board of Directors must approve any loan over $500,000.

Because the entity making the loan probably assumes that the president has full authority to enter into the agreement on the corporation's behalf, it can argue that the corporation is bound by the loan agreement. So, the corporation could be responsible for the loan.

This brings up a key aspect of due diligence. *Whenever you enter into a contract you want to be sure that the party on the other side has the actual authority to enter into the agreement.* Eliminate any doubt as to exactly who has authority to do what.

Rarely, a CEO will be terminated for inappropriate management, and, immediately after termination, the CEO will enter into some sweetheart deals for himself, claiming he represents the corporation. Essentially, he's committing fraud, pretending that he's still the CEO.

Due to this possibility, if a CEO is replaced, it's important to contact major vendors and clients and let them know the CEO has been replaced. Letting them know the previous CEO no longer has authority to bind the corporation prevents the corporation from being held liable for contracts that it appeared the ex-CEO had authority to make, because it appeared he was still the CEO.

Of course, such correspondence is usually phrased politely and from a positive viewpoint. For example, the incoming CEO might write a nice letter introducing himself or herself as the new CEO and thanking the past CEO, who it is mentioned is no longer with the company, for his past years of service.

The new CEO will probably briefly espouse his or her vision for the company and say he/she looks forward to working with the vendor or client. You probably wouldn't write: "We just canned Harry as the CEO, and, so, if that sneaky bastard claims he's still CEO, he's lying. He has no authority to act for this company anymore." Harsh language can lead to harsh lawsuits. So, be generous, even if some bum doesn't deserve it.

Suppose that before departing, the CEO loaned his brother-in-law $200,000 from the corporation (or paid an overly-generous price to his brother-in-law for some useless inventory). If the loan wasn't appropriate, the corporation could sue the ex-CEO.

Derivative Shareholder Lawsuits (Optional)

Shareholders can also sue the ex-CEO for breach of fiduciary duty. Such lawsuits are often called derivative lawsuits, because the shareholders sue the ex-CEO, but any financial verdict for the corporation will benefit the corporation, not the suing shareholders directly. Derivative lawsuits mean you're suing on behalf of someone else. In this case, the shareholders are suing for the corporation.

Derivative lawsuits for breach of fiduciary duty against key officers often happen while the officers still have powerful roles in the corporation. This happens because, in practice, many times, the CEO and other key officers have strong influence upon who is elected to the board of directors, and, often, the board of directors consists of people who will support the individual officer. So, a minority shareholder may lack the voting power to replace an officer who has breached his fiduciary duty. The shareholder could still sue the corporation, or the officer, or the officer on behalf of the corporation.

Because officers can be sued by shareholders for breach of fiduciary duty, some corporations purchase insurance to defend officers from shareholder or other lawsuits that arise from their role as an officer in the corporation. This is more common in large corporations.

It's possible for a shareholder to have a derivative lawsuit on behalf of a corporation being defended by money from the corporation. In this case, the shareholders are essentially paying the legal fees of both sides.

Entrepreneurs must be sure investors know all relevant facts about the business in which they are investing to minimize the danger of being sued by unhappy shareholders. Investments from experienced angel investors, who understand the normal risks of business, are usually better than investments made by non-business people, who might feel they've been wronged, even if they haven't been. Such individuals may sue the corporation, the president, or others, even if nothing malicious has happened.

Identifying Your Corporate Role

It's important parties negotiating with the CEO know the CEO is acting for the corporation, and not in an individual capacity, when he is acting on behalf of the corporation.

Suppose John Johnson is the CEO of Alpha-Beta Corporation. Suppose Alpha-Beta enters into a contract with Gamma-Delta Corporation to purchase $1 million worth of light emitting diodes from Gamma-Delta. John Johnson will probably sign the contract as the authorized agent of Alpha-Beta.

John Johnson will want to sign the contract as "John Johnson, President of Alpha-Beta Corporation" or just "John Johnson, President." Otherwise, it might look as if John Johnson is personally committing to purchase $1 million in light emitting diodes.

As a corporate officer, get into the habit of signing corporate contracts using a signature that makes it clear you're an officer acting on behalf of the corporation. In some cases, lenders, such as banks, will not approve a loan to a small corporation. But, they might approve the loan if someone with sufficient financial resources agrees to pay the loan if the corporation fails to do so.

If you cosign a loan for the corporation, you are personally responsible for that loan. This doesn't mean that you'd be personally responsible for other debts incurred by the corporation. Some small corporations will need to have a shareholder cosign a loan. However, as your corporation grows, seek a banking relationship where individuals do not need to personally guarantee corporate loans. If the corporation possesses sufficient assets and cash flow to cover the loan, there's little reason an individual should expose personal assets to risk. Usually, you'll want to have the "person" entering into contracts be the corporation, not an individual. Don't sign a contract with your personal name, rather than the corporation's name, listed as the contracting party. For example, the diode contract should be between Alpha-Beta Corporation and Gamma-Delta, not between John Johnson and Gamma-Delta.

Treasurer, Secretary, And Vice President

The treasurer is another key officer. The treasurer usually writes the checks for the corporation and prepares financial reports. Sometimes, the treasurer is also known as a controller or the chief financial officer (CFO).

The secretary is the officer who keeps corporate records, such as minutes of a directors' meeting.

The vice president steps into the president's role if the president is incapacitated. Often, the vice president has little authority to act, unless he or she becomes president. One-person corporations won't have a vice president.

Most states allow one person to hold all corporate offices. So, if you form a one-person corporation, you can be president, treasurer, and secretary, all rolled into one. Some states may still require certain officers to be different people. For example, maybe, the same person couldn't be both president and treasurer. This is one case where you might want to seek incorporation in another state which allows a single person to hold all corporate offices.

Officers are usually elected annually. Each director usually casts one vote for each office, and the person with the most votes wins. When a small corporation is first formed, it's good to decide in advance who the president, treasurer, and secretary will be.

Chapter 11
A Resolution For Everything

A scene in the film *Fiddler on the Roof* has a group of men asking the Rabbi if there's a prayer for the Czar. The Rabbi says there's a prayer for everything. When asked for a prayer for the Czar, he says: "May God bless and keep the Czar far, far away from here."

Corporate resolutions are a bit like prayers. There's a resolution for everything or nearly so. If your corporation wishes to start a qualified retirement plan, the board will approve a resolution to start it. If the board decides to adopt a medical reimbursement plan, there is a resolution for that.

Most business attorneys should have template resolutions to cover the gamut of possibilities. Some books give several template resolutions. *The Corporate Minutes Book: A Legal Guide to Taking Care of Corporate Business* by Anthony Mancuso has sample corporate resolutions.

Corporate start-up kits, which include stock certificates, a corporate seal, etc., also include many resolutions which are fill-in-the-blank.

Accountable Plan To Reimburse Employee-Paid Expenses

One resolution your board of directors might want to adopt is an accountable plan which reimburses employees for legitimate corporate expenses that employees pay using personal funds.

For example, suppose the corporation needs to mail a corporate letter certified and you, as corporate officer, forgot your corporate checkbook when you went to the post office. You could pay for the postage with a personal check and have the corporation reimburse you later.

In general, such reimbursements should be used sparingly, if at all, to prevent blurring of corporate and personal use of funds. But, if reimbursements occur, it's best if you have a corporate resolution authorizing such reimbursements.

Reimbursement plans are useful because you might want your employees to be able to make certain purchases for the corporation, but you don't want them handling the corporate checkbook.

For example, if Andy is an agent with Upstart Talent Agency, maybe, Andy will take clients and producers to dinner or lunch. Andy would expect to be reimbursed for such expenses. So would the other Upstart agents. But, you might not have a corporate charge card or checkbook for Andy. Many small business owners follow a policy that they're the only one to write business checks and have access to the company's money. In addition, they insist that they're the only one to balance the corporate checkbook. Such a policy minimizes the danger of embezzlement. The treasurer is the one who usually cuts corporate checks.

Reimbursing employees who aren't shareholders (and who aren't related to shareholders) usually doesn't pose the danger that the corporate veil will be pierced because corporate and personal expenses are being inappropriately commingled.

You can limit the reimbursement plan to certain employees and to a certain maximum dollar amount that will be reimbursed. You can have the plan authorize select employees to make purchases for corporate use and have the corporation reimburse the employees for the exact amount of their expenses, provided the employees document the expenses.

For every reimbursement made, have the corporation retain the receipts showing what was purchased by the employee for the corporation. All businesses must keep careful records documenting their expenses. Keep the original receipts. The more clearly you can show the IRS what was purchased, the less likely you'll run into audits and questions about the validity of expenses.

Which sounds more reasonable for business expenses? $1,000.01 in miscellaneous expenses? Or, $1,000.01 in postage expense? The IRS might wonder what's included in the miscellaneous expenses, while postage expense is rather clear. Just keep the postal receipts. Some accountants say the more detail provided on tax returns, the less likely the company will be audited.

In addition to a receipt, Agent Andy should probably provide information about who was wined and dined and what business matters were discussed at the dinner. If a sale was made, so much the better! But, a lonely receipt for two steaks with wine might or might not be a business expense.

As I mention in *How To Start And Run A Small Book Publishing Company*, publishing is one area where entertainment and travel expenses are common and justifiable. Agenting is another such business. Alas, due to abuse of the category of travel and entertainment expenses, this is one expense area that tends to draw IRS audits. If your business inherently must use travel and entertainment expenses, read IRS Publication 463, which covers entertainment and travel expenses.

One good book to help you understand how to document expenses correctly and minimize the likelihood of an audit is *Minding Her Own Business: The Self-Employed Woman's Guide To Taxes and Recordkeeping* by Jan Zobel.

While you can't pass a resolution that will keep the IRS far, far away, if you follow proper business procedure, you minimize the likelihood of an audit, and you'll be fully prepared if you're company is ever audited to document your expenses and show why the expenses are tax deductible.

Sample Resolution For Opening
A Corporate Bank Account

A copy of your resolutions should be kept in your corporate folder. A copy of this resolution is also given to the bank where you wish to open an account. To make it look more "official," you can stamp your corporate resolution with your corporate seal! Whenever possible, I believe it's usually better to write your own simple resolutions than blindly accept template resolutions which are handed to you by various institutions.

Joe's Pottery Emporium, Ltd.
c/o Joe Plaster
1234 Kiln Lane
...

On January 1, 2012 by the board of directors it was

Resolved, that the treasurer, Joe Plaster, be and hereby is authorized to open a bank account on behalf of Joe's Pottery Emporium with ABC Bank, located at 666 Financial Blvd.

Employer ID number: xx-xxxxxxx

Chapter 12
Workers' Compensation

As a corporate officer, you're an employee of the corporation, and the laws regulating employee-employer relationships apply to your corporation. However, because the government recognizes that corporate officers who are significant shareholders are more "owners" than "employees," there are some exceptions to employment law when the employee is an officer and a major shareholder.

Workers' compensation is designed to compensate workers who are injured on the job. One of the purposes of workers' compensation is to eliminate expensive litigation against employers by injured workers. Employers are required by law to carry insurance to compensate injured workers. The penalties for failure to comply with workers' compensation requirements are usually stiff.

Workers' compensation laws are highly state specific, so contact your state for more information. But, most states allow corporate officers to be exempt, so the corporation will not have to purchase insurance for certain corporate officers.

Depending upon your state, there are two ways exemptions to workers' compensation work. Either, as an officer and major shareholder, you will automatically be exempt from state workers' compensation. For example, in Minnesota, Minnesota Statutes, Chapter 176, addresses workers' compensation, but it doesn't apply to executive officers of closely-held corporations which have fewer than 22,800 hours of payroll, as long as the officer owns 25% or more of the corporate stock. However, officers may elect coverage if desired.

In Wisconsin, a form must be filed with the Workers' Compensation Division by officers who wish to be exempt. Check with your state to see how workers' compensation affects the officers of your corporation.

Officers may not wish to be covered by workers' compensation. Just because an officer is covered by a policy doesn't mean that collecting in the event of an injury will be trivial. For example, insurance companies don't want one-person corporate owners falsely claiming an injury and collecting workers' compensation. Cases are often closely scrutinized, and insurance premiums are high for sole business owners. And, many corporate owners won't be subject to any real on-the-job risks. There is little reason to pay for insurance you can't use and which won't benefit you.

Some corporate officers may elect coverage. For example, workers' compensation rates are dependent upon the danger of the work. Covering roofers is expensive, because a fall from a rooftop could cause serious injury. However, if you're the owner of a roofing company and you go on the roofs yourself, you probably *want* to be covered, because a fall could end your career.

Incidentally, workers' compensation rates are affected by an "experience factor" for the corporation. For example, if you're in the roofing business, but if your workers have had few injuries relative to your industry statistics, you can wind up paying less for your workers' compensation insurance than other roofing companies. On the other hand, if your workplace seems particularly dangerous, based upon its history, the corporation will pay higher rates.

Whenever you become aware of an employment issue you think shouldn't apply to a corporate officer, be sure to investigate it with your state. You might find exceptions apply. In the case of workers' compensation insurance requirements, you, as a corporate officer and shareholder, can save yourself money by opting out if such coverage really isn't useful to you.

Unemployment Insurance (FUTA)

Unemployment Insurance (also known as Reemployment Insurance) is a government program to pay people money while they're out of work. While workers' compensation requires the corporation to purchase a private insurance policy, unemployment insurance is administered directly by your state government and by the federal government (Federal Form 940). The federal program is known as The Federal Unemployment Tax Act or FUTA. Chapter 20 goes over Form 940 in detail.

Typically, the employer pays a small percentage of wages up to some wage limit into the state's pool of unemployment funds. Federal unemployment charges 6% on the first $7,000 of an employee's wage ($420). However, if the corporation pays into state unemployment, the corporation may deduct that amount (up to 5.4%) from the federal amount. So, if you pay 5.4% in state unemployment insurance, you'll pay 0.6% in federal unemployment insurance. Unemployment is paid by the employer. It cannot be deducted from the employee's paycheck.

Because corporate officers are employees, you'll need to examine your state's position regarding unemployment insurance payments for corporate officers. Unemployment insurance isn't designed to compensate business owners if business slows down. Rulings have said that owners of seasonal businesses can't collect unemployment during the slow seasons. Further, unemployment benefits can be denied if certain criteria are not met.

Sole proprietors typically don't pay unemployment insurance. It's possible a one-person business owner would never be eligible for unemployment insurance, regardless of the business's structure. Many states deny unemployment benefits to business owners.

Do you need to pay unemployment insurance for corporate officers? Check with your state government concerning your state's policy. For example, California allows a sole shareholder to file a form to be exempt from paying unemployment insurance. It's important to check with your state on topics such as this, because you don't want your one-person corporation to pay into a program, if you can't receive any benefit as a corporate employee for the payments the corporation makes. Ask and you may find an exemption that saves you money.

Unfortunately, IRS publications say corporate officers are subject to FUTA. This is one disadvantage to operating as a corporation. As mentioned, sole proprietors don't have to pay FUTA. Further, sole proprietors' spouses and children are also exempt from paying federal unemployment taxes if they're employed by the sole proprietor. (For more about this, employers should examine IRS Publication 15 *Circular E: Employer's Tax Guide*.) Corporate employees are subject to FUTA. So, if your company hires your child and you operate as a sole proprietor, you can save just a bit of money by not needing to pay FUTA.

Because payments made to state unemployment insurance are deducted from your federal unemployment insurance payments, the state exemptions may not be as valuable as they first appear.

Workers' compensation and unemployment insurance show one of the disadvantages of incorporation for a one-person company. Once you incorporate, you are an *employee* of your corporation, and many laws, taxes, etc., that govern employee-employer relationships must be evaluated. In many cases, exceptions do exist which recognize that a corporate officer who is a major shareholder is as much a business owner as an employee.

Just as you can influence your business's workers' compensation rate, you can influence the percentage of tax you pay into unemployment insurance. Companies that hire and fire a lot and have many workers who go through unemployed periods typically pay higher unemployment rates. So, unemployment insurance is one more reason to take your time when making a hire. If your business needs to hire new people, you'll want to learn about the exemptions concerning who is eligible for unemployment and who isn't. Your hiring, termination, and evaluation policies might be influenced by the dates employees become entitled to unemployment insurance and/ or other benefits.

Personally, I feel it is fundamentally unfair to force corporate officers who own 100% of their corporation to pay into FUTA for themselves. As explained, the officer-owner will probably never collect FUTA and, so, shouldn't be forced to pay for a benefit which isn't available. Such entrepreneurs should be allowed to opt out at the federal program, just as they often can at the state level. I highly recommend writing to your Senators and Representatives and asking them to create an exemption to FUTA for corporate officers who own at least 25% of their corporation.

Self-Insurance

Sometimes, business slows down. Due to this, it's important for business owners to build a cash cushion to see them through slow business periods. The cash will be acquired during more profitable business times. Employees generally have regular paychecks. But, as the owner of a business, your income is much more closely tied to the success or failure of your company. If your corporation pays you a regular wage, you want to be sure your corporation has a modest financial reserve to pay you during a down time.

If you form an S-corporation, paying yourself a modest wage has the advantage of not forcing you to readjust your wage downward during a slowdown. But, during good times, you can withdraw more money with shareholder distributions.

Bonuses

For C-corporation owners, in addition to wages, bonuses can be paid. Bonuses are useful, because they give more flexibility as to how much is paid. More can be paid to yourself during profitable operations and less during downturns.

You must be careful the IRS doesn't reclassify your "bonus" as a dividend if you operate a C-corporation. Have a corporate resolution that sets the bonus conditions at the beginning of the year. A bonus that is "declared" at the end of the year is more likely to be disallowed and reclassified as a dividend. If, however, an officer receives a bonus based upon conditions set earlier in the year, there's less likelihood the bonus will be disallowed. Bonuses can be based upon a percentage of any net profits the corporation earns, usually paid to the officer if profits are above some given level.

Of course, to an S-corporation owner, a bonus could also come in the form of dividends (For IRS purposes they are technically called "distributions."). As long as the S-corporation officer is receiving a reasonable wage, extra money withdrawn from the corporation may as well be distributed as non-wages. If an excessive bonus is paid to a shareholder-employee of an S-corporation, the IRS doesn't care. Remember, for an S-corporation, distributions to shareholders must be in proportion to their percentage of corporate ownership. So, if you own less than 100% of the corporation, bonuses shouldn't be paid as distributions, unless you're OK with distributing cash to the other shareholders.

Chapter 13
Employees And Employee Benefits

After forming a corporation, you'll need to learn a bit about employment issues because officers are employees of the corporation. You must pay Social Security for the employees and withhold the proper amount from their wages for income taxes. As discussed elsewhere, you'll also need to pay into federal unemployment (FUTA) for corporate officers. For the single shareholder-officer-employee, this is one disadvantage of operating your business as a corporation, rather than as a sole proprietorship.

Every entrepreneur should decide if he/she plans to hire non-shareholder, non-officer employees. This is important, because you might not want to adopt too generous a fringe benefit policy if you plan to grow your company by hiring employees.

For example, in addition to providing health insurance to employees, some corporations pass a resolution which reimburses all employee medical expenses not covered in the insurance plan. This is one reason some entrepreneurs prefer C-corporations. C-corporations can offer full reimbursement of medical expenses to employees, including the officers. All corporations can offer deductible health insurance, as discussed elsewhere.

However, most large corporations, while providing health insurance, do not reimburse out-of-pocket employee medical expenses not covered in the health insurance. This can become a very costly fringe benefit if you have many employees.

With any employment benefit, ask several questions: Is the benefit available to officers who are major shareholders in the company, and is it tax-deductible to the corporation? Is the benefit taxable as income to the employee receiving the benefit? (See IRS *Publication 525: Taxable And Nontaxable Income*) Is there a problem if the benefit is made available to officers or highly-compensated employees *only*? For example, some retirement plans are deemed to be "top heavy," if they unfairly benefit owners of a corporation while denying benefits to line-level employees.

Most smaller corporations try to provide as many deductible fringe benefits as possible to officers. However, if you anticipate hiring workers, be sure to consult with a tax advisor and/or employment attorney to be certain your fringe benefit package is legally acceptable.

Here's typically how entrepreneurs learn about deductible benefits: The entrepreneur learns some company offers a benefit to its employees. For example, the entrepreneur's son worked at a computer consulting firm, and he received nearly $5,000 reimbursement for college tuition. (IRS *Publication 970* covers *Tax Benefits For Education*. Especially see Chapter 12: Business Deduction For Work-Related Education) This was a tax-deductible expense to the company, and no income needed to be reported by the student.

The entrepreneur decides he'd like to take some classes in art history and wonders if he can have the corporation pay for them. Just because workers at other companies can receive a benefit doesn't mean the same benefit will be available as a deductible expense to a major owner of a small corporation. That all depends upon what the IRS decides.

So, the entrepreneur contacts his tax attorney and learns that corporations can offer qualified tuition plans which reimburse employee college tuition. However, if over 5% of the benefits go to major shareholders, the college expenses aren't deductible. The entrepreneur learns courses and study related to his field of business are always deductible as long as they aren't necessary to meet minimum educational or certification requirements for the industry.

Oddly enough, education required to meet minimum industry requirements isn't deductible.

The entrepreneur thinks for a moment and asks, if he hires his son, can he deduct his son's tuition as a legitimate business expense? Also, if the entrepreneur's business is plumbing, can he take a history class if he writes a paper about the history of plumbing? Will the course be deductible, then? Even if the course isn't deductible, can it be paid for by the corporation and have the corporation report the value of the course as income to the employee?

Of course, if the entrepreneur has 200 employees, he might not want to reimburse tuition for all his employees. That could prove too costly and drive him out of business.

Some companies offer cafeteria plans, which offer employees the choice between higher wages or lower wages combined with a choice of certain fringe benefits. This allows the employees to choose the benefits they like. Hence, the name "cafeteria plan."

The entrepreneur can consider his/her workforce and decide if certain benefits would be highly desirable to employees. When offering benefits, it's important to note that the cost of the benefit to the corporation might be much less than the perceived value of the benefit to the employee.

For example, suppose many employees would like the corporation to offer free health club memberships. The entrepreneur might look into this and realize that individuals have little bargaining power and often pay several thousand dollars for a health club membership. The entrepreneur, on the other hand, represents many people, is good at negotiation, and works out a lower rate for his corporate purchase of the benefit. The employee sees the value of the benefit as the cost he/she would pay to acquire it.

Of course, some employees might not want a health club membership. Hence, the desirability of cafeteria plans. Retirement plans, such as a 401(k), are desired by many knowledgeable employees, and companies specialize in providing the administration of such plans to small and mid-sized businesses. Of course, you'd need to inquire as to the cost of the plan and determine if it's worth the cost. If you only have a few employees, you may find many fringe benefits offered by large corporations are prohibitively expensive for a small corporation.

Once you have employees, you'll want to get a copy of IRS *Publication 15: Circular E: Employer's Tax Guide.* Some states offer free classes about employment taxes. Minnesota, for example, offers a free publication *Course Guide: Introduction To Employment Taxes And Employer Issues And Responsibilities.* Your state might offer a similar publication.

As I wrote in *Thinking Like An Entrepreneur,* the huge growth in entrepreneurial activity will create many opportunities for companies to provide important services to small and growing companies. Employee benefit management is one of these areas. Many firms allow you to outsource employee payroll functions. So, if you feel a bit overwhelmed by all the employee-reporting requirements, don't feel too bad. An entire industry has been created to deal with the reporting requirements!

If you decide to outsource payroll functions or employee benefit management, I'd suggest getting references from several companies who utilize the firm. Also, if you want a local company, ask other local business owners who they recommend. Payroll taxes are one liability for which corporate officers, directors, and shareholders will often be held liable.

Chapter 14
Business Expenses

When you start a business, you'll produce products or services to sell to customers. In doing so, you'll generate costs which are tax-deductible business expenses. The profit your business earns is the revenue generated less your business expenses. Revenue is also known as Sales.

Profit = Revenue - Expenses

Most individuals are forced to pay for things with after-tax dollars. Assume you're in a 34% personal income tax bracket (say, 28% Federal and 6% State income tax rates). Of every dollar you earn, only $0.66 remains after income tax. *Every personal purchase made actually costs you the purchase amount divided by 0.66 in pretax earnings.* That's how much you must earn to buy something.

For example, consider purchasing a 46¢ stamp. Dividing 46¢ by 0.66, we see the stamp cost you 70¢. You needed to earn 70¢ in personal, pretax earnings to pay for it. This is how most individuals purchase things, even necessary things, like the stamp to mail your electric bill.

Generally, tax-deductible business expenses are thought of as costs necessary to market, sell, produce, and deliver your product to the customer. The costs do not need to be absolutely "necessary." But, they should be reasonable. A business could pay its electric bill online, thereby saving a stamp. But, if the company chooses to use snail mail, the stamp is tax deductible. A company doesn't "need" new office furniture, but it's a *reasonable* thing for a business to purchase. Advertising and marketing expenditures are reasonable for any business.

Running a business and trying to make money is one of the few tax-deductible hobbies! If you take up photography and purchase $2,000 worth of camera equipment, you'll need to pay for it with after-tax dollars. If you start a sideline business and try to earn some money with your camera equipment, the stuff usually becomes tax-deductible and is paid for with pre-tax dollars.

Because the IRS doesn't want every hobby photographer to claim their hobby as a business and save hundreds or thousands of dollars in taxes, the IRS has "hobby loss rules." In general, the IRS wants to see you're making a good faith effort to try to earn money with your camera equipment. It's best if your business can show a slight profit. At the least, you want to document that you've tried to make money. You've tried to market and sell your service.

If your business purchases a lot of fun equipment that you also use for your hobby or recreation, learn about the IRS concepts of hobby loss rules and listed property. Of course, a mechanic's tools are fully tax-deductible, even if one of his hobbies is rebuilding old cars. A professional tournament fisherman can deduct the cost of his fishing tackle. A travel writer can deduct the cost of trips. Any cost that is necessary and reasonable *for the particular business* is usually legitimate. You should be able to explain why a given expense is appropriate for your business.

Let's assume you use your camera 100% for your business. It's clearly fully deductible. However, the matching principle of accounting says expenses should be paired up with the resulting revenue they generate. The camera will serve you for many years. Property that has a lifetime longer than a year must often be depreciated. This means the cost of the item is deducted over several years.

Amortization is similar to depreciation. For example, when you start your business, you'll have business start-up costs that were generated before the company's first year of operation. Currently, those costs are typically amortized over 15 years. One fifteenth of the cost would be tax deductible each year for the company's first 15 years. This is comparable to straight-line depreciation, where equal dollar amounts are deducted each year until the item is fully expensed. Accelerated depreciation deducts larger amounts in the first years and smaller amounts in the following years until the item is fully expensed.

See IRS *Publication 535: Business Expenses* for more about amortizing startup costs. Deprecation and Amortization is reported on IRS *Form 4562: Depreciation And Amortization*. For every year you put new capital property into service, you'd fill out Form 4562 and attach it to your corporate tax return. If you're merely continuing to depreciate or "deduct" property already reported on previous year's forms 4562s, you'd just enter the amount on your tax return. You wouldn't need to attach another Form 4562 to your return.

You can see that as the years go on and you put more and more capital equipment into service, each depreciated under different schedules, that depreciation can become somewhat of a record-keeping chore. To help you, the IRS has a nice one-page Depreciation Worksheet on Page 23 of the Instructions for Form 4562 (reprinted at end of chapter).

One way of getting the full tax deduction immediately is to look into expensing the capital asset under Section 179. Section 179 allows you to treat capital expenditures as current year fully-deductible expenses. Tangible personal property and off-the-shelf computer software are some of the things you can immediately expense in the year purchased when you claim a Section 179 deduction for them. Section 179 deductions are also reported on IRS Form 4562.

Because our hypothetical camera is used 100% for business, it's not listed property. It's also tangible personal property. So, its cost could be fully deducted in the year of purchase by using a Section 179 deduction. Not only do you get a larger current tax deduction, but your future tax returns are simplified: You don't have to remember to include depreciation for this item in the future, because it's already been fully expensed.

Some items which are usually classified as currently tax-deductible expenses do provide future benefit. A common example is year-end marketing efforts. Those are just an ordinary business expense. Suppose it's approaching year end, and your company will have great earnings for the year.

Suppose your company is going to launch a direct mail campaign to locate new customers. Neglecting seasonal effects of responses to direct mail, there's a clear advantage to launching the marketing campaign *before* the current tax year ends.

By launching the campaign before year's end, you acquire a current tax deduction, lowering your reported income. Hopefully, the effort will increase next year's profit!

Legitimate, tax-deductible expenses which are investments creating future company value are especially desirable and should be sought.

Notice, while tax effects are significant, the decision whether or not to undertake the marketing promotion (or any other business decision for that matter) is only dependent upon whether or not the promotion will likely be profitable, neglecting all tax effects. If you spend $1 pretax on the promotion, then you should generate more than $1 pretax in the resulting earnings.

For more information about tax-deductible business expenses, I suggest getting a copy of IRS *Publication 535, Business Expenses.*

State Use Tax And Audits

When a business purchases inventory for resale, the inventory isn't usually subject to state sales tax. Only the end buyer will pay state sales tax. When a business purchases an item for its own use (and is the final user of the item), it's usually subject to state sales tax. If this sales tax hasn't been collected (for example, for an online sale of office supplies), it's the responsibility of the company to calculate and pay the tax. This tax is called "use tax." Paying use tax on items purchased for business is important. If your corporation were ever audited by your state, one of the easiest things for an auditor to do is look over your business expenses and ask: "Did you pay sales tax on this item?" The auditor knows you purchased this item, because you claimed it as an expense!

Fringe Benefits Paid To The Owner Of The Corporation

In the last chapter we introduced the concept of fringe benefits paid to employees. Fringe benefits are usually deductible to the corporation paying them. They're an ordinary business expense. Depending on the benefit, the employee often reports no income for them. They're provided as a form of compensation to help retain desirable workers.

The IRS is alert to the fact that some corporate owners might try to game the system and give themselves or family members all sorts of tax-favorable corporate fringe benefits. Because of this, if you own more than 2% of a corporation, you'll need to research the specific benefit you contemplate providing. Some fringe benefits will be treated as income when provided to the owner of a corporation.

Depreciation Worksheet (Keep for your records.)

Description of Property	Date Placed in Service	Cost or Other Basis	Business/ Investment Use %	Section 179 Deduction and Special Allowance	Depreciation Prior Years	Basis for Depreciation	Method/ Convention	Recovery Period	Rate or Table %	Depreciation Deduction

Page 23 of IRS Instructions For Form 4562.
Depreciation Worksheet.

Chapter 15
Tax Strategies

Here are some common corporation tax strategies:

1) Using an S-corporation to reduce employment taxes for the founder of a corporation. Collectively, according to the IRS, this tax strategy saves entrepreneurs billions of dollars a year.

Suppose a small business owner, operating as a sole proprietor, earns $50,000 per year. That $50,000 is subject to self-employment tax at a rate of 15.3%. So, the owner pays $7,650 in self-employment taxes. Now, self-employment taxes aren't entirely bad. They give the owner the right to collect Social Security, which is an important source of retirement income for many people.

However, suppose the business owner would rather pay less into Social Security and invest the rest of the money for himself. By forming an S-corporation, having the corporation pay the owner a wage of $25,000 per year, and giving the other $25,000 to the owner as S-corporation dividends, which are only taxed once to the shareholder, a tax savings is achieved. In this case, the savings is 15.3% of $25,000. That's $3,825 per year.

Through the power of compounding, investing this $3,825 annually in a personal retirement account can lead to a significant amount of money upon retirement. For example, over 35 years, at a 10% rate of return, $3,825 invested annually becomes $1.14 million dollars.

If you wish to read more about compounding and investment, I recommend my own book, *Becoming An Investor: Building Wealth*

By Investing In Stocks, Bonds, And Mutual Funds. I also recommend all business owners read some books about retirement planning, because small business owners are responsible for financing their own retirement. Planning ahead often means retiring a multimillionaire, while a failure to plan can lead to disastrous results.

Some readers are probably thinking, "Hey, why not pay the entire $50,000 as dividends and save more money?" The IRS expects shareholder-officers of an S-corporation to pay themselves a reasonable salary. If you're rendering services to a corporation, the IRS expects the corporation to put a fair value on those services and pay the appropriate Social Security tax. If the IRS feels your S-corporation is grossly underpaying your salary and paying large dividends solely to avoid Social Security taxation, the IRS can reallocate some of your dividends as salary and make you pay the appropriate Social Security tax.

What's an appropriate salary? If your salary is comparable to others doing similar work, that will probably be considered acceptable. Even if it's just a bit less, you probably won't be hassled by the IRS. People working full-time will generally be paid more money than those working part-time. So, for example, if you're a computer consultant working 1,000 hours per year, $30,000 might be an appropriate salary, because it corresponds to a full-time salary of $60,000, which is well within the range paid to other programmers. So, even though your salary appears low relative to what you do, it can be argued that it really isn't.

What the IRS doesn't want to see is a $5,000 salary and $55,000 in dividends for an officer-employee-shareholder who is clearly working hard. The IRS is aware of saving employment taxes by paying dividends, and this is a legal and effective strategy. Just don't overdo it. (Incidentally, for sole proprietors, the money paid into Social Security is called self-employment tax. Employees of a corporation are not self-employed. They are employees of the corporation, so they pay employment taxes, not self-employment taxes.)

In 2012 a major court case addressed appropriate compensation for shareholder-employees (Watson v. Commissioner, 668 F.3d, 1008,

8th Cir., 2012). The IRS challenged a successful CPA who paid himself $24,000 in salary while withdrawing $375,000 in distributions from his S-corporation. The court decided the appropriate compensation was $93,000 for a CPA rendering professional services.

Of course, if your company is struggling and not paying dividends, there is no obligation to pay yourself a wage. Low wages become an issue primarily when dividends are paid to employee-shareholders and when the corporation is profitable.

2) Use a corporation to legitimately turn some expensive non-deductible expenses into tax-deductible expenses.

Deductible expenses are usually considered any expense that is ordinary and necessary to operate the business. Deductible expenses include expenses, such as marketing, that help the business grow.

Most legitimate business expenses are deductible to *all* business structures, including sole proprietorships. For example, if you operate a small publishing company, some expenses might be employee salaries, rent, postage, advertising, cost-of-goods-sold, packaging material, and royalties paid to authors.

Some restrictions on tax-deductible *benefits* are placed upon sole proprietorships and even S-corporations. Benefits that can become non-deductible are sometimes called "fringe benefits," and they are usually not absolutely necessary to the business, but these benefits are desired by the owner.

C-corporations can generally offer slightly better tax-deductible benefits to employees than can other business structures, including S-corporations. As an officer of a corporation, you're an employee of the corporation, which means you're usually entitled to participate in benefit plans the corporation offers its employees. You must be very careful that certain benefits aren't "top heavy" in that they only benefit highly-compensated employees while neglecting rank-and-file workers.

Some entrepreneurs abuse tax-deductible expenses, and this often brings them trouble. For example, some entrepreneurs might have their corporation purchase a company car for the entrepreneur's use. If the car's a Porsche and it's mainly used for personal trips, and if it's claimed the car is a 100% deductible business expense, the entrepreneur is just asking for an audit.

It's important to point out that hiding personal expenses as corporate expenses is a quick way to run amuck with the IRS and even have the liability protection of incorporation disallowed.

Today, health insurance is tax-deductible to *all* small business owners, including C-corporations, sole proprietorships, limited liability companies, and S-corporations. 100% of health insurance premiums are tax-deductible to C-corporations, sole proprietors, partnerships, S-corporations, and LLCs. So, the deductibility of health insurance should not affect which business structure you choose.

Suppose an individual paid $3,000 a year in health insurance and paid 28% in federal income taxes and another 9% in state income taxes. A total of 37% of the individual's income went to income tax. Personal health insurance isn't tax-deductible and is paid with after-tax earnings. (Only if your health insurance expense is greater than 7.5% of your adjusted gross income is health insurance currently deductible to individuals.) *To earn $3,000 after-tax to pay the health insurance, the individual needed to earn $4,761.50 pretax.* And, this neglects that the money earned to pay for the health insurance was probably also subject to employment taxation at 15.3%!

However, if the health insurance had been tax-deductible, only $3,000 in *pretax* income would have been necessary to pay for it.

As Andrew Tobias, author of *The Only Investment Guide You'll Ever Need*, argues, a dollar saved *isn't* a dollar earned. Back when Ben Franklin came up with the saying that a dollar saved is a dollar earned, there was no income tax. There was no employment tax. Today, allowing for income tax and other taxes, a dollar saved is more like *two* dollars earned. To have one dollar to spend on something, you'll need to earn much more than a buck on a pretax basis.

In my opinion, individuals who don't operate businesses who purchase their own health insurance shouldn't be forced to pay for health insurance with after-tax earnings either! That's fundamentally unfair. If you purchase your own health insurance, by operating a modestly profitable small business, you'll be able to take advantage of the deduction and save thousands of dollars a year.

By the time you read this, you'll need to figure in the effects of any implementation of Obama-Care that occur. For example, some lower or moderate income individuals might receive subsidies for their health insurance. These subsidies would only be available to individuals and not to businesses. For those individuals, it might make sense to purchase health insurance individually and receive the subsidy.

The new law will also mandate that individuals who don't have health insurance will be forced to purchase it or face penalties. The law will also place extra surtaxes on some corporate health insurance plans. You'll need to balance all of these factors to decide whether you should have your corporation pay for your health insurance or whether you should purchase it as an individual. For many entrepreneurs, having your corporation provide your health insurance is probably still the best option.

If you have a business with fifty or more employees working full-time (defined for this law as 30 hours per week), you'll need to provide health insurance to your employees under the new law.

If you form an S-corporation, you'll be able to treat your health insurance as a justifiable, tax-deductible expense. According to the current rules, money the corporation pays for health insurance premiums for its shareholder-employees is fully deductible to the corporation. The amount is reported on form W-2 to the employee, but is then subtracted as a "self-employed health insurance deduction" on the employee's 1040 tax return. (See Chapter 19). The overall effect is that the income used to purchase health insurance isn't taxed as income to either the company or to the employee. Money paid for health insurance premiums is not subject to Social Security, Medicare, or unemployment tax. It's paid with pretax earnings.

I personally feel that the ability of a C-corporate structure to turn non-tax-deductible expenses into deductible expenses is overrated. One notable exception is the advantage to a family with substantial *out-of-pocket* medical expenses not covered by insurance. C-corporations can provide tax-deductible reimbursement of medical expenses paid out-of-pocket. Be sure to distinguish between providing *health insurance* as a benefit and providing *reimbursement of out-of-pocket medical costs not covered by health insurance* as a benefit.

I probably wouldn't choose a business structure based upon which fringe benefits are considered deductible. However, the laws are constantly changing, and it's possible some fringe benefit you desire is a legitimate tax-deductible expense to a C-corporation, but not to a sole proprietor or to an S-corporation.

The Disadvantages/Advantages Of A C-Corporation

So, what about the doubly-taxed dividends of a C-corporation? If you're earning a great deal of money and paying that money out to yourself, an S-corporation is probably the better option. You might not achieve the same fringe benefits of a C-corporation, but you'll more than offset this by eliminating taxation at the corporate level.

Suppose your company earns $400,000 per year before subtracting a salary for the CEO. Suppose a reasonable salary for you, as CEO, is $100,000 per year. You will pay personal income tax on that salary, but it's a legitimate tax-deductible expense for the corporation. Salaries are applicable to both C-corporations and S-corporations. Both types of corporations have employees and pay employees in a similar fashion. That leaves $300,000 that can be paid from the corporation to you as S-corporation dividends. An S-corporation is a pass-through entity from a taxation standpoint, while a C-corporation is taxed as a separate entity.

Just as a person pays taxes based upon tax brackets, so does a C-corporation. Currently, the tax-bracket structure for C-corporations is:

Earnings Amount	Tax Bracket
Up to $50,000	15%
$50,001 to $75,000	25%
$75,001 to $10 million	34%

It gets funky above $10 million, so check with your tax advisors!

A 5% surtax on earnings above $100,000, but less than $335,000, is also added to corporate profits to phase out the lower incremental tax rates for larger corporations. Essentially, the surtax means any corporation earning more than $335,000 pays a flat 34% income tax rate. So, to account for the surtax, sometimes, the corporate tax rates are written:

Earnings Amount	Tax Bracket
Up to $50,000	15%
$50,001 to $75,000	25%
$75,001 to $100,000	34%
$100,001 to $335,000	39%
$335,001 to $10 million	34%

For a C-corporation earning $300,000, the taxes are as follows:

$50,000 x 15% = $7,500   (First $50,000)

$25,000 x 25% = $6,250   ($25,000 falls into the bracket $50,001 to $75,000)

$25,000 x 34% = $8,500   ($25,000 falls into the bracket $75,001 to $100,000)

$200,000 x 39% = $78,000 ($200,000 falls into the bracket $100,001 to $335,000)

Total Tax: $100,250

In this case, the company pays a overall rate of 33.4%.

Sometimes, the rate tables are written to include the total amount of tax that can fall into each of the lower tax brackets:

Earnings Amount	Tax Bracket	Total Maximum Tax
Up to $50,000	15%	$7,500
$50,001 to $75,000	25%	$6,250
$75,001 to $100,000	34%	$8,500
$100,001 to $335,000	39%	$91,650
$335,001 to $10 million	34%	

So, if a corporation's taxable income is $150,000, we could add up the amounts in the lower brackets to get $7,500 + $6,250 + $8,500 = $22,250. This is the amount of income tax that must be paid due to income falling into the lower tax brackets. Then, $50,000 of income falls into the bracket between $100,001 to $335,000 which adds ($50,000 x 39%) = $19,500 more in tax. Thus, the total tax is $41,750. The overall tax rate is 27.8%.

If a company earns $500,000, the overall tax rate is 34%, and the C-corporation pays $170,000 in taxes.

Companies classified as "personal service corporations" are taxed at a flat rate of 35%. Personal service corporations include firms rendering professional services, such as accounting. Personally, I feel companies offering personal services shouldn't favor the C-corporation structure due to this flat rate. (Large salaries can, however, be paid to professionals in high-salary occupations, and salary escapes corporate-level taxation, because it's a tax-deductible business expense to the corporation. For a C-corporation, you must not pay too *high* a salary or the IRS might feel you're trying to disguise C-corporation dividends as salary.)

Recall, for the C-corporation earning $300,000, we paid $100,250 in federal income taxes, bringing the net after-tax income to $199,750. That money has been taxed to the C-corporation, because the C-corporation is a separate taxable entity. If the money is then paid to shareholders as C-corporation dividends, the shareholders will also pay personal income taxes on the dividends. This is the infamous double taxation of C-corporations that people wish to avoid.

In the past, C-corporation dividends were taxed higher, because they were taxed at the individual's federal income tax rate, as high as 39.6%. Today, the tax rate on corporate dividends is lower. See Appendix A3. For individuals in the 10% and 15% tax brackets, the tax rate on dividends is now 0%. For individuals in the 25%, 28%, 33%, and 35% income tax brackets, the dividend tax rate is 15%. For individuals in the 39.6% income tax bracket, the dividend tax rate is 20%.

If an individual shareholder is in the 33% personal income tax bracket and receives all $199,750 in dividends, at the personal dividend tax rate of 15%, the tax is $29,962. After all federal income taxation, the C-corporation owner is left with $169,788. This amounts to only about 56% of the original $300,000 in pretax income. Forty-four percent went to federal income tax.

We have neglected income taxation at the state level. That can lob off a good deal more. A C-corporation will probably pay taxes at the state level. Then, the shareholder will also pay taxes at the state level. This can lob off nearly another 20% in some states. We don't need to work specific state income tax rates to show just how badly C-corporation dividends are taxed. Being able to keep only 56% of your money is bad enough to illustrate the point.

Small C-corporations usually want to avoid paying any dividends. C-corporation dividends are simply too heavily taxed. Some entrepreneurs who form C-corporations try to pay themselves huge wages. Wages are an expense of the corporation and not doubly-taxed as dividends. The IRS frowns upon this and can reclassify excessive C-corporation wages as dividends.

If you operate a C-corporation and pay yourself a large salary, document the justification for doing so. In particular, show that your salary isn't out of line when compared to officers in other similar-sized companies. Show your responsibilities justify the wage. This can help keep the IRS from reclassifying a large salary as dividends. Also, be sure not to let your salary rise and fall with corporate earnings. That's a key factor the IRS examines to see if wages (and bonuses) are dividends in disguise. Bonus formulas should be set in advance and not decided at year-end. And, bonus formulas obviously cannot be based upon proportionate stock ownership.

In one case (Alpha Medical, Inc.), the tax court said that compensation of $4.4 million dollars was reasonable. The medical management company entrepreneur built the company from an investment of only $1,000 to annual profits of $7 million in five years. He turned down a $1-million-a-year position to build the company, and the investors in such a company would receive an excellent return, even with the high salary. So, many factors are used to determine a reasonable compensation.

For really high, *justifiable* wages, FICA (Social Security tax) is less of an issue. FICA taxation is made up of two components. One part covers Social Security retirement benefits and is taxed at the rate of 12.4% (half paid by the employer and half paid by the employee) *up to a maximum wage base* ($113,700 in 2013). The other component covers Medicare and is taxed at the rate of 2.9% (half paid by the employer and half paid by the employee). Starting in 2013, wages for highly-compensated employees includes an extra additional Medicare tax of 0.9% paid by the employee. Wages above $200,000 are subject to this new 0.9% tax.

There is no wage base for Medicare. *All compensation is subject to Medicare taxation.* Thus, the first $113,700 in earnings are taxed at 15.3% for Social Security and Medicare. But, wages above $113,700 are only taxed at an additional 2.9%, not 15.3%. Starting in 2013, wages above $200,000 will be taxed at 2.9% + 0.9% = 3.8%. There is no Social Security tax for wages above the wage base.

So, on compensation of $4.4 million, we could calculate the total FICA tax that would be due today. First, 15.3% of $113,700 is $17,396. Then, 2.9% of *$4.4 million minus $113,700* is $124,302. Finally, there is the new 0.9% tax on $4.2 million. That is $37,800. Total FICA tax is $179,498, which represents 4% of the $4.4 million.

Years ago, I showed on thinkinglike.com how then Presidential candidate John Edwards used an S-corporation to save $600,000 on Medicare taxation on $26.9 million he earned as a trial attorney.

It's important to note that the Social Security wage base is subject to change. There is political talk about shoring up Social Security in the future by removing the wage base entirely. This would mean all compensation would be subject to the 12.4% Social Security tax.

S-Corporation

If you wish to pay a great deal of profits from a corporation to shareholders, you'll probably prefer the S-corporation structure to the C-corporation structure. Suppose $300,000 is earned in pretax S-corporation income. This money isn't taxed at the corporate level and passes through to be taxed only once as personal income to the shareholder. (S-corporations are almost never subject to double taxation. The exception is if you first operated as a C-corporation, had accumulated earnings, and then switched to an S-corporation. Then, those accumulated C-corporation earnings would involve extra taxation when distributed.)

Neglecting personal deductions, $300,000 in personal income would correspond to a net tax of about $83,129. That's an overall tax rate of 27.7%. You'd get to keep 72.3% of your earnings, which is much better than keeping only 56%.

Thus, an S-corporation gives the liability protection of incorporation, while eliminating the infamous double taxation. It also allows a big chunk of your earnings to escape Social Security and Medicare tax.

Income Splitting

While corporations earning a great deal of money and wishing to pay that money out to shareholders will probably prefer the S-corporation status, consider the case of a moderately profitable company earning $50,000 before allowing for any wages paid to the owner, who is also a corporate officer. Suppose the owner pays himself/herself $40,000 in wages, but wishes to retain $10,000 within the company for corporate growth.

If the entrepreneur forms an S-corporation, that $10,000 is treated as pass through income to the shareholder, whether or not it is received. In this case, that $10,000 would be taxed at the incremental personal tax rate of 27.5%. However, if that $10,000 had remained within a C-corporation, it would only have been taxed at the rate of 15%. Splitting income between two different entities to lower the incremental tax bracket that income falls into is called "income splitting."

Income splitting is splitting income among multiple, taxable entities so as to reduce the maximum incremental tax bracket that income falls into. The idea is to pull some income from a higher bracket in one entity and shift it into a lower bracket in another entity.

One form of income splitting some people recommend is shifting some adult income to children, who are usually in a lower tax bracket. For example, if children are given shares of an S-corporation, they're entitled to their pro rata share of the corporate earnings, and those earnings will probably be taxed at the child's lower rate.

However, the children will also be entitled to their pro rata share of any distributions. The S-corporation may or may not distribute those earnings. Distribution of dividends is at the discretion of the corporation.

The IRS does not want to see parents claiming the child is the owner of S-corporation shares, when, in fact, the parent is the real owner. So, the transfer of S-corporation shares to children should not be taken lightly. Do you really want to give part ownership of the company to your younger children? If not, I'd probably avoid income splitting in this fashion.

Surprisingly, the IRS has ruled that one class of stock may have multiple types with respect to voting rights. So, you could have Type A stock with one vote per share and Type B stock with no voting rights. (Be sure not to call your stock Class A and Class B!) Then, you can give non-voting shares to your children. This allows corporate control to be held by the entrepreneur and not his eight-year-old.

Other entrepreneurs, running sole proprietorships or corporations, employ their children and pay them wages to shift taxable income to lower tax brackets. If you do this, be certain the wages are reasonable and the work is real. Otherwise, you could get into trouble with the IRS by claiming children employees. Also, for corporations, those child earnings are subject to employment taxation.

Accumulated Earnings

While income splitting between a C-corporation and the owner leads to saving money in current taxes, two factors must be examined in regard to income splitting. First, is the money to be used to grow the corporation? Because the IRS is aware of income splitting and wants to prevent people from forming C-corporations solely for the purpose of income splitting, the IRS imposes an extra tax on "excessive" accumulated earnings. A C-corporation can only retain $250,000, unless it has plans to use the money to fuel corporate growth. For personal service corporations, the amount is only $150,000. This tax on excessive accumulated earnings isn't an issue for an S-corporation.

A tax on "excessive" accumulated earnings has always seemed unfair to me. Who's to say the money won't be used to grow the business? Many large companies sit on tremendous financial reserves measured in the billions of dollars, but, if a smaller non-growth company does so, it might be treated as an attempt to avoid taxation. This tax is an extra 15% tax on "excessive" accumulated earnings above $250,000.

However, if you're initially only accumulating a few thousand dollars per year, it will take many years before "excessive" accumulated earnings become an issue. Plus, during bad years, if you fail to earn money, you can continue to pay yourself a wage, drawing on your saved surplus. This can be used to even out your personal income.

The ability to split income and health insurance tax-deductibility are two reasons many small companies operated as C-corporations prior to 2000. If a company was earning only $40,000 or so, before allowing for the owner's salary, most of that money was probably paid out as wages. Wages are taxed the same for both S-corporations and C-corporations. So, the S-corporation had little advantage for a moderately profitable small business. The small amount retained by the C-corporation would be taxed at a lower rate, and a great deduction was allowed for health insurance (Health insurance became fully deductible to S-corporations in 2003). No dividends were ever paid, because it could all be justified as a reasonable salary.

Growing A Business

If a company plans to reinvest and grow itself, either a C-corporation or an S-corporation will probably work. Large, publicly-traded corporations are C-corporations. Many pay little or nothing in the way of dividends. The earnings are reinvested and used to grow the corporation's sales and earnings. The goal is to create a business that has substantial value.

For some businesses, building the business to a substantial size so that the business can be sold is a great exit strategy. When you sell a business to another company or to an individual, the gain you realize is often taxed as capital gains, which is taxed at a lower rate than income. Further, when a desirable business is sold, it often is sold for several times annual earnings.

Suppose you've built a corporation earning $400,000 per year. That company might be sold for five or eight times earnings or about $2 million to $3.2 million (of course, it could also be sold for much less or much more depending upon many factors). The capital gains tax rate will only be 20% or, maybe, even only 10%. (See the discussion of IRC 1202 stock.)

The profits retained by the corporation will have been taxed during the years the corporation was growing. However, much money could have been reinvested on a pretax basis, growing the company during the corporation's earlier years.

Due to aggressive growth, some growth companies don't have large earnings. For example, amazon.com spent tremendous amounts of money on advertising to grow its revenue and gain new customers. Even while the company was losing money, it was creating a company that had value to investors. Money spent on advertising is tax deductible. Of course, a corporation must be careful to be sure that money spent to grow the company actually *does* lead to meaningful growth. For example, if money is spent on advertising that doesn't lead to acquiring profitable, long-term customers, the money spent has little value for building the future earnings power of the company.

Company Valuation: Buying And Selling A Company

Many entrepreneurs forming a corporation will want to know a bit about buying and selling a business. You might be forming a corporation to purchase the assets of another business, or you might plan on selling your corporation in the future.

I discuss buying and selling a company in more detail in *Thinking Like An Entrepreneur: How To Make Intelligent Business Decisions That Will Lead To Success In Building And Growing Your Own Company*. There are also many other books written especially for people buying and selling a business. Because buying or selling a company is probably the biggest financial decision you'll make in your life, I highly recommend going into negotiations for buying or selling a business thoroughly prepared and knowledgeable. A business attorney can help you with the legal aspects of buying or selling a business. And, an appraiser can help you establish the value of a company.

When you buy a business, there are two different ways to go about it. First, you can purchase the company's assets, such as the company's inventory and intellectual property. Secondly, you can purchase a company by acquiring its stock, which gives you ownership of all company assets, contracts, and liabilities. In either case, be sure it's clearly specified exactly what you are buying or giving up.

Buying assets usually involves less liability exposure. If you purchase a milling machine, you own the milling machine, but you aren't responsible for a lawsuit against the company that claims the milling machine lobbed off a visitor's hand long before you purchased the machine. If you had purchased the company's stock, you would also acquire all of the company's liabilities, unless provisions were made in the sales contract that stated otherwise.

The biggest danger in buying a business is purchasing a liability headache that makes the business worth much less than you paid. This is why you'll need an experienced business attorney to help you create a sold sales contract. Some profitable businesses have gone bankrupt after an acquisition because of unanticipated liabilities of the acquired business.

Similarly, when you sell a business, if you sell stock, rather than just assets, that generally exposes you to less future liability. For example, if a corporation is liquidated and the assets sold, and an unexpected lawsuit develops against the original company, an important question is: Who will the suit name as defendant? Who will be responsible for the liability? Sometimes, liquidating corporations set aside funds for future liabilities.

For many businesses, future liability isn't an issue, but if you think it could be for your company, be sure to address these questions and seek expert legal advice.

Valuation is the other key factor that a business buyer or seller must understand. What's a business worth? That's not an easy question to answer.

There are two primary ways to value a business. The first is to treat the business as a collection of assets and liabilities and value those independently. By calculating the net asset value at fair market value, you have the liquidation value of a company. If you were to sell all corporate assets, pay all liabilities, what remains would be available for distribution to the owners of the business.

We should point out the basic accounting equation (Assets - Liabilities = Owner's Equity) applies. However, to use this equation for company valuation, we must use the fair market value of the assets, not the stated book value of the assets, which is merely a way to account for expensing the assets over time.

Suppose a company purchases a machine for $10,000. Assume the machine has a useful life of four years. The depreciation on this machine is $2,500 per year for four years. After the first year, the machine has a book value of original cost minus accumulated depreciation or $7,500. After two years, the machine has a book value of $5,000. That's the "worth" of the asset as recorded in the company books. However, suppose the machine is sold at the end of year two. There is no assurance the machine will fetch $5,000 when sold on the market. Maybe the machine is outdated and only fetches $2,000. When valuing the assets of the company for sale, the proper value to use for the machine is its fair market value of $2,000.

Many business buyers/sellers hire professional business appraisers to help them value the assets of a business. If you're buying a machine, you want to be sure you're not paying too much, because you can always buy the machine from another source. And, many companies that claim to offer substantial "goodwill value" aren't worth squat.

The other way to value a company is as an "ongoing" enterprise. This assumes the company has some value above and beyond the fair market value of its net assets. For a business to be properly valued as a going concern, the company should have some ability to generate income profitably.

Consider a service company earning $300,000 per year regularly like clockwork. Suppose the company is a small dating service. The net assets of the company might be quite small. Possibly, it rents offices. So, it owns no real estate. It owns a few computers, some chairs, pens, paper, and other relatively trivial assets. (It also has a customer database, which might be highly-valued by other companies.) Suppose those physical assets have a net market value of $15,000.

Clearly, a business owner wouldn't sell the company for the net asset value. Why sell a business that consistently generates $300,000 a year in profits for only $15,000? Within a month after purchasing the company, a buyer would have earned back the full purchase price of the business and also own a company generating $300,000 per year.

This is an example of a business which would be more appropriately valued as a going concern. The question becomes: How much should a buyer pay for those $300,000 in annual profits? That depends upon exactly how stable the current profits seem to be and the future market, i.e., whether those profits are likely to grow or deteriorate. It also depends upon what is deemed to be a fair rate of return on an investment in the business. For example, does the buyer demand a 10%, 15%, 40%, or a 50% rate of return on her investment in the company?

In this case, maybe, the company is valued at three to four times earnings or about $1 million. (If we assumed a fair rate of return, given the risks, on such an investment of 25%, and we valued the business as an annuity, the value would be $300,000/0.25 or $1.2 million.) That's considerably more than the net asset value. Here the value of the business lies in its ability to continue to generate profits. Paying $1 million, a buyer could still do well. After a few short years of owning the business, the buyer would recover his/her initial investment and then also own a wealth-producing company worth a great deal of money. Because the company has value in continuing to do what it does, it's valued as a going concern.

Another way to value a business is to examine any intellectual capital within a business. Trademarks, patents, copyrights, proprietary processes, proprietary databases of information, customer lists, etc., all can have value to a buyer. Possibly, the buyer just wants the intellectual capital within the business. Sometimes, it's something quite esoteric, such as a patented way to store data on a disk or some other thing that makes most people yawn. I discuss intellectual capital in *Thinking Like An Entrepreneur: How To Make Intelligent Business Decisions That Will Lead To Success In Building And Growing Your Own Company.*

Intellectual property valuation isn't the same as valuing a going concern. For example, in *Becoming An Investor: Building Wealth By Investing In Stocks, Bonds, And Mutual Funds,* I briefly mention that Cisco Systems purchased a new start-up company called NuSpeed for $450 million. NuSpeed had no revenue at the time, and an initial investment of only $2.6 million was made in the company. Clearly, this wasn't a "going concern," but Cisco saw some value within the company that it wanted to acquire. The same is true for some medical research companies. The companies have little or no revenue, but may have value to a buyer because of proprietary process, patented genes, etc., that the acquiring company can utilize.

Valuation of Intellectual Property and Intangible Assets by Gordon Smith and Russell Parr discusses intellectual property valuation in more detail.

When you build a business to sell, you'll probably work to create a company that has value either as a going concern or due to owning proprietary intellectual property.

While selling a business is a great exit strategy for many companies, other companies will have little sales value. For example, maybe, you're a one-person company providing a professional service, such as accounting. When you retire, the business essentially ends. This businesses will probably wish to generate as much income as possible and remove it from the company. An S-corporation might be the best option.

For businesses that plan to grow and retain earnings, it's often a toss up between an S-corporation and a C-corporation. Businesses being created to be sold often operate as C-corporations. You'll need to examine both options carefully and see which suits your company best.

Selling a business is often the most tax-favorable way to extract wealth from a company, and many entrepreneurs have become extremely wealthy by building and growing a company. Sometimes, buying a business offers a great entry strategy into entrepreneurship. Be sure to learn about purchasing/selling a company before you make such a large financial decision.

Phantom Income

A growing S-corporation that's reinvesting earnings can pose a problem for shareholders. *For income taxation, S-corporation income is treated as if it passed through to the shareholders. This is true whether or not they receive the income.* Income a person is taxed on, but which is not received, is sometimes called "phantom income."

Suppose S-corporation ABC, Ltd., earns $400,000 in 2013. John owns 60% of the shares, while Tom owns 40%. From a taxation standpoint, the $400,000 income passes through on a pro rata basis. This means each shareholder is taxed on his percentage ownership of the company multiplied by the corporation's net income. John is taxed on 60% of $400,000. Tom is taxed on 40% of $400,000. John is taxed on $240,000. Tom is taxed on $160,000. This is true whether or not ABC actually distributes the earnings to John and Tom. Tom might need to come up with $80,000 or more to pay his tax liability.

One possibility would be for ABC to pay out a reasonable dividend to cover the tax burden of the shareholders. For example, assuming an overall tax rate of about 35%, if we calculate 35% of $400,000, we see ABC could pay a dividend of $140,000. John would receive a dividend of $84,000. Tom would receive a dividend of $56,000. Those amounts would just about cover the personal income tax liability. (There is a psychological blow in being handed a check for $84,000 and knowing that it's all going to the IRS!)

It's important to note a corporation is under no obligation to pay dividends or distribute earnings. This is one reason all shareholders must initially agree to S-corporation status. If the company plans to reinvest nearly all earnings to grow the business, there is very little current difference between operating as an S-corporation or a C-corporation. In each case, the corporation retains about 65% of its income for reinvestment (we neglect state taxes and recall the C-corporation tax rate would be 34%).

Personal Holding Company

A company which generates 60% or more of its earnings from passive sources and which is held by a very small number of people is sometimes called a personal holding company. As with taxation on excessive retained earnings, extra taxes on personal holding companies do not apply to S-corporations. This is because there is no tax at the corporate level for an S-corporation and the shareholder has already paid her portion of taxes on the S-corporation income.

Personal holding companies have been used to time the realization of income and gains to a single shareholder. Because the IRS felt such companies were being used to avoid individual income taxes, it created an extra tax on personal holding companies. Most C-corporations with an active business shouldn't run into problems with being labeled a personal holding company. The great bulk of a company's earnings should come from its active business.

To Invest In Other Stocks And Bonds Within Or Outside The Business

Often a single-shareholder corporation owner wonders if he/she should invest money within or outside the corporation when purchasing stocks and bonds of large publicly-traded companies. With an S-corporation, from a tax standpoint, it makes little difference. My personal feeling is that if you wish to invest earnings into the stocks and bonds of other businesses and you operate as an S-corporation, you should pay the money to yourself, as wages or dividends, and then invest from your personal account. If you've formed an SIMPLE-IRA or other tax-deferred retirement savings account, you probably should max out that account first, if possible, before using a non-tax-deferred account so that you gain the advantages of tax-deferred compounding.

Money and investments held by the corporation are corporate assets which could be lost due to a major liability of the corporation. Your personal assets are not at risk, unless the "corporate veil is pierced" and it's deemed you didn't properly distinguish the corporation's business from your own personal business. So, if you're building a huge investment portfolio, it may as well be in a private account.

With a C-corporation, some incorporation books tout the value of the dividends-received deduction. This means that C-corporations holding stock in other dividend-paying corporations can exclude 70% of those dividends from taxation.

Suppose ABC, Inc., a C-corporation, owns 100 shares of XYZ, Inc., which pays annual dividends of $1,000. Of that $1,000, only 30% of those dividends are subject to taxation. At a 15% dividend tax rate, this implies that the effective tax rate on dividends paid to the corporation by other corporations is only about 4.5% (we get this by multiplying 30% by 15%). In our example, 15% tax is due on $300. That's $45. Relative to the total amount of dividends received, this is only 4.5%.

The dividends-received deduction is one reason high-dividend preferred stock of publicly-traded companies is desirable to corporations wishing to hold income-producing investments. Seventy percent of those dividends are tax free. If the corporation had invested in bonds (of another company or treasuries), bond interest received would be fully taxable.

For building personal wealth, however, I think the dividends-received deduction of a C-corporation is overrated, because ultimately that money must come out of the C-corporation and flow to the individual shareholder. (The ability of a corporation to provide fringe benefits is greatly overrated in many incorporation books also. So, the argument that corporate wealth can be used to provide *personal* benefits and pay for a person's *personal expenses* has some real limitations.) If the money is paid in wages, it's hit with Social Security tax and personal income tax. If the money is paid as C-corporation dividends, it's hit with personal income tax, after first being hit with corporate income tax, albeit at a very low overall rate due to the dividends-received deduction.

From the example, after paying $45 in C-corporation tax, $955 remain within the corporation. If that money is paid in wages, 15.3% is lobbed off, bringing the amount received by the officer to $809. And, that money is fully taxable as personal income. Suppose the rate is 28%. That leaves $582. Similarly, if the money is paid as a dividend, it has already been taxed at the corporate level (at the 4.5% effective "dividend-received" rate), but it is also taxed as personal income. If, on the other hand, the money had been sitting in a private investment portfolio, it would only have been taxed as personal income.

Further, any capital appreciation becomes taxable at both a corporate and a shareholder level. If your dividend-paying stocks appreciate in value over the years, you need to contemplate how the money from the sale of those stocks flows to you and how it will be taxed both at a corporate level and at a personal level.

After working it out, you'll find there is little advantage to putting a great deal of money into a C-corporation, just so you can invest it in high-dividend paying stocks and take advantage of the dividends-received deduction. While the tax rate on dividends to a C-corporation is low, if that money is ultimately to come back to the shareholder, it will suffer another *level* of taxation.

If a C-corporation pays dividends to another C-corporation which then pays dividends to a shareholder, that money has been taxed three times. When evaluating alternative ways to be taxed and options for saving tax dollars, it's important to "run the numbers" through a spreadsheet or calculator to see the results of each option. Often, what sounds like a logical way to save money turns out to be less than desirable when the numbers are actually calculated.

If you want to invest in stocks and bonds to build personal wealth, consider the tax-advantaged retirement plan options which we'll cover in the next chapter.

Tax Strategy Summary

Choosing the optimal business structure helps minimize your taxation. Consider these strategies:

* Instead of operating as a sole proprietor, use an S-corporation to save thousands of dollars a year in self-employment taxes. S-corporation distributions avoid employment taxation.

* Be sure to pay yourself a reasonable salary before you withdraw substantial S-corporation distributions.

* Use the corporate business structure to make your health insurance fully tax deductible and paid with pre-tax dollars. This can save entrepreneurs substantial tax dollars.

* Carefully examine the IRS rules for any specific fringe benefit you wish to provide to yourself via your own corporation. Trying to make too many of your personal expenses "tax-deductible" is a quick way for small business owners to run amuck of the IRS.

* Building and growing a business that is sold for a multiple of earnings is one of the most powerful ways to build wealth. It allows you to benefit from lower capital gains tax rates.

* If you're building a business to sell it, learn about business valuation. If your company creates intellectual property, invest some time understanding how to value it. Don't overlook the value of customer lists and other non-tangible assets.

* Highly profitable businesses, which don't need to reinvest the money into the business, should consider the S-corporation to avoid the double taxation of C-corporation dividends.

* Be aware of "phantom income" which can raise your personal tax liability.

* If you operate as a C-corporation and if you retain "excessive" accumulated earnings, be prepared to explain why your corporation needs those earnings for contingencies and future growth.

* If you wish to remove larger amounts of money from a C-corporation without paying heavily-taxed dividends, consider increasing officer salary. Be prepared to justify the high salary to the IRS.

* Once your business is sufficiently profitable, consider starting a tax-deferred retirement account for yourself. Especially, if you're a younger entrepreneur and investor, learn about the power of compounding and how money can grow over time. See Chapter 16.

Chapter 16
Retirement Plans (Optional)

Qualified Plans

Corporations can adopt qualified retirement plans which allow the corporation to save money for employee retirements. Qualified plans are deductible to the corporation, and the employee typically doesn't pay taxes on money contributed by the employer. Qualified plans are valuable, because the money contributed to the plan generally grows tax-deferred. Other retirement plans allow employees to save a portion of their income in a tax-deferred savings account. The cost of administering retirement plans is usually tax deductible.

There are two basic types of qualified retirement plans—defined contribution plans and defined benefit plans. Defined benefit plans fix the retirement benefit to be received by the employee. For example, maybe the employee is to receive $1,000 per month at retirement. How much must be saved each year to provide $1,000 per month at retirement is calculated based upon the estimated rate of return achieved on invested sums, life expectancy, and the number of years the employee has until retirement. I feel defined benefit plans should be avoided by small corporations.

Disadvantages of defined benefit plans include complexity. To predict how much currently needs to be saved to provide an income of $1,000 per month fifteen years from now depends upon many actuarial assumptions, such as what rate of return will be achieved on the money invested. Such plans will require professional help and constant evaluation.

A bigger disadvantage of defined benefit plans is that you must save a certain amount, regardless of whether or not the corporation has earnings and is capable of saving for employee retirement. If actuarial assumptions suggest you must save $5,000 this year to meet the future benefit, but the corporation loses money during the year, that creates a problem. In practice, the best entrepreneurs can ever really do is save what they can. It does little good to calculate that you should save $5,000 this year if you simply don't have the money.

Defined benefit plans could be the right choice for entrepreneurs who have solid corporate cash flow and high earnings. Defined benefit plans allow large sums of money to be contributed toward retirement.

Defined contribution plans define how much can be contributed to the plan. The actual benefit received during retirement is a function of how much has been invested and how well that money has grown due to good investments. Often, 1% to 25% of an employee's wages and bonuses may be contributed to a qualified retirement plan. All plans set a maximum amount that can be contributed annually.

Many plans have template versions that are IRS qualified and available through brokerage firms, such as Vanguard and Charles Schwab. Brokerage firms can help you set up your plan.

S-Corporation Issues And The SIMPLE-IRA

If you run an S-corporation and pay yourself a modest but reasonable salary, you might find a SIMPLE-IRA is a desirable choice. Remember, the amounts that can be saved toward retirement plans are usually based upon salary, and S-corporation owners often pay relatively low salaries. One advantage of a higher salary is the ability to contribute more to a tax-deferred retirement plan.

A SIMPLE-IRA is allowed if you have 100 or fewer employees. In 2013, up to $12,000 can be saved by employees from their salary. And, employees can save the full $12,000, even if their salary is only $12,000. Employees over fifty can save slightly more. The maximum contribution amounts for all retirement plans are subject to increase over the years due to cost of living adjustments.

For smaller companies, a SIMPLE-IRA might be a better choice than a 401(k), because it costs less to administer. The employee contributions reduce the employee's taxable income, and plan expenses are deductible to the corporation.

Large companies will want to examine the 401(k) option, because many employees desire 401(k)s. If you need more options, there is also a SIMPLE 401(k).

Suppose your S-corporation pays you a modest but reasonable salary of $50,000. Any additional income is paid as dividends to minimize Social Security taxes. The most any defined-contribution retirement plan will allow you to save is typically about 25% of $50,000 or about $12,500. This is very close to the SIMPLE-IRA maximum, making the SIMPLE-IRA an attractive option for modest-salaried corporate owners.

SIMPLE stands for Savings Incentive Match Plan for Employees. "Incentive Match" is a key phrase. The employer is usually required to match the employee's contribution dollar for dollar up to 3% of the employee's compensation. Other matching options are also allowed.

Employer matching contributions and deposits of deferred compensation to all retirement plans must be made in a timely fashion. If you want to look into a SIMPLE-IRA, download IRS Publication 4334: *Simple IRA Plans For Small Businesses.*

The employee is allowed to have a personal IRA in addition to the SIMPLE-IRA. After two years' participation in a SIMPLE-IRA, you're allowed to roll the money over into a conventional IRA. If you contemplate closing your corporation, you'll probably want to transfer your SIMPLE-IRA money into your personal IRA, so you can continue to receive the benefits of tax-deferred compounding.

To establish a SIMPLE-IRA, the board of directors approves the plan, and the president completes IRS Form 5305-SIMPLE. Another form, IRS Form 5304-SIMPLE allows each individual employee to select the financial institution to hold his/her personal account.

Of course, if you're a one-person corporation, or if you have a limited number of employees, you might just choose one reliable, low-cost brokerage account. Because Vanguard offers a range of low-cost index funds and other investment choices, I'd examine Vanguard as one possibility. More active stock traders might choose Charles Schwab or another discount brokerage firm. Forming a retirement plan couldn't be simpler.

SEP-IRA

The SEP-IRA is another option. As of 2013, the SEP-IRA allows *employers* to save up to 25% of an employee's income, up to $51,000 in annual savings. For an entrepreneur receiving an S-corporation salary of $40,000, the SEP-IRA allows the employer to save only $10,000, which is less than the SIMPLE-IRA. However, a corporate officer earning $100,000 per year could have the corporation contribute $25,000 per year with an SEP-IRA.

The SEP-IRA is clearly more valuable for officer-employees earning large salaries. Large officer salaries are typically more desirable when paid from a C-corporation. So, if you form a C-corporation, you might want to look into the SEP-IRA, rather than the SIMPLE-IRA. Other qualified plans might be more desirable for a highly-profitable company, so you might want to check with a financial advisor who can help explain your range of options.

If you want to start a SEP-IRA, download IRS Publication 4333: *SEP Retirement Plans For Small Businesses.*

As with most deferred retirement plans, there is usually a stiff penalty for early withdrawal of retirement funds. If you're under age 59 1/2 and you withdraw your money within two years of starting the SIMPLE-IRA, you're hit with a whopping 25% penalty for early withdrawal. If you've participated in the plan for more than two years, but withdraw the money before age 59 1/2, you're subject to a ten percent penalty.

This brings up an important point about saving for retirement. While some qualified retirement plans allow hardship withdrawals and allow borrowing money from the plan, SIMPLE-IRAs and SEP-IRAs do not have these provisions. Thus, you should first establish a comfortable savings cushion outside of the SIMPLE-IRA to meet emergency needs. Be sure your corporation is adequately financed, so that it can be successful.

The One-Person 401(k)

The Economic Growth and Tax Relief Reconciliation Act of 2001 added yet one more retirement plan to consider—The One-Person 401(k). It's also called a Solo 401(k). The one-person 401(k) is available to corporations, sole proprietors, and other business structures. *In this context, "one-person" includes companies where the only employees are the owners of the business or the spouses of owners.*

Prior to 2002, a one-person 401(k) wasn't the best option, because the costs and paperwork to administer it were excessive. It was treated as any other 401(k). However, if your company is a one-person business, or if all employees are also owners, the 2001 act simplifies the requirements for a 401(k) plan, making them feasible.

The one-person 401(k) has several advantages:

1) It allows tax-deferred savings up to a maximum of $51,000 per year. Some financial experts argue you'll be able to save more tax-deferred money with a one-person 401(k) than with other retirement accounts. Both the employee and employer contribute to the 401(k). As of 2013, the employee can tax-defer up to $17,500 of his salary. The corporation can contribute up to 25% of the employee's compensation.

Suppose Joe pays himself $50,000 in salary from his S corporation (reported on W-2). Joe can contribute $17,500 to his 401(k) from these wages. The corporation can contribute 25% of his $50,000 in compensation or $12,500 to his 401(k). Thus, Joe socks away $30,000 tax deferred, a whopping 60% relative to his salary.

2) You may borrow money from the one-person 401(k). I'm not a fan of borrowing from retirement accounts, but some entrepreneurs may find this feature useful.

3) The paperwork for a one-person 401(k) has been simplified and amounts to filing IRS Form 5500-SF, the short-form, or the easy-version, 5500-EZ annually. The information on Form 5500 is shared with the Department Of Labor. Filings of the full Form 5500 are made public and are available by searching the Department of Labor's website. Your return won't appear on searches if you file online (efast.dol.gov) with 5500-SF. If total plan assets are below $250,000 you're exempt from the annual filing requirement.

Because of the simplification of filing, costs to administer a one-person 401(k) are now low. Filing your own forms will save the most, while having a brokerage firm do the paperwork might cost $150 per year. That's considerably less than the $2,000 per year you might spend to administer a traditional 401(k), which can include non-owner employees.

The disadvantage of one-person 401(k)s is that if you hire employees who are not owners of the business or their spouses, your 401(k) is no longer classified as a one-person 401(k). You'll need to make the 401(k) benefit available to your employees and, suddenly, you'll be subject to the full reporting and paperwork requirements that accompany a typical 401(k). So, for companies hiring a few non-owner employees, the one-person 401(k) probably isn't the best option.

If you operate a "one-person" corporation, with no non-owner employees, I recommend examining the one-person 401(k) option. Companies with many employees may want to offer the traditional 401(k) to employees, because it's such a highly-desired benefit and will help your company retain a quality workforce.

For more information about 401(k) plans, download IRS Publication: 4222: *401(k) Plans For Small Businesses.*

The Roth IRA and The Roth 401(k)

There is one more retirement plan option entrepreneurs should know about. That's the Roth IRA and the Roth version of the solo 401(k). Most qualified retirement plans allow a portion of a person's salary to be tax-deferred. The contributions to the plan reduce taxable income and the earnings on the investment grow tax-deferred. This is a powerful savings force. When money in these accounts is withdrawn, it is then taxed as ordinary income. You wind up with substantially more money saved because of tax-deferral.

A newer version of the basic IRA is the Roth IRA, which works somewhat differently. With a Roth IRA, your contributions to the Roth IRA do not receive tax deferral. You pay income tax on the money you contribute to the plan. In other words, Roth IRAs are funded with after-tax dollars.

However, the promise is that all money withdrawn from a Roth IRA will be tax free. So, if you contribute $200,000 to your Roth over the years and it grows into $1 million, you won't pay taxes on $800,000 of your savings.

Due to the power of compounding, Roth IRAs are probably most desirable for younger entrepreneurs. Roth IRAs have another important benefit: Because income tax has already been paid on the contributions, there aren't penalties for early withdrawals on the contributions.

If you have no employees for your corporation, other than yourself, you can form a Roth version of the solo 401(k).

Is Your Retirement Plan Safe From Judgments And Bankruptcy?

Some entrepreneurs ask: If my company goes bankrupt, will my retirement plan be protected? If I personally go bankrupt, will my retirement plan be protected or could I lose it?

Before 2005, whether or not an IRA was protected during bankruptcy was largely determined by state law. In 2005, the Bankruptcy Abuse Prevention and Consumer Protection Act (BAPCPA) shielded IRA assets from bankruptcy. Just before this, in Rousey v. Jacoway, the Supreme Court ruled that IRAs are shielded from bankruptcy up to amounts that were "reasonably necessary" for retirement.

Thus, today, IRAs are shielded from bankruptcy. Traditional and ROTH IRAs are protected up to $1 million. SIMPLE-IRAs and SEP IRAs are protected, for up to unlimited amounts. Other qualified retirement plans that weren't previously protected from bankruptcy by ERISA are now protected.

The protections of the 2005 Bankruptcy Act and Supreme Court decision only apply to bankruptcies and do not extend to non-bankruptcy-civil-judgments. So, if your corporation fails and goes bankrupt, or even if you personally go bankrupt, your retirement assets should be safe.

Profit-Sharing Plans And Other Options

It's possible to save more than $51,000 annually (tax-deferred) toward retirement than is possible with the SEP-IRA. Qualified profit-sharing plans tend to be more complex and require more administrative overhead. The cost of the plan is often fully funded by the corporation, including the contributions made to the plan.

I'd recommend examining IRS *Publication 560: Retirement Plans For Small Business*. IRS *Publication 590: Individual Retirement Accounts* is also useful. Also, Request literature about company retirement plans from several brokerage firms. Then, consult with your accountant to explore your retirement account options. If you change your mind later, one plan can usually be converted into another.

The Power Of Tax-Deferred Compounding

If your corporation is profitable and, especially, if you're the sole employee, you should examine qualified retirement plans and other retirement plan options. Tax-deferred compounding of retirement savings is a huge benefit. For those who want to understand tax-deferred compounding better, I recommend my own book, *Becoming An Investor: Building Wealth By Investing In Stocks, Bonds, And Mutual Funds.*

Both entrepreneurship and investing involve the growth of wealth by compounding. Compounding is exponential growth, where previous gains are reinvested. In investing, an investment is made and a rate of return is achieved over some compounding interval, typically taken to be a year. The return could be interest received or stock price appreciation.

In entrepreneurship, an investment is made to produce and sell products. After some period of time, the invested amount is returned with profits. In operating a business, the effective compounding period is often less than a year. This allows the rapid accumulation of wealth.

Consider book publishing where payments are typically received 90 days after a sale is made. This three-month cash flow cycle implies there are effectively four possible compounding periods within a year.

It's good for a well-versed businessperson to understand the mathematics of compounding and how it relates to cash flow and bootstrapping. It will help an entrepreneur make better financial decisions when confronted with a rapidly growing business or a very successful product.

As an investor, you don't need to understand the mathematics of compounding to benefit from it. All you need to know: Get started investing as early as possible, and let your money grow over time. Over a working lifetime, even modest annual contributions to a retirement plan can add up to millions of dollars.

To illustrate this, here's a simple calculation. Assume you receive an annual rate of investment return of 12%. How much money must be invested today as a lump sum to have $1 million in 40 years? The answer: Only $10,753.

Solution: $1,000,000 = (Initial Investment)(1.12)^{40}$ and solve for initial investment. Initial Investment is $10,753.

Of course, because you'll be making annual contributions to your investment portfolio, your wealth will actually grow much faster than calculating only a one-time contribution.

With any compounding problem, there are four key variables: 1) The initial investment made or the annual contributions; 2) The compounding interval involved; 3) The number of compounding intervals; and 4) The rate of return anticipated.

In predicting the growth of your retirement portfolio, the anticipated rate of return is the most difficult thing to estimate. Reasonable return estimates might range from 7% to 12% depending upon how successful and aggressive your investments are.

To demonstrate the importance of investing as early as possible, here's another simple calculation. How much must your initial lump sum investment be to have $1,000,000 if you again receive a 12% rate of return but only have 20 years to invest? The answer: $103,626. At a 12% return, cutting your investment time frame by half required contributing nearly ten times as much for your initial investment!

Chapter 17
Introducing Schedule M-2 And
The AAA

The S-corporation tax return 1120S contains a Schedule M-2, which refers to all earnings/losses and distributions of an S-corporation that affect the amount of tax-free distributions the S-corporation can typically make in the future. Essentially, Schedule M-2 via the AAA tracks a cumulative "basis" created by earnings that have been previously taxed.

I put "basis" in quotes, because the corporation doesn't have a basis. Each shareholder has an individual basis. Further, for the first year of the corporation, the AAA starts at zero. This is unlike the individual shareholder's basis, which starts as his/her initial investment in the company.

AAA: The Mother Of All "Basis" Accounts

AAA refers to the Accumulated Adjustments Account. This account is a running total of all income minus distributions of that income made to shareholders. Unlike basis accounts, the AAA account doesn't belong to any particular shareholder. It belongs to the corporation. It also doesn't record investments made to the corporation. It starts at zero.

Line 8 of Schedule M-2 for the AAA is the balance of S-corporation profits that have not been distributed. Because these S-corporation profits haven't been distributed, but because they have already been taxed to the individual shareholders, any distributions made from the AAA account are typically tax-free.

Important Note: Whether or not a distribution to a shareholder is tax-free depends upon the *shareholder's basis* relative to the amount of the distribution. A particular shareholder will have to pay taxes if his/her pro rata share of the distribution is in excess of his/her basis in the stock. So, conceivably, if a new shareholder purchased stock cheaply from an existing shareholder, the new shareholder's basis might be low, even while the AAA is high, and the distribution could still be taxable to *that* new shareholder. This is why I qualify the previous paragraph with "typically." The AAA doesn't allow for factors such as change of stock ownership. The AAA only measures a collective amount of income which has been previously taxed to *some* shareholders. In our hypothetical example of sale of shares, the stockholder who *sold* shares cheaply probably had a higher basis, partially coming from earnings, which also added to the AAA. When this stockholder sold his shares cheaply, he probably received an amount less than his basis in the stock and he reported a capital loss. Each shareholder is responsible to track his/her own basis in his/her S-corporation stock.

Stockholders usually don't have to pay additional taxes on distributions they receive, as long as the distribution amount is less than the amount in the AAA and as long as the earnings that added to the AAA account have been taxed pro rata to those particular stockholders receiving the distribution. Distributions larger than the balance in the AAA can trigger extra taxes. Many new corporations will not pay distributions larger than the balance in the AAA.

From a business standpoint, not paying distributions in excess of the AAA account usually makes sense. A company earns a certain amount of money and, then, pays dividends/distributions from earnings. Paying dividends in excess of earnings isn't a sustainable business policy.

An S-corporation without C-corporation earnings and profits (E&P) isn't required to compute an AAA account. But, it's considered good accounting practice to do so. Due to losses and other reductions, the balance of the AAA can fall below zero. A shareholder's basis will never be negative.

Other Adjustments Account

For many small corporations, this account will not be used. It typically tracks income (and expenses associated with that income) which have a tax-free nature. Distributions from this account can also typically be made without incurring additional taxation to the shareholder, as long as the amount of the distribution is less than or equal to the net balance in the account. The IRS instructions for S-corporation tax return 1120S give an example showing how the OAA works.

Shareholder's Undistributed Taxable Income Previously Taxed

This account doesn't apply unless your corporation was an S-corporation prior to 1982. Because you're reading this book after 2013, I assume you weren't incorporated back then and weren't an S-corporation. If so, you'll never use this account.

This account has a horrible name, because if you read "Shareholder's Undistributed Taxable Income Previously Taxed," and if your corporation has undistributed taxable income, which was previously taxed to the shareholders because of the pass through nature of the S-corporation, it sounds like this account should apply to you. The account should read something like: "Shareholder's Undistributed Taxable Income Previously Taxed Prior To 1982."

The AAA and the account "Shareholder's Undistributed Taxable Income Previously Taxed" are very similar accounts. Both measure the balance of profits that have not been distributed (but due to the nature of S-corporations being a pass-through tax entity, those profits have already been taxed). It's just that with a change in tax laws, the IRS wanted to differentiate the periods before 1982 and after 1982 and have a separate account for each period.

Earnings And Profits (E&P)

In addition to AAA, OAA, and "Shareholder's Undistributed Taxable Income Previously Taxed," some corporations have "Earnings And Profits" also known as E&P. Now, it's important not to rely upon an English definition of "Earnings And Profits," because you might think: "Yes, my corporation has earnings and profits. It better have, because earnings and profits are the whole purpose of running a business, and I'm doing well!"

The IRS definition of "Earnings And Profits" for S-corporation tax purposes is very specific. The E&P account refers to earnings a corporation had while it was a C-corporation. Distributions from the E&P account are taxable to shareholders, even if the corporation is an S-corporation. This is because those profits were earned while the corporation was a C-corporation and the individual corporation owners *haven't* paid income taxes on these earnings and profits.

The purpose of the E&P account is to track earnings from a C-corporation that have not been distributed and to be certain that when they are distributed, they don't escape taxation at the individual income tax level. Distributions from the E&P account are called dividends and are doubly taxed. If an S-corporation previously operated as a C-corporation and paid dividends from E&P, the corporation would file 1099-DIV to report those dividends.

The E&P account shows the flaw in many incorporation books that suggest you operate as a C-corporation for your first several years until you approach the maximum accumulated earnings. Then, these books casually suggest switching to an S-corporation structure to pay out income. All of those accumulated profits the corporation had while it was a C-corporation cannot be paid out without incurring double taxation. This may not be a problem, because many corporations desire to retain capital for funding future business growth. But, if the corporation wishes to distribute this money to shareholders, starting in a C-corporation mode and, then, switching to an S-corporation is no magic solution. C-corporation earnings are essentially earmarked for double taxation when the corporation switches to S-corporation status.

The Order Of Distributions From The Accounts

If you plan to operate as an S-corporation, I'm a big fan of making the election as soon as you incorporate. That way you'll always operate as an S-corporation, and you don't need to worry about things like "E&P" or how the existence of previous C-corporation earnings affects your S-corporation. The worst situation is a mid-year switch from one type of corporation to another. Then, essentially, you have two short tax years, and you'll get to fill out tax forms for *both* an S-corporation and a C-corporation. What fun!

Now that you understand the AAA, the IRS instructions for Schedule M-2 become more readable (instructions for Form 1120S, Page 38):

> The accumulated adjustments account (AAA) is an account of the S corporation that generally reflects the accumulated undistributed net income of the corporation for the corporation's post-1982 years. S corporations with accumulated E&P must maintain the AAA to determine the tax effect of distributions during S years and the post-termination transition period. An S corporation without accumulated E&P does not need to maintain the AAA in order to determine the tax effect of distributions.

> Nevertheless, if an S corporation without accumulated E&P engages in certain transactions to which section 381(a) applies, such as a merger into an S corporation with accumulated E&P, the S corporation must be able to calculate its AAA at the

time of the merger for purposes of determining the
tax effect of post-merger distributions. Therefore, it
is recommended that the AAA be maintained by all S
corporations.

Notice, if you've never operated as a C-corporation, the IRS
instructions for S-corporation return 1120S say you don't need to
maintain an AAA to determine the tax effect of distributions, but the
IRS recommends the AAA be maintained anyway. Many
entrepreneurs have a professional accountant maintain the AAA.

If you've never operated as a C-corporation (you have no E&P),
the pass through nature of the S-corporation is simple. The corporation
reports income which is (from a tax standpoint) passed through to
the shareholders who pay tax on it. At this point, distributions of
that previously-taxed income should be tax-free to those individuals
already taxed on the income. Thus, you don't need the AAA account
(unless you merge with or purchase a company that has E&P).

What happens if you have E&P (i.e., you operated as a C-corporation
or you acquired a company with E&P), a balance in the OAA, a
balance in the "Shareholder's Undistributed Taxable Income
Previously Taxed," and a balance in the AAA? You'll probably want
to seek professional accounting help.

In this case, distributions are made from the accounts in the
following order (See the instructions for IRS Form 1120S):

1) AAA account
2) Shareholder's Undistributed Taxable Income Previously Taxed
3) E&P
4) OAA
5) Return of Initial Investment Capital (This reduces that part of
    the basis acquired when shares were purchased. It's sometimes
    called a return of basis.)

The corporation can elect to first distribute from the E&P. The
treatment of S-corporations with E&P with regard to passive income
is slightly different, so, sometimes, it's advantageous to pay the double

taxation to deplete the E&P account. Incidentally, the IRS defines "passive income" differently with respect to different parts of the Internal Revenue Code (IRC).

The order of distributions above is adequate for many S-corporations. See the IRS instructions for Schedule M-2 for more information. New corporations that have always operated as S-corporations don't need to worry about items 2) and 3).

You may now understand more about the accounts on IRS Schedule M-2 than you'll ever need. You'll see an example of an M-2 in the next chapter, where we go over a sample 1120S tax return to help us understand some of the concepts of S-corporations.

Dividends And Distributions

English, again, plays tricks on us. Typically, investors and entrepreneurs call income received from a corporation "dividends." Nearly everyone refers to S-corporation "dividends." However, technically, we should call them *distributions* or even *distributions of previously taxed income* when we're discussing taxation.

Further, if we have a company that earns money and pays this money to us, we usually think of the money received as a return on investment. However, due to the nature of S-corporations, i.e., because the money has already been taxed, it looks as if we are having a portion of our investment returned to us—a return *of* investment.

Chapter 18
Sample 1120S Return: Joe's Pottery Emporium

Because many entrepreneurs forming corporations will operate as S-corporations, we'll go over a basic 1120S income tax return. The 1120S is usually due March 15 for corporations which use the calendar year for their tax year. A sample C-corporation return is included in IRS *Publication 542: Corporations*. You might want to go to the IRS website IRS.gov and download IRS Form 1120S and its instructions.

For our example, suppose Joe starts a new S-corporation called Joe's Pottery Emporium, Ltd. (JPE). He plans to sell pottery through mail order. He contributes $10,000 to the corporation for 100 shares of stock. Thus, his initial basis in the corporation is $10,000 or $100 per share.

Joe's corporation purchases $5,000 worth of inventory, buying 100 pottery bowls at $50 each. He sells 50 of the bowls for $100 each. Joe then purchases $3,000 worth of pottery cups, buying 100 for $30 each. The corporation sells 80 of them for $60 each.

Joe's corporation spends $100 on advertising, has other expenses of $200, and earns $5 interest on its corporate checking account. Joe creates a website for his corporation, links to amazon.com, and the corporation earns $2 in Amazon associate referral fees. Joe then decides to pay himself a bonus of $500.

Here's a summary of the activity of Joe's corporation for its first year:

Initial Cash: $10,000
Initial Inventory: $0
Purchases Of Inventory: $8,000
Cost Of Goods Sold: (50 x $50) + (80 x $30) = $4,900
Value Of Inventory At End Of Year:
        (50 x $50) + (20 x $30) = $3,100
Sales Revenue: ($100 x 50) + ($60 x 80) = $9,800
Other Income: $5 interest + $2 referral fee

Expenses:
    Advertising: $100
    Other Expenses $200
    Salary/Bonus To Joe $500
_____

Total Expenses $800

Assume Joe's corporation doesn't have any outstanding liabilities at the beginning of the year or at the end of the year. For example, Joe's corporation has no accounts payable at year end. It doesn't owe money to any wholesalers, nor has the corporation borrowed any money.

Of the $9,800 sales revenue generated, assume $7,800 has been paid in cash, while $2,000 remains in accounts receivable at the end of the year (recall, accounts receivable is money we are owed). The $2 owed by Amazon is also an account receivable.

We can quickly calculate the cash in Joe's company at year end:

$10,000
- $8,000 inventory purchases
+ $7,800 cash received for sales
- $100 advertising expense paid for in cash
- $200 in other expenses paid for in cash
- $500 bonus/salary paid to Joe by his corporation
+ $5 received in interest

$9,005.00

Reading the instructions, Joe fills out his 1120S return. First, he notices that he must enter some very basic information about the corporation, such as its Employer ID Number, the date of incorporation, and the date the election was made to become an S-corporation.

Joe notices that he must enter a business code (Line B) to describe what his company does. The instructions for the 1120S give some codes (page 41 and page 42 of the 2012 1120S instruction booklet). He chooses Code 454110 under "Non-store retailers" which is "Electronic Shopping And Mail Order Services." Joe debated using Code 453220 under "Miscellaneous Store Retailers" which is "Gift, Novelty & Souvenir Stores." But, Joe's corporation isn't really a store retailer, although he occasionally sells products from the trunk of his car.

Notice that for most smaller S corporations, Line C will be unchecked, because the special Schedule M-3 applies to corporations with over $10 million in assets. For most corporations, most of the lines on 1120S will be left blank.

Because this is Joe's first year of business, he should select "Yes" on Line G "Is the corporation electing to be an S corporation beginning with this tax year?" We assume Joe already filed form 2553 to elect S-corporation status. In his second and following years, Line G will be left blank.

Next, Joe comes across "H. Check if." which offers selections: 1) Final Return, 2) Name change, and other choices. Notice that "Check if" doesn't mean that any boxes are applicable to your corporation. For Joe, no boxes will be checked. If a line of the 1120S doesn't apply to your corporation, it should be left blank. If you are closing an S-corporation and this is the company's last tax return, "Final Return" would be selected.

Joe sees he must enter the corporation's total assets at year end (Line F). The amount is $14,107.00. This line should correspond to the value on Page 4, Line 15, "Total Assets" in the end of the year column at the far right. (At year end, the only assets in Joe's corporation are: Cash, $9,005.00; accounts receivable, $2,002.00; and inventory of $3,100.00)

For Line I, Joe enters the number 1 because he was the only shareholder during the year. The number is entered after the little, cute triangle.

For Line 1a) Joe enters the company's sales revenue of $9,800. To calculate the cost-of-goods-sold (Line 2), Joe must download IRS Form 1125-A (IRS.gov).

Form 1125-A

For Item 9a) on Form 1125-A, Joe sees "Cost" as an option for valuing inventory, so he selects that. Other questions are a bit more perplexing to Joe. He reads: "Do the rules of section 263A apply to the entity [Joe's Corporation] (see instructions)?"

There is a "Yes," and there is a "No" answer. "Maybe" or "I Have No Clue" are not options. It's often simple lines like this that get entrepreneurs to go see an accountant. Fortunately, once you've filled out tax forms for one year, the rest of the years will become trivial, because it's like retaking the same test.

In Joe's case, he looks at the instructions and reads: "**Exceptions.** Section **263A does not apply** to: Personal Property acquired for resale if the taxpayer's average annual gross receipts for the 3 prior years are $10 million or less." So, Joe, can safely check "No." Section 263A doesn't apply. It doesn't matter if Joe understands the exact definition of "Personal Property," because Joe knows his revenue isn't near $10 million. The answer for box f) is also "No." There wasn't a change in inventory valuation during the year.

For taxation purposes, the cost-of-goods-sold is calculated as:

Inventory At Start Of Year
+ Purchases
+Any Other Costs That Are Capitalized Into Inventory
- Ending Inventory Value
_____

cogs

For Joe who values inventory at cost:

$0
+ $8,000
- $3,100
_____

$4,900

Meanwhile On Page 1

After using Form 1125-A to compute cogs, Joe subtracts cogs ($4,900) from the company's sales revenue ($9,800) to get $4,900 as the gross profit for Joe's company. Joe decides to include the $2 in referral revenue under "Other Income" on Line 5. He attaches a short description of the source of the $2 revenue. When assembling returns, it's good to review each line of the return looking for the words "attach schedule" where you haven't.

Incidentally, while manufacturing companies, wholesalers, retailers, publishers, and many other companies have inventory and cost-of-goods-sold, many companies don't have cogs. For example, service companies may have no inventory. In that case, you can safely ignore Line 2 for cogs or fill in a zero. All your expenses of running the service can be filled-in on other lines between Line 7, "Compensation of Officers," and Line 19, "Other Deductions."

Line 19 is especially useful, because you can collect all of your other expenses that don't belong on other lines. Be sure to attach the schedule of the deductions. We put the advertising expense on Line 16. We could just as easily have included it under Line 19 "Other deductions."

For JPE, maybe the schedule of other deductions reads something like this:

Other Deductions: Line 19

Postage Expense $142.00
Web Domain Name Expense $20.00
Office Supplies, Pens, Paper, Etc., Expense $20.00
Magazine Subscription To "Pottery Seller Today" $18.00
_____

Total Other Deductions $200.00

Be sure to double check your math. Many taxpayers who are audited by the IRS simply make an addition or subtraction error somewhere on their tax form. If your accounting data is in a computer accounting program, be sure to print out copies of your profit and loss statement, your balance sheet, and any other pages relevant to figuring your taxes. It's also good to save a copy of your accounting data at year end. You'll probably never need it, but it's there just in case.

It's important to realize that every item under "Income" on Page 1 of the 1120S refers to *operating income*. Joe's company has $5 in interest it earned, but that doesn't appear on Page 1. It will be entered elsewhere on the return and passed through to the shareholders as "interest income." (Note: According to the instructions for 1120S, if "Interest income is derived in the ordinary course of the corporation's trade or business, such as interest charged on receivable balances," it may be entered on Line 5 of Page 1 of the 1120S under "Other Income.")

If you peek ahead to Schedule K, you'll see some of the income items that won't ever appear on Page 1, including interest income, royalty income, ordinary dividends (paid by other corporations to your corporation), etc. It's not that these items aren't taxed to the shareholder, it's just that they won't contribute to the ordinary operating income reported on Line 21 of Page 1. Don't make the mistake of believing that Line 21 of Page 1 collects and summarizes *all* taxable income passed through by the S-corporation. Only "Ordinary income (loss)" from trade or business activities is recorded there. Separately stated items go straight to Schedule K.

On Page 1, we see a large section of "Deductions," Line 7 through Line 19. Deductions are subtracted from income to determine the net taxable operating income. Notice officer compensation is a deduction. Joe's salary/bonus of $500 will reduce the taxable income reported by JPE. However, this salary *will* be reported as wage income to Joe. It will appear on his W-2, which the corporation will provide for him. Even though Joe is the only person working for the corporation, he is an employee of the corporation and must be treated like an employee for wage reporting. Wages paid to non-officer employees are reported on Line 8.

For those who want to learn more about wage reporting, W-2's, etc., I recommend *Small Time Operator: How To Start Your Own Small Business, Keep Your Books, Pay Your Taxes, And Stay Out Of Trouble!* by Bernard B. Kamoroff. Also, see Chapter 20.

Incidentally, Joe didn't need to pay himself a wage this year. With $500 in wages, 15.3% will go to Social Security taxes and 6% will go to Federal Unemployment. So, low wages are particularly heavily taxed. What Joe could *not* do is pay no wage and declare a cash distribution.

Of course, Line 13 "Interest" is a tax deduction for interest *paid*, not interest *received*, by the corporation. JPE didn't pay any interest during the year. Interest paid is a tax-deductible expense to businesses. Interest received is entered on Schedule K.

After entering the information for income and deductions, JPE shows an ordinary income from operations of $4,102.00 on Line 21 of Page 1.

While Lines 1 through Line 21 are the heart and soul of reporting S-corporation operational income, Lines 22 through Line 27, "Taxes and Payments," are often left blank, because the corporation, itself, will usually owe no tax. Most S-corporations will leave this section blank. Line 22 may be invoked if there are net passive earnings. This applies to corporations that previously operated as C-corporations.

Finally, Joe signs and dates his return. The section under "Paid Preparer's Use Only" is left blank, unless an accountant did your taxes. After completing your 1120S, you might still wish to have an accountant do the corporation's taxes. Then, you can compare your return with the accountant's return and learn a bit more about taxation. It's also a great chance to ask questions like: "What exactly is Section 263A, anyway?"

Moving On To Page 2 Of The 1120S (Schedule B)

Moving to Page 2, we next confront Schedule B "Other Information." JPE uses accrual accounting. After the arrow and above the dots, Joe fills in his company's principal business activity. If you follow the dots after the arrow, they won't lead anywhere, so you simply write above the dots.

Schedule B "Other Information" will generally ask a series of questions to which you answer "yes" or "no" with a checkmark. The questions vary from year to year, so read this section carefully, looking for changes from last year.

Joe answers "No" to Question 3, because he (as the only shareholder) isn't a "disregarded entity" a trust or a similar creature. Because JPE doesn't own stock in any other corporations and his company didn't own any partnership interest in another business, the answers to Question 4 parts a) and b) are "No."

Joe selects "No" for question 5a. The corporation doesn't have any restricted stock.

Restricted stock is an alternative to employee stock options. Joe also checks "No" for question 5b. JPE doesn't have stock options or anything similar.

The answer to question 6 is "No." The corporation isn't a "material adviser to a reportable transaction." It hasn't filed Form 8918. Because Joe doesn't really understand what is meant by "material advisor to a reportable transaction," he downloads the instructions for Form 8918. After reading them, he's more confused then ever. But it's clear it doesn't apply to him or his company.

This question illustrates why it's always prudent to prepare your taxes well before they're due. Don't put taxes off until the last day. If you do and you have questions, you'll have less time to get answers. (Incidentally, on IRS.gov, you'll find a link for e-mailing questions to the IRS.)

Line 9 "Enter the accumulated earnings and profits of the corporation..." only applies to companies that operated as C-corporations.

Line 10 says Joe does not have to fill out Schedule L and M-1. Just to show how these schedules work, we'll work them out anyway.

Line 13a asks about Forms 1099. To learn more about 1099 forms, you can download the IRS instructions for them. 1099's are the IRS's way of tracking income paid to individuals. Corporations can receive millions of dollars in transactions that aren't reported to the IRS by any entity, but the IRS cracks down on tracking individual income. Employee's wage income is reported by W-2s. 1099's report common sources of income to individuals like royalty income and dividends. There are many versions of the basic 1099 form. 1099's are usually filed with the IRS by February 28 and are sent to the person who received the reportable income.

If Joe had an artist design a special pottery piece, and if Joe paid the artist a royalty for each one sold, Joe would use Form 1099-MISC. That form is also used to report royalties paid to book authors. Having your corporation pay you royalties is another way you can remove money from a corporation. If a contract with your corporation pays you a royalty, this contract usually remains in effect if you sell your company. Joe didn't pay anybody anything reportable on any 1099s, so he selects "No" to question 13a.

One aspect of Form 1099-DIV should be mentioned: This form applies to dividends paid by C corporations. If your corporation always operated as an S-corporation, Form 1099-DIV doesn't apply. Distributions of S-corporation profits aren't reported on 1099s. They're reported on Schedule K and K-1 under "Items Affecting Shareholder Basis" (Line 16d) Because you've already been taxed on your flow-through S-corporation income, distributions aren't taxed. Only if your company pays dividends from earnings and profits (E&P) *from operating as a C-corporation* will you ever need to file 1099-DIV.

While we're discussing tax forms you probably don't need to know about, we should introduce one other form you probably don't need to know about: IRS Form 5452. This form applies to non-dividend distributions to shareholders under 1368(c)(3).

One of the more pleasurable aspects of doing your own taxes is coming across a complex tax form you think you need to fill out and then realizing it doesn't apply to you!

Schedule K (Pages 3-4 of 1120S)

Schedule K starts on Page 3 of the 1120S. Schedule K records income, credits, and deductions that will be passed through to the shareholders. Schedule K items will be copied pro rata onto Forms K-1 which are shareholder specific. The corporation will provide each shareholder with his/her K-1. Copies of K-1's will also be sent to the IRS and will be kept on file with the corporation for its own records. Don't forget to keep copies of all your tax forms!

Schedule K, Line 1: "Ordinary Income (loss) from trade or business activities (page 1, line 21)" is copied directly from Page 1, Line 21 of the 1120S. This is the ordinary business income that will be "passed through" to shareholders for taxation purposes.

Rental income, interest income, charitable contributions, and Section 179 deductions are some of the items that are passed on to the shareholders while retaining their nature. Some Schedule K's won't have anything entered between Line 2 and Line 17. For example, "Foreign Transactions" won't apply to many small U.S. corporations.

The Section 179 deduction is especially interesting (Line 11). Section 179 allows a company to immediately expense assets that are usually depreciated. This often leads to a bigger tax deduction. The purpose of passing through Section 179 deductions on Schedule K is to limit the amount of capital assets that one individual can immediately expense. So, if a person operates a sole proprietorship and is also partial owner of four S-corporations, the total Section 179 deduction is capped, just as if the person filed one tax form and operated one business that encompassed the activities of all of those businesses. If you have Section 179 deductions, don't forget to attach Form 4562.

For JPE, the $5 interest income is entered on Line 4. Line 18 reads $4,107.00.

A few other lines of Schedule K are noteworthy. Line 16c records non-deductible expenses the corporation absorbed. For example, possibly, meals or travel expenses were only partially deductible to the corporation. Non-deductible expenses reduce the profitability of a corporation, but non-deductible expenses cannot appear on Page 1 of the tax return under "Deductions," or they will reduce taxable income.

Distributions are recorded on Line 16d, "Distributions." This is usually cash paid to shareholders. While entrepreneurs are fond of saying they were paid "dividends" from their corporations, with S-corporations, these "dividends" are more properly classified as "distributions" when discussing taxes.

Line 17c reads: "Dividend distributions from accumulated earnings and profits." As you recall, "accumulated earnings and profits" refer to accumulated earnings and profits *while operating as a C-corporation*. Thus, if you've always operated as an S-corporation and haven't acquired other corporations, Line 17c won't apply.

Schedule L (Page 4 of 1120S)

Schedule L is a balance sheet for the corporation which includes two columns. One column is for the beginning of the year and one column is for the end of the year. Each year's balance sheet is, itself, divided into two columns. The first column allows various accounts to be reduced by stated amounts.

For example, Line 2a lists: "Trade notes and accounts receivable" and below it is a space for entering "Less allowances for bad debts." For the end of the year, Joe enters $2,002.00 as accounts receivable. He's confident he'll collect the money, so he enters $0.00 as the allowance for bad debts and carries the full $2,002.00 to Column D. (If, however, JPE anticipated it would never collect $60.00 from one nefarious customer, Joe would enter $60.00 as the allowance for bad debts. Bad debts are those obligations it appears won't ever be paid to the corporation. In that case, the final value in Column D is reduced by $60.00. Bad debts also reduce taxable income.)

Depreciable assets and intangible assets, which are amortized, also make use of an adjustment account. Depreciation reduces the book value of capital assets, while amortization is a yearly reduction in the value of intangible assets.

Line 15 lists the total assets at the start of the year and also at the end of the year. The basic accounting equation says Assets = Liabilities + Shareholders' Equity, so the total assets on Line 15 should match Line 27, "Total liabilities and shareholders' equity" for each year. One way to read the accounting equation is to say that assets are financed either by borrowing or else by equity.

For the start of the year, the only asset is $10,000 in cash, which exactly equals the $10,000 Joe paid in for his capital stock. At the end of the year, total assets are $14,107.00.

In this case, the growth in asset value of the corporation wasn't the result of borrowing money (if JPE borrowed $5,000 right before the end of the year, cash would be increased by $5,000, but there would also be $5,000 in liabilities, which would be reported on one of the lines between Line 17 and Line 21).

Also, the growth in asset value over the year wasn't the result of raising more investment in the corporation (if Joe had convinced his uncle to invest $20,000 in JPE right before the end of the year, cash would be increased by $20,000, but capital stock would also be increased by $20,000).

The growth in asset value of JPE was the result of business operations and savvy investments. Such amounts are added to retained earnings on Line 24. This year, JPE earned $4,107.00 which added to the retained earnings. Of this, $4,102 comes from operations reported on Line 21 of Page 1 of the 1120S. The other $5 comes from interest earned on JPE's checking account, which was also reported on Schedule K.

Just as income increases the retained earnings account, losses reduce the retained earnings account. You can think of retained earnings as a running total of money earned or lost by the corporation.

We can rewrite the basic accounting equation as: Assets = Liabilities + Paid-In Capital + Retained Earnings. We see that income that is not distributed increases the company's asset value. This retained income is also called "Retained Earnings." Retained earnings could be in the form of cash or other assets.

Schedule M-1

Schedule M-1, "Reconciliation of Income (Loss) per Books With Income (Loss) per Return," exists because many corporations have accounting records that differ slightly from the values reported on the tax return. Schedule M-1 reconciles and explains the differences to the IRS.

Differences between the corporation's books and tax return are most often due to non-deductible expenses or due to differences in how depreciation is treated on the corporation's books versus how it's treated for taxation purposes.

** Non-Deductible Expenses **

Suppose JPE had $50 in non-deductible expenses. (Non-deductible expenses would be reported on Line 16c of Schedule K. *In the sample return, there are no non-deductible expenses, and the reconciliation is trivial because taxable income and corporate book income are exactly the same.*) Non-deductible expenses can't be lumped together with expenses reported on Page 1 of the 1120S, or they would be deducted from taxes. Yet, non-tax-deductible expenses are a real expense of the business.

So, JPE's books would record the non-deductible expense of $50, reducing the company's income (as reported on its own books) to $4,057.00. The income as reported to the IRS is $4,107.00.

Line 1 of Schedule M-2 would be $4,057.00, the company's book income. Line 3, "Expenses recorded on books this year not included on Schedule K, lines 1 through 12, and 14l (itemize):" would include the $50 non-deductible expense. And, Line 4 would add this non-deductible expense to the book income. The result should be the taxable income as reported to the IRS.

**

Companies can also treat depreciation differently on their corporate books from how it's treated for taxation. This is more common for larger companies, and, especially, for publicly-traded C-corporations, where corporate officers want to make the company look more profitable to investors, while also paying as little as possible in taxes.

Suppose a corporation purchases a capital asset worth $200,000 which has an estimated life of five years. One way to depreciate this asset would be linearly, which would depreciate (write-off as an expense) one-fifth of the asset's value for each of the five years. For straight-line depreciation, $40,000 would be subtracted from the company's income each year as depreciation expense.

The IRS also accepts various other depreciation schedules, often referred to as "accelerated depreciation," which means the asset is depreciated more rapidly than it would be treated under straight-line depreciation.

Suppose $80,000 were allowed as the tax depreciation for the item's first year of depreciation under an accelerated depreciation schedule.

On the corporation's books (which are on straight-line depreciation), the asset's year-end value is $200,000 minus $40,000 depreciation, or $160,000, and income is reduced by $40,000. So, if the company had $100,000 in income before depreciation of this machine, after depreciation expense of this machine, the company reports income of $60,000 on its own books.

For tax purposes, however, the machine is carried as having a value of $200,000 minus $80,000 or $120,000. And, taxable income is reduced by $80,000. So, the net income reported to the IRS is $20,000. You can see the tax advantage to accelerated depreciation on the tax return and that a company wishing to "look" more profitable to investors would use slower depreciation on its corporate books.

This difference in depreciation between the company's books and the tax return would be entered on Line 6 of Schedule M-1, "Deductions included on Schedule K, lines 1 through ... not charged against book income this year (itemize):"

While different depreciation schedules can be kept for internal purposes and for tax purposes, for small companies, there's little if any advantage to having one depreciation schedule for taxation and another for your internal, corporate books. I'd recommend choosing one depreciation schedule for taxation purposes and, then, use the same schedule for your company's books.

Incidentally, if you purchase a company, notice that depreciation methods chosen affect a company's stated book value. This is why it's important to have assets appraised and not rely upon book value as an accurate measure of a current asset's worth. For more about buying a business, I refer you to *Thinking Like An Entrepreneur: How To Make Intelligent Business Decisions That Will Lead To Success In Building And Growing Your Own Company.*

Getting back to Joe's company, Schedule M-1 is trivial. Line 1 (book income) already matches the income reported to the IRS (Line 8 of M-1). Some people become intimidated by Schedule M-1, because they don't know what to put where. But, often, the reason for this confusion is that there isn't anything to do. It's like the tricky word problem with a lot of complex-looking information that has a trivial answer.

Schedule M-2

Schedule M-2 is discussed in more detail elsewhere. For JPE, columns (b) and (c) don't apply. Joe leaves them blank. Column (a), "Accumulated adjustments account," is relatively simple.

The start of the AAA account is zero, because it measures earnings which have already been taxed and which can usually be distributed tax-free in the future. When the corporation starts as a new S-corporation, there haven't been any earnings. So Line 1 is zero. Line 2 is the ordinary income reported on Page 1 of the 1120S. That's $4,102.00. Line 3, "Other additions," includes the $5.00 interest received. The balance of the AAA at the end of the tax year is $4,107.00.

Notice Line 7, "Distributions Other than dividend distributions." Remember that "dividends" apply to C-corporations. While entrepreneurs informally say, "I received $40,000 in *dividends* from my S-corporation," you'll confuse yourself really quickly if you think of them as "dividends" when filling in tax forms. They're considered "distributions." And, perhaps surprisingly, because the money being distributed has already been taxed, it's considered a return *of* capital rather than a return *on* your investment in the company. Line 7 shows us that distributions reduce the AAA account (just as a shareholder's pro rata portion of the distribution reduces his/her basis).

So, if the board of directors of JPE decided to issue a "dividend" payment of $200, this $200 would be reported on Line 7 of Schedule M-2 (and, also, on Line 16d of Schedule K). *In our sample return, we have assumed no distributions*. Note: We're neglecting any issues of the wage being too low to be valid compensation for Joe. As a rule, reasonable wages must be paid to shareholder-employees before distributions should be made to shareholders.)

Incidentally, because Joe is the only shareholder, the AAA account and his initial basis of $10,000 tell us that Joe's basis at the end of the tax year in his S-corporation stock is $14,107.00. Joe's basis could also be easily calculated using the basis worksheet we provide in another chapter, or by simply adding Joe's pro rata share of income

($4,107.00) to his initial basis. (If a distribution of $200 had been made, his basis would be reduced by $200.)

Notice Line 5 allows reductions to the AAA when necessary. For example, if JPE had $50 in nondeductible expenses, that $50 would be entered on Line 5 (and it would reduce the retained earnings account). Nondeductible expenses would also reduce Joe's basis. *In our sample return, there are no nondeductible expenses.*

Form K-1

For shareholders to figure their personal income taxes, they'll need to receive information from their S-corporations. Corporations send each shareholder *Form K-1 for the Form 1120S.* Partnerships also use a form called K-1, so be sure to get the K-1 for S-corporations. Because shareholders need this information to do *their* taxes, your corporation should get K-1s out right after the tax year ends. Also, be sure each shareholder gets IRS *Shareholder's Instructions for Schedule K-1 (1120S)* to help him/her understand the purpose of the K-1. Schedule K-1 is based on Schedule K, but the amounts on K-1 are scaled to the shareholder's percentage of ownership in the corporation.

Schedule K-1 starts with basic information. The corporation's EIN, name, and address are entered in parts A and B. For Line C, "IRS Center where the corporation filed [its income tax] return," you can consult the instructions for 1120S. If Joe's corporation is in Texas, for example, he'd enter "Ogden, UT 84201-0013."

Information about the shareholder who is receiving the K-1 is entered in parts D and E: The shareholder's social security number, name, and address. Under part F, the percentage ownership of the S-corporation is listed for the shareholder. Be sure to double check your math so that all shareholders collectively own 100% of the corporation. (A small round-off error is, of course, allowed. For example, three shareholders each owning one-third of the company might each list 33.33% ownership.) If this is the corporation's last tax year, the little box at the very top of the page "Final K-1" applies.

Line 1 through Line 10 list income or losses that are passed through to the shareholder, and the amounts come from Schedule K. Line 11 to Line 12 list pass-through deductions. Line 11 is for the common Section 179 deduction.

Each item from Schedule K is given to the shareholder on a pro rata basis, which means in percentage to his/her ownership in the corporation. Think of each item of income or deduction on Schedule K as flowing through to the shareholders (in Schedule K-1) in proportion to their ownership of the corporation. For each line on Schedule K, be sure to double check that the total reported on all the shareholder K-1 forms add up to the total stated on Schedule K.

Line 1 is the most important, because it lists the ordinary income or loss from the business. For Joe, who owns 100% of the corporation, all ordinary income—$4,102.00—passes through to him (Line 1 of Schedule K and Schedule K-1 are the same). Similarly, all interest income flows through to Joe. Line 4 shows $5.00. Be sure to double check that amounts which are a loss and are therefore negative are in parentheses ().

**

When filling out Schedule K-1, to give to shareholders and to send to the IRS, the most important thing to keep in mind is that it's a pro-rated replication of Schedule K. Schedule K has 17 lines where items are entered. K-1 also has 17 corresponding lines. So if there's an entry on, say, Line 16a) through 16e) of Schedule K, there should be a corresponding entry on Line 16 of Schedule K-1.

To "simplify" the appearance of the K-1 tax form, the IRS decided to delete the specific letters under each number. While Schedule K has specific lines 16a, 16b, 16c, 16d, and 16e, the corresponding Schedule K-1 just has the number 16 followed by a bunch of blank lines. You need to write in the letters you need!

So, if Joe had nondeductible expenses entered on Line 16c and distributions entered on Line 16d of Schedule K, Joe would enter the "Codes" on Schedule K-1 (i.e., the letters "c" and "d" which just correspond to the specific line numbers on Schedule K). On one line under "16" just write "c" and on the next line, write "d." Joe's K-1 shows where the "Codes" are entered. Then the dollar amounts for the nondeductible expenses and distributions could be entered. In the example, Joe has no nondeductible expenses and no distributions. He doesn't need to "code" or customize any of his lines on K-1.

If you're a shareholder receiving a K-1 and you don't know what a line on the K-1 refers to, consult the shareholder's instructions for form 1120S.

** Multiple Shareholders **

Suppose Joe had two business partners, Tim and Hank. Suppose Tim owns 20 shares and Hank owns 50 shares. Joe has 100 shares. Three K-1 forms are filled out. In this case, the three K-1s would read:

Joe's percentage ownership = 100/170 = 58.824%
Tim's percentage ownership = 20/170 = 11.765%
Hank's percentage ownership = 50/170 = 29.412%

Joe's Pro Rata Share of Ordinary Income
$= (100/170) \times \$4,102.00 = \$2,412.94$
Tim's Pro Rata Share of Ordinary Income
$= (20/170) \times \$4,102.00 = \$482.59$
Hank's Pro Rata Share of Ordinary Income
$= (50/170) \times \$4,102.00 = \$1,206.47$

$$\overline{}$$
$$\$4,102.00$$

Similarly, each other item from Schedule K would be pro rated among the shareholders, including the $5 in interest income which appears on Line 4 (again, Line 4 of Schedule K matches up with Line 4 of Schedule K-1):

Joe's Pro Rata Share of Interest Income
$$= (100/170) \times \$5.00 = \$2.94$$
Tim's Pro Rata Share of Interest Income
$$= (20/170) \times \$5.00 = \$0.59$$
Hank's Pro Rata Share of Interest Income
$$= (50/170) \times \$5.00 = \$1.47$$

$$\overline{\qquad\qquad}$$

$$\$5.00$$

**

Much of Schedule K-1 will be blank for many corporations, because many of the items don't apply. As mentioned previously, Section 179 expense deduction and charitable contributions flow through to the shareholders. These are reported on Line 11 and Line 12, respectively.

Line 16 "Items affecting shareholder basis," is where nondeductible expenses are pro rated among the shareholders (Line 16 "Code C" on Schedule K-1 corresponds to Schedule K Line 16c). Nondeductible expenses reduce a shareholder's basis in her stock, so it's necessary for shareholders to have that information. Plus, investors will want to know what nondeductible expenses are being generated. The majority of expenses should be deductible.

Line 16 "Code D" "distributions" on Schedule K-1 corresponds to Line 16d on Schedule K. This is where distributions of the typical S-corporation are reported. These distributions (S-corporation "dividends") are usually not taxable. They are not reported on 1099-DIV. The shareholder will not receive Form 1099-DIV for tax-free distributions from an S-corporation.

Earnings Per Share Per Day And Ownership Changes (Optional)

K-1s become more complex if there is a change of ownership in the corporation during the year. Assume the entrepreneur who owned 100% of the corporation sells 20% of the corporation to an angel investor during the year. In this case, earnings are usually allocated to shareholders based upon both their percentage ownership and the number of days the stock has been held.

The Instructions for 1120S explain: "If there was a change in shareholders or in the relative interest in stock the shareholders owned during the tax year, each shareholder's percentage of ownership is weighted for the number of days in the tax year that stock was owned."

Suppose Angel Andy buys 20% of JPE on March 31. Looking at the calendar, we see Joe owned 100% of the company for all of January, February, and March. There are 90 days in those months. (Andy's "ownership" from a taxation standpoint starts the day after he gets the stock.) The other 275 days of the year, Joe owned 80% and Andy owned 20%.

Calculating earnings on a per day basis, we get $4,102.00 divided by 365 days which is $11.238 per day. For the first three months, all of those earnings are allocated to Joe. That amount is 90 times $11.238 or $1,011.42. The total earnings for the next 275 days is 275 times $11.238 or $3,090.45. Joe is allocated 80% of those earnings or $2,472.36, while Andy is allocated $618.09, which is his total share of pass-through earnings. Joe's total is $3,483.78.

Another way to calculate this is to do as the IRS instructions for 1120S show. Joe owned 100% of the corporation for 90 days. Then, Joe owned 80% and Andy owned 20%.

We calculate weighted percentage ownership:

First Period Of Ownership (90 days):

> Joe: 100% ownership times 90 days/365 days = 24.66%
> Andy: 0% ownership

Second Period (275 days):

> Joe: 80% ownership times 275 days/365 days = 60.27%
> Andy: 20% ownership times 275 days/365 days = 15.07%

Totals:

> Joe: 24.66% + 60.27% = 84.93%
> Andy: 15.07%

Joe's pro rata share of earnings is 84.93% of $4,102.00 or $3,483.83. Andy's pro rata share of the earnings is 15.07% times $4,102.00 or $618.17.

The values don't exactly equal the values calculated the first way. For example, the first way, Joe's portion of the earnings is $3,483.78. The second way, Joe's pro rata share is $3,483.83. The difference of 5 cents represents round-off error. While the difference might seem large, it represents only a 0.0014% difference.

Had we carried the percentage ownership more decimals, we would have calculated:

Joe: 100% times 90/365 = 24.6575%
      80% times 275/365 = 60.2740%

Andy: 20% times 275/365 = 15.0685%

And, Joe's total weighted average is 84.9315%, which gives him $3,483.89 as his pro rata share of the earnings. If under the first calculation method, we calculate earnings per day to more decimal places, we'd have earnings per day = $11.23836. With this higher precision in the calculation, Joe's total is $1,011.45 + $2,472.44 = $3,483.89. And, the calculations agree.

Round-off error might at first shock you. As the comedy *Office Space* points out, small fractions of a cent added up many, many times can become significant. So, you should usually round-off later in such a calculation, rather than sooner. Carry more decimal places. That provides more accuracy to the final result. All business people need a calculator. Depending upon the precision in your calculation, Joe's total portion of the earnings is $3,483.89, $3,483.78, or $3,483.83. The round-off differences probably won't bother the IRS, Joe, or Andy, and either calculation should be acceptable. Whenever you calculate two things that should agree by different methods, and they differ slightly, in addition to errors in calculation, look for round-off errors to help you understand why the calculations disagree slightly.

JPE originally issued Joe 100 shares of stock. If Andy purchased 20 of those shares, the number of shares to use in any calculation of earnings per share per day is 100. But, let's assume Andy received new shares from JPE. In this case, calculating as we did above is usually superior to calculating on a per share per day basis, because the number of shares has increased during the year. So, divide the year into multiple periods, each new period occurring when there is a percentage change in ownership of the company. Then, allocate earnings for each period.

If a shareholder sells his/her entire interest in an S-corporation, an election can be made to treat the tax year as two separate and shorter tax years. For example, suppose Joe decided to get out of the pottery business, and Andy purchased 100% of the corporation on March 31. The first 90 days could be treated as one "tax year," while the next 275 days become the second "tax year."

Analysis

Regardless of your business structure, you should analyze your operating results to give insight into your business. As long as we have the JPE tax return handy, we could calculate many important business ratios and other useful information.

For example, the pretax profit was $4,107 on sales revenue of $9,800, which represents a net pretax profit margin of $4,107/$9,800 = 41.9% which is incredibly good. That's because we only filled in a few key expenses of a typical business to illustrate the forms! Further, the income of $4,107 was generated on an initial investment of $10,000. That's a 41% return on investment, which is also great. You could also evaluate your expenses as a percentage of revenue and calculate other key ratios that help give insight into your operations.

In particular, it's useful to examine every expense as a percentage of sales revenue and compare your results to similar companies and to last year's performance. For JPE:

Revenue	$9,800.00	100.0%
Cogs	4,900.00	50.0%
Advertising	100.00	1.0%
Other Deductions		
Postage Expense	142.00	1.4%
Web Domain	20.00	0.2%
Office Supplies	20.00	0.2%
Trade Journal	18.00	0.2%
Net Pretax Profit	$4,600	46.9%

(Neglecting Joe's Salary, Other Income & Interest)

Notice we excluded Joe's salary because he's the only shareholder and, in a sense, that money went to him. We could have added his salary as another expense for our evaluation, if desired.

Angel investors and entrepreneurs might want to get further information and calculate some other ratios, such as revenue per employee and the growth in earnings from last year. As I mention in *Thinking Like An Entrepreneur*, I'm a big fan of calculating revenue per employee because it gives you a measure of how effective your company and its employees are in generating sales and fulfilling them.

Many smaller companies calculate such information quarterly or monthly to help them evaluate how their business is doing. If these calculations are new to you, I highly recommend *Keeping The Books: Basic Record-Keeping and Accounting For The Small Business* by Linda Pinson and Jerry Jinnett.

Conclusion

I hope you now feel more comfortable with S-corporation return 1120S and the associated K-1 form. Many successful S-corporation entrepreneurs have their accountants fill out tax forms, and they'd be hard pressed to explain exactly what an AAA is or what many of the lines on the tax form mean. So, don't feel bad if it seems a bit complex. Once you've seen these forms a time or two, they'll become easier to deal with.

** 1120S Tax Tips **

* Give yourself plenty of time to complete your tax return or find an accountant. The less time pressure the better!

* Have a printed copy of your balance sheet and profit and loss statement for the current tax year handy. These will provide information you need to complete your 1120S return.

* Page 1 of 1120S is generated from your profit and loss statement. Revenue (or "Income") minus expenses (or "Deductions") equals profits (or "Ordinary Business Income").

*Schedule L is a breakdown of your balance sheet or the basic accounting equation: Assets = Equity + Liabilities. Line 15 "Total Assets" should equal Line 27 "Total Liabilities and Shareholders' Equity." This equality holds true at the beginning of the tax year. It also holds true at the end of the tax year.

* Check your math at least twice. Math errors lead to tax audits!

* Make a copy of your tax return and all attachments and attached tax forms.

* If this isn't your first tax year, dig out your copy of last year's tax return for comparison. Note: On Schedule L, the values for last year's "End of tax year" should match the "Beginning of tax year" values for the new year. The end of last year is the beginning of this year.

* Look for any changes in the current tax form from last year. Especially look for new questions in Schedule B "Other Information." Usually, the forms will be the same. But new questions are added from time to time. Example: Question 13a) asking about 1099 forms didn't exist when the first edition of this book was published.

* I like to put a small mark under any lines which require an attachment as a reminder not to forget the attachment. Example, Line 19 "Other Deductions" says "attach statement." Forgetting to attach statements leads to audits.

Form 1120S

U.S. Income Tax Return for an S Corporation

▶ Do not file this form unless the corporation has filed or is attaching Form 2553 to elect to be an S corporation.

▶ Information about Form 1120S and its separate instructions is at *www.irs.gov/form1120s*.

Department of the Treasury
Internal Revenue Service

OMB No. 1545-0130

20**12**

For calendar year 2012 or tax year beginning _____, 2012, ending _____, 20____

A S election effective date	**TYPE**	**Name** Joe's Pottery Emporium, Ltd.
B Business activity code number (see instructions) 454110	**OR**	**Number, street, and room or suite no. If a P.O. box, see instructions.**
C Check if Sch. M-3 attached ☐	**PRINT**	**City or town, state, and ZIP code**

D Employer identification number

E Date incorporated

F Total assets (see instructions) $ 14107 00

G Is the corporation electing to be an S corporation beginning with this tax year? ☒ Yes ☐ No   If "Yes," attach Form 2553 if not already filed

H Check if: **(1)** ☐ Final return **(2)** ☐ Name change **(3)** ☐ Address change **(4)** ☐ Amended return **(5)** ☐ S election termination or revocation

I Enter the number of shareholders who were shareholders during any part of the tax year . . . . ▶ 1

Caution. Include **only** trade or business income and expenses on lines 1a through 21. See the instructions for more information.

Income

1a	Gross receipts or sales	1a	9800 00	
b	Returns and allowances	1b	0 00	
c	Balance. Subtract line 1b from line 1a			1c	9800 00
2	Cost of goods sold (attach Form 1125-A)			2	4900 00
3	Gross profit. Subtract line 2 from line 1c			3	4900 00
4	Net gain (loss) from Form 4797, line 17 (attach Form 4797)			4	
5	Other income (loss) (see instructions—attach statement) Amazon Associate Revenue			5	2 00
6	**Total income (loss).** Add lines 3 through 5 . . . . ▶			6	4902 00

Deductions (see instructions for limitations)

7	Compensation of officers	7	500 00
8	Salaries and wages (less employment credits)	8	
9	Repairs and maintenance	9	
10	Bad debts	10	
11	Rents	11	
12	Taxes and licenses	12	
13	Interest	13	
14	Depreciation not claimed on Form 1125-A or elsewhere on return (attach Form 4562)	14	
15	Depletion **(Do not deduct oil and gas depletion.)**	15	
16	Advertising	16	100 00
17	Pension, profit-sharing, etc., plans	17	
18	Employee benefit programs	18	
19	Other deductions (attach statement)	19	200 00
20	**Total deductions.** Add lines 7 through 19 . . . . ▶	20	800 00
21	**Ordinary business income (loss).** Subtract line 20 from line 6	21	4102 00

Tax and Payments

22a	Excess net passive income or LIFO recapture tax (see instructions) . .	22a		
b	Tax from Schedule D (Form 1120S)	22b		
c	Add lines 22a and 22b (see instructions for additional taxes)		22c	
23a	2012 estimated tax payments and 2011 overpayment credited to 2012	23a		
b	Tax deposited with Form 7004	23b		
c	Credit for federal tax paid on fuels (attach Form 4136)	23c		
d	Add lines 23a through 23c		23d	
24	Estimated tax penalty (see instructions). Check if Form 2220 is attached . . . . . . ▶ ☐		24	
25	**Amount owed.** If line 23d is smaller than the total of lines 22c and 24, enter amount owed . .		25	
26	**Overpayment.** If line 23d is larger than the total of lines 22c and 24, enter amount overpaid . .		26	
27	Enter amount from line 26 **Credited to 2013 estimated tax** ▶ _____	Refunded ▶	27	

Under penalties of perjury, I declare that I have examined this return, including accompanying schedules and statements, and to the best of my knowledge and belief, it is true, correct, and complete. Declaration of preparer (other than taxpayer) is based on all information of which preparer has any knowledge.

Sign Here

▶ Joe's Signature

Signature of officer   Date

▶ President

Title

May the IRS discuss this return with the preparer shown below (see instructions)? ☐ Yes ☐ No

Paid Preparer Use Only

Print/Type preparer's name	Preparer's signature	Date	Check ☐ if self-employed PTIN
Firm's name ▶			Firm's EIN ▶
Firm's address ▶			Phone no.

For Paperwork Reduction Act Notice, see separate instructions.

Cat. No. 11510H

Form **1120S** (2012)

Schedule B   Other Information (see instructions)

		Yes	No
1	Check accounting method: **a** ☐ Cash **b** ☒ Accrual		
	c ☐ Other (specify) ▶ _____		
2	See the instructions and enter the:		
	a Business activity ▶ **454110** **b** Product or service ▶ **Pottery**		
3	At any time during the tax year, was any shareholder of the corporation a disregarded entity, a trust, an estate, or a nominee or similar person?		X
4	At the end of the tax year, did the corporation:		
a	Own directly 20% or more, or own, directly or indirectly, 50% or more of the total stock issued and outstanding of any foreign or domestic corporation? For rules of constructive ownership, see instructions. If "Yes," complete (i) through (v) below		X

(i) Name of Corporation	**(ii)** Employer Identification Number (if any)	**(iii)** Country of Incorporation	**(iv)** Percentage of Stock Owned	**(v)** If Percentage in (iv) is 100%, Enter the Date (if any) a Qualified Subchapter S Subsidiary Election Was Made

		Yes	No
b	Own directly an interest of 20% or more, or own, directly or indirectly, an interest of 50% or more in the profit, loss, or capital in any foreign or domestic partnership (including an entity treated as a partnership) or in the beneficial interest of a trust? For rules of constructive ownership, see instructions. If "Yes," complete (i) through (v) below		X

(i) Name of Entity	**(ii)** Employer Identification Number (if any)	**(iii)** Type of Entity	**(iv)** Country of Organization	**(v)** Maximum Percentage Owned in Profit, Loss, or Capital

		Yes	No
5 a	At the end of the tax year, did the corporation have any outstanding shares of restricted stock?		X
	If "Yes," complete lines (i) and (ii) below.		
	(i) Total shares of restricted stock . . . . ▶ _____		
	(ii) Total shares of non-restricted stock . . . . ▶ _____		
b	At the end of the tax year, did the corporation have any outstanding stock options, warrants, or similar instruments? .		X
	If "Yes," complete lines (i) and (ii) below.		
	(i) Total shares of stock outstanding at the end of the tax year ▶ _____		
	(ii) Total shares of stock outstanding if all instruments were executed ▶ _____		
6	Has this corporation filed, or is it required to file, **Form 8918**, Material Advisor Disclosure Statement, to provide information on any reportable transaction?		X
7	Check this box if the corporation issued publicly offered debt instruments with original issue discount . . . . ▶ ☐		
	If checked, the corporation may have to file Form 8281, Information Return for Publicly Offered Original Issue Discount Instruments.		
8	If the corporation: **(a)** was a C corporation before it elected to be an S corporation **or** the corporation acquired an asset with a basis determined by reference to the basis of the asset (or the basis of any other property) in the hands of a C corporation **and (b)** has net unrealized built-in gain in excess of the net recognized built-in gain from prior years, enter the net unrealized built-in gain reduced by net recognized built-in gain from prior years (see instructions) . . . . ▶ $ _____		
9	Enter the accumulated earnings and profits of the corporation at the end of the tax year. $ _____		
10	Does the corporation satisfy **both** of the following conditions?		
a	The corporation's total receipts (see instructions) for the tax year were less than $250,000		
b	The corporation's total assets at the end of the tax year were less than $250,000 . . . . · . . .	X	
	If "Yes," the corporation is <u>not required to complete Schedules L and M-1.</u>		
11	During the tax year, did the corporation have any non-shareholder debt that was canceled, was forgiven, or had the terms modified so as to reduce the principal amount of the debt?		X
	If "Yes," enter the amount of principal reduction $ _____		
12	During the tax year, was a qualified subchapter S subsidiary election terminated or revoked? If "Yes," see instructions .		X
13 a	Did the corporation make any payments in 2012 that would require it to file <u>Form(s) 1099?</u>		X
b	If "Yes," did the corporation file or will it file required Forms 1099?		

Schedule K		Shareholders' Pro Rata Share Items		Total amount

Income (Loss)

	1	Ordinary business income (loss) (page 1, line 21)	1	4102 00
	2	Net rental real estate income (loss) (attach Form 8825)	2	
	3a	Other gross rental income (loss)	3a		
	b	Expenses from other rental activities (attach statement) . .	3b		
	c	Other net rental income (loss). Subtract line 3b from line 3a	3c	
	4	Interest income	4	5 00
	5	Dividends: **a** Ordinary dividends	5a	
		b Qualified dividends	5b		
	6	Royalties	6	
	7	Net short-term capital gain (loss) (attach Schedule D (Form 1120S))	7	
	8a	Net long-term capital gain (loss) (attach Schedule D (Form 1120S))	8a	
	b	Collectibles (28%) gain (loss)	8b		
	c	Unrecaptured section 1250 gain (attach statement)	8c		
	9	Net section 1231 gain (loss) (attach Form 4797)	9	
	10	Other income (loss) (see instructions) . . Type ▶	10	

Deductions

	11	Section 179 deduction (attach Form 4562)	11	
	12a	Charitable contributions	12a	
	b	Investment interest expense	12b	
	c	Section 59(e)(2) expenditures **(1)** Type ▶ _____ **(2)** Amount ▶	12c(2)	
	d	Other deductions (see instructions) . . . Type ▶	12d	

Credits

	13a	Low-income housing credit (section 42(j)(5))	13a	
	b	Low-income housing credit (other)	13b	
	c	Qualified rehabilitation expenditures (rental real estate) (attach Form 3468)	13c	
	d	Other rental real estate credits (see instructions) Type ▶ _____	13d	
	e	Other rental credits (see instructions) . . . Type ▶ _____	13e	
	f	Alcohol and cellulosic biofuel fuels credit (attach Form 6478)	13f	
	g	Other credits (see instructions) . . . Type ▶	13g	

Foreign Transactions

	14a	Name of country or U.S. possession ▶ _____		
	b	Gross income from all sources	14b	
	c	Gross income sourced at shareholder level	14c	
		Foreign gross income sourced at corporate level		
	d	Passive category	14d	
	e	General category	14e	
	f	Other (attach statement)	14f	
		Deductions allocated and apportioned at shareholder level		
	g	Interest expense	14g	
	h	Other	14h	
		Deductions allocated and apportioned at corporate level to foreign source income		
	i	Passive category	14i	
	j	General category	14j	
	k	Other (attach statement)	14k	
		Other information		
	l	Total foreign taxes (check one): ▶ ☐ Paid ☐ Accrued	14l	
	m	Reduction in taxes available for credit (attach statement)	14m	
	n	Other foreign tax information (attach statement)		

Alternative Minimum Tax (AMT) Items

	15a	Post-1986 depreciation adjustment	15a	
	b	Adjusted gain or loss	15b	
	c	Depletion (other than oil and gas)	15c	
	d	Oil, gas, and geothermal properties—gross income	15d	
	e	Oil, gas, and geothermal properties—deductions	15e	
	f	Other AMT items (attach statement)	15f	

Items Affecting Shareholder Basis

	16a	Tax-exempt interest income	16a	
	b	Other tax-exempt income	16b	
	c	Nondeductible expenses	16c	
	d	Distributions (attach statement if required) (see instructions)	16d	
	e	Repayment of loans from shareholders	16e	

Form **1120S** (2012)

Schedule K	Shareholders' Pro Rata Share Items (continued)		Total amount	
Other Information	**17a**	Investment income	**17a**	
	b	Investment expenses	**17b**	
	c	Dividend distributions paid from accumulated earnings and profits	**17c**	
	d	Other items and amounts (attach statement)		
Recon-ciliation	**18**	**Income/loss reconciliation.** Combine the amounts on lines 1 through 10 in the far right column. From the result, subtract the sum of the amounts on lines 11 through 12d and 14l	**18**	4107 00

Schedule L	Balance Sheets per Books	Beginning of tax year		End of tax year	
	Assets	(a)	(b)	(c)	(d)
1	Cash		10,000.00		9,005.00
2a	Trade notes and accounts receivable . . .	0.00		2,002.00	
b	Less allowance for bad debts	(0.00)	0.00	(0.00)	2,002.00
3	Inventories		0.00		3,100.00
4	U.S. government obligations				
5	Tax-exempt securities (see instructions) . .				
6	Other current assets (attach statement) . . .				
7	Loans to shareholders				
8	Mortgage and real estate loans				
9	Other investments (attach statement) . . .				
10a	Buildings and other depreciable assets . . .				
b	Less accumulated depreciation	( )		( )	
11a	Depletable assets				
b	Less accumulated depletion	( )		( )	
12	Land (net of any amortization)				
13a	Intangible assets (amortizable only)				
b	Less accumulated amortization	( )		( )	
14	Other assets (attach statement)				
15	Total assets		10,000.00		14,107.00
	Liabilities and Shareholders' Equity				
16	Accounts payable		0.00		0.00
17	Mortgages, notes, bonds payable in less than 1 year				
18	Other current liabilities (attach statement) . .				
19	Loans from shareholders		0.00		0.00
20	Mortgages, notes, bonds payable in 1 year or more				
21	Other liabilities (attach statement)				
22	Capital stock		10,000.00		10,000.00
23	Additional paid-in capital				
24	Retained earnings		0.00		4,107.00
25	Adjustments to shareholders' equity (attach statement)				
26	Less cost of treasury stock		( )		( )
27	Total liabilities and shareholders' equity . .		10,000.00		14,107.00

Schedule M-1	Reconciliation of Income (Loss) per Books With Income (Loss) per Return

Note. Schedule M-3 required instead of Schedule M-1 if total assets are $10 million or more—see instructions

1	Net income (loss) per books	4,107.00	5	Income recorded on books this year not included on Schedule K, lines 1 through 10 (itemize):	
2	Income included on Schedule K, lines 1, 2, 3c, 4, 5a, 6, 7, 8a, 9, and 10, not recorded on books this year (itemize)		**a**	Tax-exempt interest $	
3	Expenses recorded on books this year not included on Schedule K, lines 1 through 12 and 14l (itemize):		6	Deductions included on Schedule K, lines 1 through 12 and 14l, not charged against book income this year (itemize):	
a	Depreciation $		**a**	Depreciation $	
b	Travel and entertainment $				
			7	Add lines 5 and 6	
4	Add lines 1 through 3	4,107.00	8	Income (loss) (Schedule K, line 18). Line 4 less line 7	4,107.00

Schedule M-2	Analysis of Accumulated Adjustments Account, Other Adjustments Account, and Shareholders' Undistributed Taxable Income Previously Taxed (see instructions)

		(a) Accumulated adjustments account	(b) Other adjustments account	(c) Shareholders' undistributed taxable income previously taxed
1	Balance at beginning of tax year	0.00		'
2	Ordinary income from page 1, line 21 . . .	4,102.00		
3	Other additions	5.00		
4	Loss from page 1, line 21	( )		
5	Other reductions	( )	( )	
6	Combine lines 1 through 5	4,107.00		
7	Distributions other than dividend distributions	0.00		
8	Balance at end of tax year. Subtract line 7 from line 6	4,107.00		

Form **1120S** (2012)

Cost of Goods Sold

► Attach to Form 1120, 1120-C, 1120-F, 1120S, 1065, or 1065-B.
► Information about Form 1125-A and its instructions is at *www.irs.gov/form1125a.*

OMB No. 1545-2225

Name	Employer identification number
Joe's Pottery Emporium, Ltd.	

1	Inventory at beginning of year	1	0	00
2	Purchases	2	8000	00
3	Cost of labor	3		
4	Additional section 263A costs (attach schedule)	4		
5	Other costs (attach schedule)	5		
6	**Total.** Add lines 1 through 5	6	8000	00
7	Inventory at end of year	7	3100	00
8	**Cost of goods sold.** Subtract line 7 from line 6. Enter here and on Form 1120, page 1, line 2 or the appropriate line of your tax return (see instructions)	8	4900	00

9a Check all methods used for valuing closing inventory:

    (i) ☒ Cost

    (ii) ☐ Lower of cost or market

    (iii) ☐ Other (Specify method used and attach explanation.) ► ------------------------------------

  b Check if there was a writedown of subnormal goods   ► ☐

  c Check if the LIFO inventory method was adopted this tax year for any goods (if checked, attach Form 970)   ► ☐

  d If the LIFO inventory method was used for this tax year, enter amount of closing inventory computed under LIFO | 9d | |

  e If property is produced or acquired for resale, do the rules of section 263A apply to the entity (see instructions)?   ☐ Yes   ☒ No

  f Was there any change in determining quantities, cost, or valuations between opening and closing inventory? If "Yes," attach explanation   ☐ Yes   ☒ No

---

Section references are to the Internal Revenue Code unless otherwise noted.

General Instructions

Purpose of Form

Use Form 1125-A to calculate and deduct cost of goods sold for certain entities.

Who Must File

Filers of Form 1120, 1120-C, 1120-F, 1120S, 1065, or 1065-B, must complete and attach Form 1125-A if the applicable entity reports a deduction for cost of goods sold.

Inventories

Generally, inventories are required at the beginning and end of each tax year if the production, purchase, or sale of merchandise is an income-producing factor. See Regulations section 1.471-1. If inventories are required, you generally must use an accrual method of accounting for sales and purchases of inventory items.

Exception for certain taxpayers. If you are a qualifying taxpayer or a qualifying small business taxpayer (defined below), you can adopt or change your accounting method to account for inventoriable items in the same manner as materials and supplies that are not incidental.

Under this accounting method, inventory costs for raw materials purchased for use in producing finished goods and merchandise purchased for resale are deductible in the year the finished goods or merchandise are sold (but not before the year you paid for the raw materials or merchandise, if you are also using the cash method).

If you account for inventoriable items in the same manner as materials and supplies that are not incidental, you can currently deduct expenditures for direct labor and all indirect costs that would otherwise be included in inventory costs. See the instructions for lines 2 and 7.

For additional guidance on this method of accounting, see Pub. 538, Accounting Periods and Methods. For guidance on adopting or changing to this method of accounting, see Form 3115, Application for Change in Accounting Method, and its instructions.

Qualifying taxpayer. A qualifying taxpayer is a taxpayer that, (a) for each prior tax year ending after December 16, 1998, has average annual gross receipts of $1 million or less for the 3 prior tax years and (b) its business is not a tax shelter (as defined in section 448(d)(3)). See Rev. Proc. 2001-10, 2001-2 I.R.B. 272.

Qualifying small business taxpayer. A qualifying small business taxpayer is a taxpayer that, (a) for each prior tax year

ending on or after December 31, 2000, has average annual gross receipts of $10 million or less for the 3 prior tax years, (b) whose principal business activity is not an ineligible activity, and (c) whose business is not a tax shelter (as defined in section 448 (d)(3)). See Rev. Proc. 2002-28, 2002-18 I.R.B. 815.

Uniform capitalization rules. The uniform capitalization rules of section 263A generally require you to capitalize, or include in inventory, certain costs incurred in connection with the following.

• The production of real property and tangible personal property held in inventory or held for sale in the ordinary course of business.

• Real property or personal property (tangible and intangible) acquired for resale.

• The production of real property and tangible personal property by a corporation for use in its trade or business or in an activity engaged in for profit.

See the discussion on section 263A uniform capitalization rules in the instructions for your tax return before completing Form 1125-A. Also see Regulations sections 1.263A-1 through 1.263A-3. See Regulations section 1.263A-4 for rules for property produced in a farming business.

Note: Pages 2 & 3 of this form have not been reproduced. They're just instructions.

For Paperwork Reduction Act Notice, see instructions.   Cat. No. 55988R

671112

Schedule K-1
(Form 1120S)

2012

Department of the Treasury
Internal Revenue Service

For calendar year 2012, or tax
year beginning _____ , 2012
ending _____ , 20 _____

Shareholder's Share of Income, Deductions,
Credits, etc.   ▶ See back of form and separate instructions.

Part I	Information About the Corporation

A   Corporation's employer identification number

B   Corporation's name, address, city, state, and ZIP code

   Joe's Pottery Emporium, Ltd.

C   IRS Center where corporation filed return
   (This address is in the instructions for 1120S)

Part II	Information About the Shareholder

D   Shareholder's identifying number

E   Shareholder's name, address, city, state, and ZIP code

   Joe Plaster

F   Shareholder's percentage of stock
   ownership for tax year . . . . . .   **100** %

Part III	Shareholder's Share of Current Year Income, Deductions, Credits, and Other Items

1	Ordinary business income (loss) **4102.00**	13	Credits
2	Net rental real estate income (loss)		
3	Other net rental income (loss)		
4	Interest income **5.00**		
5a	Ordinary dividends		
5b	Qualified dividends	14	Foreign transactions
6	Royalties		
7	Net short-term capital gain (loss)		
8a	Net long-term capital gain (loss)		
8b	Collectibles (28%) gain (loss)		
8c	Unrecaptured section 1250 gain		
9	Net section 1231 gain (loss)		
10	Other income (loss)	15	Alternative minimum tax (AMT) items
11	Section 179 deduction	16	Items affecting shareholder basis
		c	
12	Other deductions	**d**	
		17	Other information

For IRS Use Only

Note: The only entries Joe has on this form are line 1) and line 4).

Under Line 16, we have entered the code "C" for nondeductible expenses and the code "D" for distributions. These "codes" correspond to line 16c) and line 16d) on 1120S Schedule K. If Joe had nondeductible expenses or distributions, this is where they're reported on K-1.

* See attached statement for additional information.

671112

Schedule K-1
(Form 1120S)
Department of the Treasury
Internal Revenue Service

For calendar year 2012, or tax
year beginning _____, 2012
ending _____, 20 _____

2012

☐ Final K-1   ☐ Amended K-1   OMB No. 1545-0130

Shareholder's Share of Income, Deductions, Credits, etc. ▶ See back of form and separate instructions.

Part III	Shareholder's Share of Current Year Income, Deductions, Credits, and Other Items

1	Ordinary business income (loss) 2412.94	13	Credits
2	Net rental real estate income (loss)		
3	Other net rental income (loss)		
4	Interest income 2.94		
5a	Ordinary dividends		
5b	Qualified dividends	14	Foreign transactions
6	Royalties		
7	Net short-term capital gain (loss)		
8a	Net long-term capital gain (loss)		
8b	Collectibles (28%) gain (loss)		
8c	Unrecaptured section 1250 gain		
9	Net section 1231 gain (loss)		
10	Other income (loss)	15	Alternative minimum tax (AMT) items
11	Section 179 deduction	16	Items affecting shareholder basis
12	Other deductions		
		17	Other information

Part I Information About the Corporation

A Corporation's employer identification number

B Corporation's name, address, city, state, and ZIP code

Joe's Pottery Emporium, Ltd.

C IRS Center where corporation filed return
(This address is in the instructions for 1120S)

Part II Information About the Shareholder

D Shareholder's identifying number

E Shareholder's name, address, city, state, and ZIP code

Joe Plaster

F Shareholder's percentage of stock
ownership for tax year . . . . **58.82** %

These three K-1's are for the Three Shareholder Case, where Joe only owns 58.82% of the company. You see the ordinary income and the interest income pass through to the shareholder in proportion to their ownership.

For IRS Use Only

* See attached statement for additional information.

For Paperwork Reduction Act Notice, see Instructions for Form 1120S.   IRS.gov/form1120s   Cat. No. 11520D   Schedule K-1 (Form 1120S) 2012

671112

| | □ Final K-1 □ Amended K-1 | OMB No. 1545-0130 |

Schedule K-1 (Form 1120S)
Department of the Treasury
Internal Revenue Service

2012

For calendar year 2012, or tax
year beginning _____ , 2012
ending _____ , 20 _____

Shareholder's Share of Income, Deductions, Credits, etc. ► See back of form and separate instructions.

Part I Information About the Corporation

A Corporation's employer identification number

B Corporation's name, address, city, state, and ZIP code

Joe's Pottery Emporium, Ltd.

C IRS Center where corporation filed return
(This address is in the instructions for 1120S)

Part II Information About the Shareholder

D Shareholder's identifying number

E Shareholder's name, address, city, state, and ZIP code

Tim Jones

F Shareholder's percentage of stock ownership for tax year . . . . **11.77** %

These three K-1's are for the Three Shareholder Case, where Joe only owns 58.82% of the company. You see the ordinary income and the interest income pass through to the shareholder in proportion to their ownership.

Part III Shareholder's Share of Current Year Income, Deductions, Credits, and Other Items

1	Ordinary business income (loss)	13	Credits
	482.59		
2	Net rental real estate income (loss)		
3	Other net rental income (loss)		
4	Interest income		
	0.59		
5a	Ordinary dividends		
5b	Qualified dividends	14	Foreign transactions
6	Royalties		
7	Net short-term capital gain (loss)		
8a	Net long-term capital gain (loss)		
8b	Collectibles (28%) gain (loss)		
8c	Unrecaptured section 1250 gain		
9	Net section 1231 gain (loss)		
10	Other income (loss)	15	Alternative minimum tax (AMT) items
11	Section 179 deduction	16	Items affecting shareholder basis
12	Other deductions		
		17	Other information

* See attached statement for additional information.

For IRS Use Only

For Paperwork Reduction Act Notice, see Instructions for Form 1120S.   IRS.gov/form1120s   Cat. No. 11520D   Schedule K-1 (Form 1120S) 2012

Schedule K-1
(Form 1120S)
Department of the Treasury
Internal Revenue Service

20**12**

For calendar year 2012, or tax
year beginning _____ , 2012
ending _____ , 20 _____

**Shareholder's Share of Income, Deductions,
Credits, etc.** ► See back of form and separate instructions.

☐ Final K-1   ☐ Amended K-1   OMB No. 1545-0130

Part III	**Shareholder's Share of Current Year Income, Deductions, Credits, and Other Items**	
1	Ordinary business income (loss) **1206.47**	13 Credits
2	Net rental real estate income (loss)	
3	Other net rental income (loss)	
4	Interest income **1.47**	
5a	Ordinary dividends	
5b	Qualified dividends	14 Foreign transactions
6	Royalties	
7	Net short-term capital gain (loss)	
8a	Net long-term capital gain (loss)	
8b	Collectibles (28%) gain (loss)	
8c	Unrecaptured section 1250 gain	
9	Net section 1231 gain (loss)	
10	Other income (loss)	15 Alternative minimum tax (AMT) items
11	Section 179 deduction	16 Items affecting shareholder basis
12	Other deductions	
		17 Other information

Part I   Information About the Corporation

A   Corporation's employer identification number

B   Corporation's name, address, city, state, and ZIP code

Joe's Pottery Emporium, Ltd.

C   IRS Center where corporation filed return
(This address is in the instructions for 1120S)

Part II   Information About the Shareholder

D   Shareholder's identifying number

E   Shareholder's name, address, city, state, and ZIP code

Hank Earl Putnam, The Third

F   Shareholder's percentage of stock
ownership for tax year   .   .   .   .   .   .   **29.41** %

These three K-1's are for the Three Shareholder Case, where Joe only owns 58.82% of the company. You see the ordinary income and the interest income pass through to the shareholder in proportion to their ownership.

For IRS Use Only

* See attached statement for additional information.

For Paperwork Reduction Act Notice, see Instructions for Form 1120S.   IRS.gov/form1120s   Cat. No. 11520D   **Schedule K-1 (Form 1120S) 2012**

Chapter 19
Joe Plaster's Personal Income Tax Return (1040 and Schedule E)

In the last chapter, we worked out a basic 1120S S-corporation tax return for Joe Plaster's company. As we saw, that tax return was largely informational; no tax was due. It is filed annually with the IRS by March 15. The 1120S allowed us to generate K-1 forms to provide to the shareholders. The corporation also sent copies of the K-1s to the IRS.

The K-1 received by the shareholder isn't filed with the IRS by the shareholder. It's used to help the shareholder compute his personal 1040 income tax return. A new shareholder should also receive a copy of the IRS publication "Shareholder's Instructions for Schedule K-1." This will help the shareholder unravel the mysteries of the K-1.

In this chapter we'll work out how Joe takes the information from the K-1 and computes his personal 1040 income tax return. He owns 100% of the company. Line 1 of the K-1 shows Joe has $4,102.00 in ordinary income from business activities. He has $5.00 in interest. He also has a modest salary from the company.

Since Joe is a paid employee of his corporation, he received a W-2 from it. His job with Joe's Pottery Emporium is like any other job. He reports his W-2 income on Line 7 of his personal 1040 tax return. This amount is $54,201.68, which we'll assume is the total wage income Joe has from his day job and his sideline pottery business.

Don't forget to attach copies of your W-2 form(s) to your 1040, including a W-2 from your corporation, if your corporation paid you a salary. In the next chapter, we'll discuss W-2s in detail.

Note: Because Joe isn't trying to remove employment-tax-free distributions from his S corporation, he isn't required to pay himself a reasonable wage yet. The first page of Joe's 1040 is at the end of this chapter.

Line 29 should be noted: "Self-employed health insurance deduction." Although technically Joe is not "self-employed," this line is where he reports his health insurance deduction. So, if Joe's W-2 included $5,000 paid for Joe's health insurance by his S-corporation, on Line 29, we would also record $5,000. This has the effect of reducing Joe's taxable income by $5,000. Joe does not pay income tax on the money he uses to purchase health insurance if it's provided by his S-corporation.

In our example, Joe's corporation doesn't pay his health insurance, so Line 29 will be blank. For more information about who is eligible to fill in Line 29, see the Form 1040 Instructions for Line 29. This line also applies if Joe operates as a sole proprietor (Schedule C business) or if he operates as an LLC.

Line 8a is "Taxable interest." This is where Joe reports the $5.00 in interest he earned from Joe's Pottery Emporium. We'll assume he has no other interest. We see how interest the corporation earns flows through to Joe's personal tax return. Just as an aside, notice, that if Joe didn't remove any money from his corporation, either as wages or distributions, this earned interest would be an example of "phantom income." He's taxed at the personal level for this interest, but it remains in his corporation, undistributed.

Joe is nearly done. He must now report his $4,102.00 in business income. This is done on Line 17. When filling out Line 17, you'll need to download 1040 Schedule E. Joe's Schedule E is shown at the end of this chapter. We didn't reproduce Page 1 of Schedule E because it doesn't apply. Only Part II "Income or Loss From Partnerships and S Corporations" and Part V "Summary" apply.

On Line 28, under "A" Joe lists the name of his S-corporation "Joe's Pottery Emporium." He writes down a big "S" to let the IRS know it's an S-corporation. Under column "d" he records the Employer Identification Number (EIN) for his corporation. "A" now refers to "Joe's Pottery Emporium."

If Joe owned another S-corporation or was a partner in a partnership, that entity would be reported under "B." Schedule E provides room for up to four partnerships or S corporations, "A" through "D."

Because Joe is actively involved in operating his company, Lines 28 columns f) and g) "Passive Income and Loss" don't apply. All of his income is Nonpassive. Under column j) "Nonpassive income from Schedule K-1" and on the line for "A" (i.e., Joe's Pottery Emporium), Joe writes down $4,102.00.

Line 30 is just the total income from all of Joe's S-corporations and partnerships. Because Joe doesn't have any partnerships or S-corporations with losses (which would have been reported in column h), Line 32 is the same as Line 30.

Following the instructions, we also record $4,102.00 on Line 41 of Schedule E and on Line 17 of Joe's 1040. Joe's personal income tax return is now completed. We see Joe will pay personal income tax on the money his S-corporation earned, regardless of if the money is distributed to him or if it remains in the corporation.

If you have a Section 179 expense deduction, that amount is reported in column i) of Schedule E. A Section 179 deduction is effectively treated as negative income on Line 31, i.e., it reduces taxable income. This is how Section 179 expense deductions flow through to shareholder tax returns.

If Joe hadn't had a profitable first year, but had incurred an operating loss, the loss would have been entered in column h) "Nonpassive loss from Schedule K-1." Line 32 and Line 41 would have been negative numbers. This negative number would be entered on Line 17 of Joe's 1040 page 1. This would have reduced Joe's personal, taxable income by the amount his corporation lost.

You now see exactly how S-corporation income and losses flow through to the shareholders, via Schedule E. You also see that Joe will pay income tax on his S-corporation's earnings (1040 Line 17), even if he didn't remove any of those earnings from the company (so called "phantom income").

Estimated Taxes (IRS Form 1040-ES)

Because from a tax standpoint, S-corporation income flows through to the shareholders, the shareholders must pay individual income tax on that income. Joe had $4,102.00 in S-corporation income in 2012. Unlike wages, where the employer withholds a portion of the wages to cover the employee's income tax on the wages, there is no withholding of S-corporation profits to cover the individual's tax liability.

What if Joe has smashing success in 2013 and earns $150,000 in profits with his new pottery business? This $150,000 is in excess of the wages he pays himself. At year end, he'd have a whopping tax bill! Because the income tax system is considered a "pay as you go" system, Joe should pay tax on this income as it's earned. He can do this by downloading IRS tax package 1040-ES for 2013. Form 1040-ES is basically just four payment vouchers which allow Joe to make quarterly estimated tax payments to the IRS.

At the end of this chapter, Page 11 of Form 1040-ES is reproduced to show you what the payment vouchers look like. They're very basic. Just fill out who you are and how much you're sending to the IRS.

Package 1040-ES contains a worksheet to help you calculate the estimated taxes you'll owe. The worksheet can help you minimize your estimated tax payments. If you use the worksheet, remember, as a S-corporation owner, you won't owe self-employment tax on your pass through income.

Rather than using the worksheet, it's simpler to just estimate your income tax rate and multiply it by the earnings for the quarter. If you overpay your estimated taxes, you can have this money refunded to you at year end or apply it to your next year's estimated taxes. It's important not to underpay, because you could face penalties.

If Joe's S-corporation profits are $37,500 in the first quarter of 2013, and he estimates he'll be in the 28% individual incremental tax bracket, he could estimate he'll owe about $10,500 in personal income tax on his first quarter's S-corporation's 2013 income.

Form **1040**
Department of the Treasury—Internal Revenue Service (99)
U.S. Individual Income Tax Return 2012 OMB No. 1545-0074 IRS Use Only—Do not write or staple in this space.

| For the year Jan. 1–Dec. 31, 2012, or other tax year beginning | , 2012, ending | , 20 | See separate instructions. |

Your first name and initial: **Joe**
Last name: **Plaster**
Your social security number:

If a joint return, spouse's first name and initial:
Last name:
Spouse's social security number:

Home address (number and street). If you have a P.O. box, see instructions.
This is page 1 of Joe's personal tax return. Not part of 1120S
Apt. no.

▲ Make sure the SSN(s) above and on line 6c are correct.

City, town or post office, state, and ZIP code. If you have a foreign address, also complete spaces below (see instructions).

Presidential Election Campaign
Check here if you, or your spouse if filing jointly, want $3 to go to this fund. Checking a box below will not change your tax or refund. ☐ You ☐ Spouse

| Foreign country name | Foreign province/state/county | Foreign postal code |

Filing Status
Check only one box.

1 ☐ Single
2 ☐ Married filing jointly (even if only one had income)
3 ☐ Married filing separately. Enter spouse's SSN above and full name here. ▶
4 ☐ Head of household (with qualifying person). (See instructions.) If the qualifying person is a child but not your dependent, enter this child's name here. ▶
5 ☐ Qualifying widow(er) with dependent child

Exemptions

6a ☐ **Yourself.** If someone can claim you as a dependent, **do not** check box 6a
b ☐ **Spouse**

c Dependents:		(2) Dependent's social security number	(3) Dependent's relationship to you	(4) ✓ if child under age 17 qualifying for child tax credit (see instructions)
(1) First name	Last name			
				☐
				☐
				☐
				☐

Boxes checked on 6a and 6b
No. of children on 6c who:
• lived with you
• did not live with you due to divorce or separation (see instructions)
Dependents on 6c not entered above
Add numbers on lines above ▶

If more than four dependents, see instructions and check here ▶ ☐

d Total number of exemptions claimed

Income

Attach Form(s) W-2 here. Also attach Forms W-2G and 1099-R if tax was withheld.

If you did not get a W-2, see instructions.

Enclose, but do not attach, any payment. Also, please use Form 1040-V.

7	Wages, salaries, tips, etc. Attach Form(s) W-2	7	54201	68
8a	Taxable interest. Attach Schedule B if required	8a	5	00
b	Tax-exempt interest. Do not include on line 8a	8b		
9a	Ordinary dividends. Attach Schedule B if required	9a		
b	Qualified dividends	9b		
10	Taxable refunds, credits, or offsets of state and local income taxes	10		
11	Alimony received	11		
12	Business income or (loss). Attach Schedule C or C-EZ	12		
13	Capital gain or (loss). Attach Schedule D if required. If not required, check here ▶ ☐	13		
14	Other gains or (losses). Attach Form 4797	14		
15a	IRA distributions 15a	b Taxable amount	15b		
16a	Pensions and annuities 16a	b Taxable amount	16b		
17	Rental real estate, royalties, partnerships, S corporations, trusts, etc. Attach Schedule E	17	4102	00
18	Farm income or (loss). Attach Schedule F	18		
19	Unemployment compensation	19		
20a	Social security benefits 20a	b Taxable amount	20b		
21	Other income. List type and amount	21		
22	Combine the amounts in the far right column for lines 7 through 21. This is your **total income** ▶	22		

Adjusted Gross Income

23	Educator expenses	23		
24	Certain business expenses of reservists, performing artists, and fee-basis government officials. Attach Form 2106 or 2106-EZ	24		
25	Health savings account deduction. Attach Form 8889	25		
26	Moving expenses. Attach Form 3903	26		
27	Deductible part of self-employment tax. Attach Schedule SE	27		
28	Self-employed SEP, SIMPLE, and qualified plans	28		
29	Self-employed health insurance deduction	29		
30	Penalty on early withdrawal of savings	30		
31a	Alimony paid b Recipient's SSN ▶	31a		
32	IRA deduction	32		
33	Student loan interest deduction	33		
34	Tuition and fees. Attach Form 8917	34		
35	Domestic production activities deduction. Attach Form 8903	35		
36	Add lines 23 through 35	36		
37	Subtract line 36 from line 22. This is your **adjusted gross income** ▶	37		

Cat. No. 11320B Form **1040** (2012)

Name(s) shown on return. Do not enter name and social security number if shown on other side. | Your social security number

Joe Plaster

Caution. The IRS compares amounts reported on your tax return with amounts shown on Schedule(s) K-1.

Part II   **Income or Loss From Partnerships and S Corporations**   **Note.** If you report a loss from an at-risk activity for which any amount is **not** at risk, you **must** check the box in column **(e)** on line 28 and attach **Form 6198.** See instructions.

27   Are you reporting any loss not allowed in a prior year due to the at-risk or basis limitations, a prior year unallowed loss from a passive activity (if that loss was not reported on Form 8582), or unreimbursed partnership expenses? If you answered "Yes," see instructions before completing this section. ☐ **Yes**   ☐ **No**

28	(a) Name	(b) Enter P for partnership; S for S corporation	(c) Check if foreign partnership	(d) Employer identification number	(e) Check if any amount is not at risk
A	Joe's Pottery Emporium	S	☐	EIN HERE	☐
B			☐		☐
C			☐		☐
D			☐		☐

	Passive Income and Loss		Nonpassive Income and Loss		
	(f) Passive loss allowed (attach Form 8582 if required)	(g) Passive income from Schedule K-1	(h) Nonpassive loss from Schedule K-1	(i) Section 179 expense deduction from Form 4562	(j) Nonpassive income from Schedule K-1
A					4102 00
B					
C					
D					
29a Totals					4102 00
b Totals					

30	Add columns (g) and (j) of line 29a	30	4102 00
31	Add columns (f), (h), and (i) of line 29b	31	( )
32	**Total partnership and S corporation income or (loss).** Combine lines 30 and 31. Enter the result here and include in the total on line 41 below	32	4102 00

Part III   **Income or Loss From Estates and Trusts**

33	(a) Name	(b) Employer identification number
A		
B		

	Passive Income and Loss		Nonpassive Income and Loss	
	(c) Passive deduction or loss allowed (attach Form 8582 if required)	(d) Passive income from Schedule K-1	(e) Deduction or loss from Schedule K-1	(f) Other income from Schedule K-1
A				
B				
34a Totals				
b Totals				

35	Add columns (d) and (f) of line 34a	35	
36	Add columns (c) and (e) of line 34b	36	( )
37	**Total estate and trust income or (loss).** Combine lines 35 and 36. Enter the result here and include in the total on line 41 below	37	

Part IV   **Income or Loss From Real Estate Mortgage Investment Conduits (REMICs)—Residual Holder**

38	(a) Name	(b) Employer identification number	(c) Excess inclusion from Schedules Q, line 2c (see instructions)	(d) Taxable income (net loss) from Schedules Q, line 1b	(e) Income from Schedules Q, line 3b

39	Combine columns (d) and (e) only. Enter the result here and include in the total on line 41 below	39	

Part V   **Summary**

40	Net farm rental income or (loss) from **Form 4835.** Also, complete line 42 below	40	
41	**Total income or (loss).** Combine lines 26, 32, 37, 39, and 40. Enter the result here and on Form 1040, line 17, or Form 1040NR, line 18 ▶	41	4102 00

42	Reconciliation of farming and fishing income. Enter your **gross** farming and fishing income reported on Form 4835, line 7; Schedule K-1 (Form 1065), box 14, code B; Schedule K-1 (Form 1120S), box 17, code U; and Schedule K-1 (Form 1041), box 14, code F (see instructions) . .	42	
43	Reconciliation for real estate professionals. If you were a real estate professional (see instructions), enter the net income or (loss) you reported anywhere on Form 1040 or Form 1040NR from all rental real estate activities in which you materially participated under the passive activity loss rules . .	43	

Form 1040-ES
Department of the Treasury
Internal Revenue Service

20`13` **Estimated Tax**

Payment Voucher 3

OMB No. 1545-0074

Calendar year—Due Sept. 16, 2013

File only if you are making a payment of estimated tax by check or money order. Mail this voucher with your check or money order payable to **"United States Treasury."** Write your social security number and "2013 Form 1040-ES" on your check or money order. Do not send cash. Enclose, but do not staple or attach, your payment with this voucher.

Amount of estimated tax you are paying by check or money order.

Dollars | Cents

Your first name and initial	Your last name	Your social security number
If joint payment, complete for spouse		
Spouse's first name and initial	Spouse's last name	Spouse's social security number
Address (number, street, and apt. no.)		
City, state, and ZIP code. (If a foreign address, enter city, also complete spaces below.)		
Foreign country name	Foreign province/county	Foreign postal code

Print or type

For Privacy Act and Paperwork Reduction Act Notice, see instructions.

Tear off here

Form 1040-ES
Department of the Treasury
Internal Revenue Service

20`13` **Estimated Tax**

Payment Voucher 2

OMB No. 1545-0074

Calendar year—Due June 17, 2013

File only if you are making a payment of estimated tax by check or money order. Mail this voucher with your check or money order payable to **"United States Treasury."** Write your social security number and "2013 Form 1040-ES" on your check or money order. Do not send cash. Enclose, but do not staple or attach, your payment with this voucher.

Amount of estimated tax you are paying by check or money order.

Dollars | Cents

Your first name and initial	Your last name	Your social security number
If joint payment, complete for spouse		
Spouse's first name and initial	Spouse's last name	Spouse's social security number
Address (number, street, and apt. no.)		
City, state, and ZIP code. (If a foreign address, enter city, also complete spaces below.)		
Foreign country name	Foreign province/county	Foreign postal code

Print or type

For Privacy Act and Paperwork Reduction Act Notice, see instructions.

Tear off here

Form 1040-ES
Department of the Treasury
Internal Revenue Service

20`13` **Estimated Tax**

Payment Voucher 1

OMB No. 1545-0074

Calendar year—Due April 15, 2013

File only if you are making a payment of estimated tax by check or money order. Mail this voucher with your check or money order payable to **"United States Treasury."** Write your social security number and "2013 Form 1040-ES" on your check or money order. Do not send cash. Enclose, but do not staple or attach, your payment with this voucher.

Amount of estimated tax you are paying by check or money order.

Dollars | Cents
10500 | 00

Your first name and initial	Your last name	Your social security number
Joe P.	Plaster	Joe's SSN
If joint payment, complete for spouse		
Spouse's first name and initial	Spouse's last name	Spouse's social security number
Address (number, street, and apt. no.)		
City, state, and ZIP code. (If a foreign address, enter city, also complete spaces below.)		
Foreign country name	Foreign province/county	Foreign postal code

Print or type

For Privacy Act and Paperwork Reduction Act Notice, see instructions.

Form 1040-ES (2013)

-11-

Joe earned $37,500 in the first quarter of 2013. On this, he estimates he'll owe $10,500 in income tax.

Chapter 20
Your Employment Taxes

If you operate a corporation, the IRS generally considers you to be an "employee" of your corporation (IRS Code Section 3121(d)(1)). The president and CEO is an employee of her corporation, if the president receives compensation for services rendered to the corporation. All salaried corporate officers are corporate employees. (Members of the board of directors and shareholders are *not* considered "employees" of the corporation in those respective roles. A corporate officer who performs only minimal services and who doesn't receive compensation is not yet considered an "employee.") As a corporate officer, you'll need to familiarize yourself with the basics of employment taxes and payroll withholding. You'll need to pay yourself a reasonable wage/salary (as a corporate officer) before you can remove distributions (as a shareholder) from your S-Corporation which are free from employment taxation.

To help you understand employment taxes, download IRS Publication 15 (Circular E) *Employer's Tax Guide* from IRS.gov. Other useful IRS publications include: Publication 15-A: *Employer's Supplemental Tax Guide*; *General Instructions for Forms W-2 and W-3*; *Instructions for Form 940* (Employer's Annual Federal Unemployment Tax (FUTA) Return); and, *Instructions for Form 941* (Employer's Quarterly Federal Tax Return). This chapter will discuss the key IRS employment tax forms. This chapter will walk you through some of the considerations when hiring a new employee.

When you hire any new employee, you must check the employee's eligibility to work in America. This is done, somewhat ineffectually, by filling out Form I-9 *Employment Eligibility Verification Form* (uscis.gov). Although it might seem silly, as a corporate officer, you're supposed to fill out an I-9 for yourself. This is a one-time deal. Fill it out, and you're done. I'd venture to guess that most new presidents of small corporations never fill out an I-9 for themselves and never have any issues. But, theoretically, the U.S. Citizenship and Immigration Services (USCIS) could ask to inspect your I-9. Surprisingly, you don't submit I-9s to USCIS. You just keep them in your file cabinet.

Because you know your own Social Security number, you won't need form W-9 *Request for Taxpayer Identification Number and Certification*. This is a form you can give to a new employee to request his Social Security Number, which will be used for wage reporting to the IRS. This form is a one-shot deal. Once you have a W-9 on file for the employee, you never need to bother the employee with this form again.

W-4

Next, you'll want to give your employee a W-4 *Employee's Withholding Allowance Certificate* to complete. This tells the employer how many dependents the employee has. This is necessary for the employer to compute the ideal level of federal income tax withholding for the employee.

The more dependents (i.e., children) the employee has, the less he'll owe in Federal income tax and the less the employer must withhold for income tax. Withholding also includes money taken out of an employee's paycheck for Social Security and Medicare. Those amounts aren't affected by the information on the W-4.

The W-4 is in effect until it's updated. As the owner of a corporation, you don't need to give yourself a new W-4 annually. If you get married or have more children, you can certainly update it, then, if you want to have less withholding. Like the W-9, the W-4 is used internally by the corporation and usually isn't sent to the IRS. It's an employee's responsibility to let their employer know if they want to change their number of dependents.

If your employee fails to give you back a W-4, you withhold at the maximum rate: single, no dependents. IRS Publication 15 shows how to use withholding tables to calculate the proper withholding amount for federal income tax.

If you claim too many dependents as an employee, you might underpay your income tax and wind up with tax penalties. If you claim too few, you'll get your money back at the end of the year. You've made an interest-free loan to the government. It's usually better to slightly overpay than to underpay your taxes.

At the end of this chapter is a sample W-4. Joe Plaster is single and claims one "withholding allowance." Note there is a line (Line 6) for any additional amount you want withheld. Joe can also fill out 1040-ES and make estimated tax payments, if he believes he'll owe the IRS more in federal income tax than he has paid in. If he wanted less withheld, he could also have entered "1" on Line E for head of household. "Withholding allowances" can exceed the number of your exemptions/dependents.

Note: Only page 1 of Joe's W-4 is shown. The W-4 contains a second page which allows you adjust your withholding based upon extra complexities, such as having a second job or having a working spouse. Those factors could push your family into higher tax brackets, so you might want to withhold more. The overall purpose of W-4 is to arrive at Line 5 and Line 6, so that the employer has these numbers to compute the employee's withholding. For Joe: Line 5 is 1. Line 6 is blank.

**

Before you have any employees, look into your state's requirements for Workers' Compensation Insurance. Workers' Compensation Insurance provides payments to workers who are injured or killed on the job.

In Minnesota, for example, corporate officers or executives who own 25% or more of a corporation are exempt from being insured by worker's compensation. You can certainly carry such insurance, if you wish, but it's not required. Your state probably has a similar exemption for corporate officer-shareholders. Even if you're exempt, if you work in a dangerous occupation, like general contracting and roofing, you might want to carry such insurance to protect yourself in the event of an injury.

IRS Form 941

Now that the I-9 and W-4 are out of the way, we can turn our attention to the employment tax forms that are filed on a regular basis. Quarterly, you'll fill out and send in Form 941, *Employer's Quarterly Federal Tax Return*. A sample 941 form is at the end of this chapter. It's pretty straightforward. This form is due one month after the quarter ends. For the previous quarter, this form is due on or before:

April 30 (for quarter: January, February, March)
July 31 (for quarter: April, May, June)
October 31 (for quarter: July, August, September)
January 31 (for quarter: October, November, December)

As with most tax forms, you can file 941 electronically. Your 941 forms will be reconciled with your W-3 and W-2s. If you pay low wages, you might be asked to file Form 944, *Employer's Annual Federal Tax Return* instead of Form 941.

IRS Form 940 (FUTA)

Annually, you'll need to fill out and file Form 940, *Employer's Annual Federal Unemployment (FUTA) Tax Return*. The FUTA tax rate is 6%, but it only applies to the first $7,000 you pay to each employee. This $7,000 is called the FUTA "wage base." If you pay into state unemployment tax, you may reduce your federal unemployment tax by a maximum credit of 5.4% bringing your FUTA tax rate to 0.6%.

Before 2011, the FUTA tax rate was 6.2% which included a 0.2% "temporary" rate passed by Congress in 1976. The 0.2% portion expired. President Obama's 2013 budget proposes increasing the FUTA "wage base" to $15,000. This would effectively double the FUTA tax.

The worksheets included in the Instructions for Form 940 have some convoluted math. Follow the worksheets step-by-step if you pay into state unemployment insurance (UI) to calculate your FUTA.

**

State UI has its own "wage base" or the amount of wages subject to state UI. The state's UI tax rate will also vary. I've had state officials vociferously point out that it's possible to pay less money overall by voluntarily choosing to pay into state UI. This is because states often have an unemployment "experience" tax rate, which can be lower than 5.4%, and you can receive a credit for the difference between the state rate you actually pay and 5.4%. In other words, you can receive a credit for money you haven't paid. In practice, I've found the lower state rates are usually more than offset by a much higher state wage base.

Many states exempt corporate shareholder-employees from paying into state unemployment. Personally, I think corporate officer-shareholders who own the majority of a corporation should be exempt at the federal level. Alas, currently, that's not the way the system works.

**

FUTA is typically deposited quarterly. The deposit due dates are one month after the end of the previous quarter:

April 30 (for quarter: January, February, March)
July 31 (for quarter: April, May, June)
October 31 (for quarter: July, August, September)
January 31 (for quarter: October, November, December)

(Notice the dates are the same as for Forms 941)

If your FUTA tax liability is less than $500, you do not have to deposit the tax. Instead, you carry it forward and make a quarterly deposit when the amount exceeds $500 or at year end. To make payments, you can use the Electronic Federal Tax Payment System (EFTPS). Year-end payments of less than $500 can be made with the payment voucher that's included with Form 940. With all the taxes discussed in this chapter, it's important to pay them in a timely fashion to avoid penalties.

At the end of the chapter is a sample Form 940. We assume Joe paid himself $25,000 in wages, of which $5,000 was paid as health insurance, which is exempt from FUTA tax. Part 1 only applies if you paid into state UI. We'll assume Joe doesn't pay into state UI. If Joe did pay into state UI, notice Line 2 "Credit Reduction." Joe would need to check if his state was subject to the credit reduction. This means his state has run low on UI funds and has borrowed money from the Federal Government. Because of this, Joe wouldn't get the full 5.4% credit.

Part 2. Joe was the only employee and received $25,000. Line 4 is $5,000. Health insurance premiums paid are considered Fringe Benefits, 4a, is checked. Line 5 is computed by subtracting wages not subject to FUTA ($5,000) from total wages paid ($25,000) and then subtracting the FUTA wage base ($7,000): $25,000 - $5,000 - $7,000 = $13,000.

Line 8 "FUTA tax before adjustments" is the 0.6% rate, which assumes you received a full 5.4% maximum credit. If you had received the full credit, this line would really represent your effective rate *after all credit adjustments have been made*!

Part 3. Because we assumed Joe didn't pay into state UI, Line 9 applies. Joe is forced to shell out another 5.4% of $7,000 or $378. Part 4 shows Joe's total FUTA tax is $420.00 which is just 6% of $7,000. Because the amount is less than $500, he may pay the tax at the end of the year with the payment voucher that is part of the Form 940 package. He also doesn't need to fill out Part 5. Part 6 doesn't apply, because Joe computed his own Form 940. Joe must sign and date Part 7 and provide his contact information.

W-2s and W-3

The two final employment tax forms are the W-2 and the W-3. Arguably, these are the most important. Form W-2, *Wage and Tax Statement*, is given to your employees at the end of the calendar year. The employee must receive the form by January 31. This form is necessary for the employee to compute her personal 1040 income tax return.

You must send all your W-2 tax forms, together with W-3, *Transmittal of Wage and Tax Statements*, to the Social Security Administration (SSA) by February 28 for the previous year. The SSA shares the W-2s with the IRS. You can file online, in which case, you don't need the transmittal form W-3. The W-3 is essentially just a running total of all of the amounts on all of your W-2s. It tells the SSA how many W-2 forms you're submitting.

If you mail in your W-2s and W-3 form, you must use the machine scannable forms provided by the IRS. They're printed in a pretty red color. Copy A goes to the SSA. As the employer, you keep Copy D. With all tax-compliance forms, you should keep a copy for your records. It's also good to have proof of the date when such forms were snail mailed. I've seen cases where the IRS or other government agency said some form was received late. The issue was quickly resolved when postal records showed that not only was the form delivered on time, but officials had signed for the mailing before the due date. If you use snail mail, consider using certified mailing, where the recipient signs for the letter. Otherwise, consider delivery confirmation, so you have proof of the date delivered.

You can request machine scannable W-2 copies from IRS.gov. Also request W-3, the transmittal form that accompanies the W-2s. W-2s come two per page, so, if you want an extra copy in case you mess up, request three W-2 forms.

At the end of the chapter, we show two sample W-2 forms. The first W-2 form is for a small amount of annual wages paid by Joe's startup company to Joe. $5,000 in wages is paid entirely as health insurance premiums for Joe. Because health insurance premiums aren't subject to Social Security or Medicare taxation, Lines 3, 4, 5, and 6 are zero. Recall, money paid for health insurance premiums is also not subject to FUTA.

If the IRS contacts Joe telling him it looks like he owes Social Security and Medicare tax on his salary, he just needs to write back explaining that his entire salary consisted of health insurance premiums paid, which aren't subject to Social Security or Medicare.

To let employees know how much their employers paid for health insurance, code "DD" can be used on Line 12 of the W-2. This is for informational purposes only. It doesn't affect the taxation of most employees. **However, my reading of the instructions says that corporate officer-shareholders who own more than 2% of their corporation aren't supposed to use code "DD."** This is ironic, because this is one of the few classes of employees where providing this information is useful to the employee, who receives a "self-employed" tax deduction. It's also useful to the IRS, because it lets them know that this portion of their wages is exempt from Social Security and Medicare.

While health insurance premiums paid to 2% or greater corporate officers are reported on W-2 Line 1 "Wages tips, other compensation," the amount isn't taxed, because of the "self-employed" health insurance deduction that appears on Form 1040. See Chapter 19 for details. Joe will owe no federal income tax on this $5,000 salary paid as health insurance.

The second W-2 shows Joe earning $10,000. In this case, all the salary is paid in cash and is fully subject to Social Security and Medicare. Social Security and Medicare consist of two parts: One part is taken out of the salary of the employee. This amount is reported on the W-2. The other part comes out of the pocket of the employer. The amounts are equal.

Both employer and employee pay 6.2% toward Social Security (up to the Social Security wage base) and 1.45% for Medicare. There is no wage base for Medicare. If you receive $10 million in salary, it's all subject to Medicare taxation. Line 4, Social Security tax withheld throughout the year should turn out to be about 6.2% x $10,000 = $620. Line 6, Medicare tax withheld is 1.45% x $10,000 = $145. These amounts are obtained by just adding up the actual amounts withheld throughout the year, calculated at the 6.2% and 1.45% rates for each paycheck. There will be round off errors, of course.

In the old days before computers, employers kept payroll ledgers on paper. Today, payroll ledgers are usually part of your computer accounting program. The payroll ledger gives you a record of every paycheck you write. The date the check was written, the payroll period, the check number, the employee's SSN and name, the amounts withheld for Social Security, Medicare, federal income tax, and state income tax should all be entered. The net amount paid to the employee is also recorded. For hourly employees, the number of hours worked is recorded as well as their hourly rate of pay. This gives a complete record of your payroll payments.

To calculate the amount that should be withheld from Joe's paycheck for federal income tax, we use Joe's number of "withholding allowances" from his W-4 and use the tax withholding tables in Publication 15. If Joe pays himself $10,000 annually or $833.33 per month, we can use the Monthly Withholding Table for a single person. With one withholding allowance, $31 is withheld from each of Joe's monthly paychecks. The total withheld over the year is thus $372. IRS Publication 15 has weekly, bi-monthly, and other payroll periods too. Page 58 of Publication 15 appears at the end of this chapter.

Your tax calendar should include the due dates for your 940, 941s, and W-2s with W-3 transmittal form. It should also include the appropriate deposit dates, when payments of withheld employment taxes must be made.

The first time you work through your employment tax forms, you might feel like ripping your hair out, because there are so many forms. But, once you get use to it, it's not really that bad. There are companies that will administer your payroll, too, if you want to go with that option.

Form W-4 (2013)

Purpose. Complete Form W-4 so that your employer can withhold the correct federal income tax from your pay. Consider completing a new Form W-4 each year and when your personal or financial situation changes.

Exemption from withholding. If you are exempt, complete **only** lines 1, 2, 3, 4, and 7 and sign the form to validate it. Your exemption for 2013 expires February 17, 2014. See Pub. 505, Tax Withholding and Estimated Tax.

Note. If another person can claim you as a dependent on his or her tax return, you cannot claim exemption from withholding if your income exceeds $1,000 and includes more than $350 of unearned income (for example, interest and dividends).

Basic instructions. If you are not exempt, complete the **Personal Allowances Worksheet** below. The worksheets on page 2 further adjust your withholding allowances based on itemized deductions, certain credits, adjustments to income, or two-earners/multiple jobs situations.

Complete all worksheets that apply. However, you may claim fewer (or zero) allowances. For regular wages, withholding must be based on allowances you claimed and may not be a flat amount or percentage of wages.

Head of household. Generally, you can claim head of household filing status on your tax return only if you are unmarried and pay more than 50% of the costs of keeping up a home for yourself and your dependent(s) or other qualifying individuals. See Pub. 501, Exemptions, Standard Deduction, and Filing Information, for information.

Tax credits. You can take projected tax credits into account in figuring your allowable number of withholding allowances. Credits for child or dependent care expenses and the child tax credit may be claimed using the **Personal Allowances Worksheet** below. See Pub. 505 for information on converting your other credits into withholding allowances.

Nonwage income. If you have a large amount of nonwage income, such as interest or dividends, consider making estimated tax payments using Form 1040-ES, Estimated Tax for Individuals. Otherwise, you may owe additional tax. If you have pension or annuity

income, see Pub. 505 to find out if you should adjust your withholding on Form W-4 or W-4P.

Two earners or multiple jobs. If you have a working spouse or more than one job, figure the total number of allowances you are entitled to claim on all jobs using worksheets from only one Form W-4. Your withholding usually will be most accurate when all allowances are claimed on the Form W-4 for the highest paying job and zero allowances are claimed on the others. See Pub. 505 for details.

Nonresident alien. If you are a nonresident alien, see Notice 1392, Supplemental Form W-4 Instructions for Nonresident Aliens, before completing this form.

Check your withholding. After your Form W-4 takes effect, use Pub. 505 to see how the amount you are having withheld compares to your projected total tax for 2013. See Pub. 505, especially if your earnings exceed $130,000 (Single) or $180,000 (Married).

Future developments. Information about any future developments affecting Form W-4 (such as legislation enacted after we release it) will be posted at www.irs.gov/w4.

Personal Allowances Worksheet (Keep for your records.)

A	Enter "1" for **yourself** if no one else can claim you as a dependent	**A** 1
B	Enter "1" if: { • You are single and have only one job; or	
	• You are married, have only one job, and your spouse does not work; or	**B**
	• Your wages from a second job or your spouse's wages (or the total of both) are $1,500 or less. }	
C	Enter "1" for your **spouse.** But, you may choose to enter "-0-" if you are married and have either a working spouse or more than one job. (Entering "-0-" may help you avoid having too little tax withheld.)	**C**
D	Enter number of **dependents** (other than your spouse or yourself) you will claim on your tax return . . .	**D**
E	Enter "1" if you will file as **head of household** on your tax return (see conditions under **Head of household** above)	**E**
F	Enter "1" if you have at least $1,900 of **child or dependent care expenses** for which you plan to claim a credit . .	**F**
	(**Note.** Do **not** include child support payments. See Pub. 503, Child and Dependent Care Expenses, for details.)	
G	**Child Tax Credit** (including additional child tax credit). See Pub. 972, Child Tax Credit, for more information.	
	• If your total income will be less than $65,000 ($95,000 if married), enter "2" for each eligible child; then **less** "1" if you have three to six eligible children or **less** "2" if you have seven or more eligible children.	
	• If your total income will be between $65,000 and $84,000 ($95,000 and $119,000 if married), enter "1" for each eligible child . . .	**G**
H	Add lines A through G and enter total here. (**Note.** This may be different from the number of exemptions you claim on your tax return.) ▶ **H**	1

For accuracy, complete all worksheets that apply.	• If you plan to **itemize** or **claim adjustments to income** and want to reduce your withholding, see the **Deductions and Adjustments Worksheet** on page 2.
	• If you are **single and have more than one job** or are **married and you and your spouse both work** and the combined earnings from all jobs exceed $40,000 ($10,000 if married), see the **Two-Earners/Multiple Jobs Worksheet** on page 2 to avoid having too little tax withheld.
	• If **neither** of the above situations applies, **stop here** and enter the number from line H on line 5 of Form W-4 below.

---------------------- **Separate here and give Form W-4 to your employer. Keep the top part for your records.** ----------------------

Form **W-4** Department of the Treasury Internal Revenue Service	**Employee's Withholding Allowance Certificate** ▶ Whether you are entitled to claim a certain number of allowances or exemption from withholding is subject to review by the IRS. Your employer may be required to send a copy of this form to the IRS.	OMB No. 1545-0074 **2013**

1 Your first name and middle initial Joe P	Last name Plaster	**2** Your social security number Joe's SSN

Home address (number and street or rural route)	**3** [X] Single ☐ Married ☐ Married, but withhold at higher Single rate.
City or town, state, and ZIP code	**Note.** If married, but legally separated, or spouse is a nonresident alien, check the "Single" box.
	4 If your last name differs from that shown on your social security card, check here. You must call 1-800-772-1213 for a replacement card. ▶ ☐

5	Total number of allowances you are claiming (from line **H** above **or** from the applicable worksheet on page 2)	**5**	1
6	Additional amount, if any, you want withheld from each paycheck	**6**	$
7	I claim exemption from withholding for 2013, and I certify that I meet **both** of the following conditions for exemption.		
	• Last year I had a right to a refund of **all** federal income tax withheld because I had **no** tax liability, **and**		
	• This year I expect a refund of **all** federal income tax withheld because I expect to have **no** tax liability.		
	If you meet both conditions, write "Exempt" here . . . . ▶	**7**	

Under penalties of perjury, I declare that I have examined this certificate and, to the best of my knowledge and belief, it is true, correct, and complete.

Employee's signature (This form is not valid unless you sign it.) ▶	Joe's Signature	Date ▶ date

8 Employer's name and address (Employer: Complete lines 8 and 10 only if sending to the IRS.)	**9** Office code (optional)	**10** Employer identification number (EIN)

For Privacy Act and Paperwork Reduction Act Notice, see page 2.   Cat. No. 10220Q   Form **W-4** (2013)

Form **941 for 2013:** Employer's QUARTERLY Federal Tax Return
(Rev. January 2013)   Department of the Treasury — Internal Revenue Service

OMB No. 1545-0029

Employer identification number (EIN) [ ] [ ] – [ ] [ ] [ ] [ ] [ ] [ ] [ ]

Name (not your trade name) **Joe's Pottery Emporium, Ltd.**

Trade name (if any)

Address

| Number | Street | Suite or room number |

| City | State | ZIP code |

Report for this Quarter of 2013
(Check one.)

[X] 1: January, February, March

[ ] 2: April, May, June

[ ] 3: July, August, September

[ ] 4: October, November, December

Instructions and prior year forms are available at www.irs.gov/form941.

Read the separate instructions before you complete Form 941. Type or print within the boxes.

Part 1: Answer these questions for this quarter.

1	Number of employees who received wages, tips, or other compensation for the pay period including: Mar. 12 (Quarter 1), June 12 (Quarter 2), Sept. 12 (Quarter 3), or Dec. 12 (Quarter 4)	1	1
2	Wages, tips, and other compensation	2	2500.00
3	Income tax withheld from wages, tips, and other compensation	3	93.00
4	If no wages, tips, and other compensation are subject to social security or Medicare tax [ ] Check and go to line 6.		

		Column 1		Column 2
5a	Taxable social security wages	2500.00	× .124 =	310.00
5b	Taxable social security tips	.	× .124 =	.
5c	Taxable Medicare wages & tips	2500.00	× .029 =	72.50
5d	Taxable wages & tips subject to Additional Medicare Tax withholding	.	× .009 =	.

5e	Add Column 2 from lines 5a, 5b, 5c, and 5d	5e	382.50
5f	Section 3121(q) Notice and Demand—Tax due on unreported tips (see instructions)	5f	.
6	Total taxes before adjustments (add lines 3, 5e, and 5f)	6	475.50
7	Current quarter's adjustment for fractions of cents	7	.
8	Current quarter's adjustment for sick pay	8	.
9	Current quarter's adjustments for tips and group-term life insurance	9	.
10	Total taxes after adjustments. Combine lines 6 through 9	10	475.50
11	Total deposits for this quarter, including overpayment applied from a prior quarter and overpayment applied from Form 941-X or Form 944-X filed in the current quarter	11	475.50
12a	COBRA premium assistance payments (see instructions)	12a	.
12b	Number of individuals provided COBRA premium assistance		
13	Add lines 11 and 12a	13	475.50
14	Balance due. If line 10 is more than line 13, enter the difference and see instructions	14	0.00
15	Overpayment. If line 13 is more than line 10, enter the difference [ ] . Check one: [ ] Apply to next return. [ ] Send a refund.		

▶ **You MUST complete both pages of Form 941 and SIGN it.**

Next ▶

For Privacy Act and Paperwork Reduction Act Notice, see the back of the Payment Voucher.   Cat. No. 17001Z   Form **941** (Rev. 1-2013)

Name (not your trade name)	Employer identification number (EIN)
Joe's Pottery Emporium, Ltd.	Joe's EIN

Part 2: Tell us about your deposit schedule and tax liability for this quarter.

If you are unsure about whether you are a monthly schedule depositor or a semiweekly schedule depositor, see Pub. 15 (Circular E), section 11.

16 Check one: ☐ Line 10 on this return is less than $2,500 or line 10 on the return for the prior quarter was less than $2,500, and you did not incur a $100,000 next-day deposit obligation during the current quarter. If line 10 for the prior quarter was less than $2,500 but line 10 on this return is $100,000 or more, you must provide a record of your federal tax liability. If you are a monthly schedule depositor, complete the deposit schedule below; if you are a semiweekly schedule depositor, attach Schedule B (Form 941). Go to Part 3.

☒ **You were a monthly schedule depositor for the entire quarter.** Enter your tax liability for each month and total liability for the quarter, then go to Part 3.

Tax liability:	Month 1	158.50
	Month 2	158.50
	Month 3	158.50
Total liability for quarter		475.50	Total must equal line 10.

☐ **You were a semiweekly schedule depositor for any part of this quarter.** Complete Schedule B (Form 941), Report of Tax Liability for Semiweekly Schedule Depositors, and attach it to Form 941.

Part 3: Tell us about your business. If a question does NOT apply to your business, leave it blank.

17 If your business has closed or you stopped paying wages . . . . ☐ Check here, and

enter the final date you paid wages   /   /   .

18 If you are a seasonal employer and you do not have to file a return for every quarter of the year . . ☐ Check here.

Part 4: May we speak with your third-party designee?

Do you want to allow an employee, a paid tax preparer, or another person to discuss this return with the IRS? See the instructions for details.

☐ Yes. Designee's name and phone number

Select a 5-digit Personal Identification Number (PIN) to use when talking to the IRS. ☐ ☐ ☐ ☐ ☐

☐ No.

Part 5: Sign here. You MUST complete both pages of Form 941 and SIGN it.

Under penalties of perjury, I declare that I have examined this return, including accompanying schedules and statements, and to the best of my knowledge and belief, it is true, correct, and complete. Declaration of preparer (other than taxpayer) is based on all information of which preparer has any knowledge.

✗ Sign your name here	Print your name here	
	Print your title here	
Date / /	Best daytime phone	

Paid Preparer Use Only   Check if you are self-employed . . . ☐

Preparer's name		PTIN	
Preparer's signature		Date	/ /
Firm's name (or yours if self-employed)		EIN	
Address		Phone	
City	State	ZIP code	

Form **941** (Rev. 1-2013)

Form **940 for 2012:** Employer's Annual Federal Unemployment (FUTA) Tax Return

Department of the Treasury — Internal Revenue Service

OMB No. 1545-0028

Employer identification number (EIN)	☐☐ – ☐☐☐☐☐☐☐

Name *(not your trade name)* **Joe's Pottery Emporium, Ltd.**

Trade name *(if any)*

Address

Number   Street   Suite or room number

City   State   ZIP code

Type of Return
(Check all that apply.)

☐ **a.** Amended

☐ **b.** Successor employer

☐ **c.** No payments to employees in 2012

☐ **d.** Final: Business closed or stopped paying wages

Instructions and prior-year forms are available at *www.irs.gov/form940*.

Read the separate instructions before you complete this form. Please type or print within the boxes.

Part 1: Tell us about your return. If any line does NOT apply, leave it blank.

1a If you had to pay state unemployment tax in one state only, enter the state abbreviation . **1a** ☐ ☐

1b If you had to pay state unemployment tax in more than one state, you are a multi-state employer . . . . **1b** ☐ Check here. Complete Schedule A (Form 940).

2 If you paid wages in a state that is subject to CREDIT REDUCTION . . . . **2** ☐ Check here. Complete Schedule A (Form 940).

Part 2: Determine your FUTA tax before adjustments for 2012. If any line does NOT apply, leave it blank.

3 Total payments to all employees **3** **25000.00**

4 Payments exempt from FUTA tax **4** **5000.00**

Check all that apply: **4a** ☒ Fringe benefits   **4c** ☐ Retirement/Pension   **4e** ☐ Other
  4b ☐ Group-term life insurance   **4d** ☐ Dependent care

5 Total of payments made to each employee in excess of $7,000 . . . . **5** **13000.00**

6 Subtotal (line 4 + line 5 = line 6) **6** **18000.00**

7 Total taxable FUTA wages (line 3 – line 6 = line 7) (see instructions) **7** **7000.00**

8 FUTA tax before adjustments (line 7 x .006 = line 8) **8** **42.00**

Part 3: Determine your adjustments. If any line does NOT apply, leave it blank.

9 If ALL of the taxable FUTA wages you paid were excluded from state unemployment tax, multiply line 7 by .054 (line 7 x .054 = line 9). Go to line 12 . . . . **9** **378.00**

10 If SOME of the taxable FUTA wages you paid were excluded from state unemployment tax, OR you paid ANY state unemployment tax late (after the due date for filing Form 940), complete the worksheet in the instructions. Enter the amount from line 7 of the worksheet . . **10** **.**

11 If credit reduction applies, enter the total from Schedule A (Form 940) . . . . . . **11** **.**

Part 4: Determine your FUTA tax and balance due or overpayment for 2012. If any line does NOT apply, leave it blank.

12 Total FUTA tax after adjustments (lines 8 + 9 + 10 + 11 = line 12) **12** **420.00**

13 FUTA tax deposited for the year, including any overpayment applied from a prior year . **13** **0.00**

14 Balance due (If line 12 is more than line 13, enter the excess on line 14.)
  • If line 14 is more than $500, you must deposit your tax.
  • If line 14 is $500 or less, you may pay with this return. (see instructions) **14** **420.00**

15 Overpayment (If line 13 is more than line 12, enter the excess on line 15 and check a box below.) . . . . **15** **.**

▶ You **MUST** complete both pages of this form and **SIGN** it.   Check one: ☐ Apply to next return.   ☐ Send a refund.

Next ▸

For Privacy Act and Paperwork Reduction Act Notice, see the back of Form 940-V, Payment Voucher.   Cat. No. 11234O   Form **940** (2012)

850212

Name *(not your trade name)*

Joe's Pottery Emporium, Ltd.

Employer identification number (EIN)

| Part 5: | Report your FUTA tax liability by quarter only if line 12 is more than $500. If not, go to Part 6. |

16 Report the amount of your FUTA tax liability for each quarter; do NOT enter the amount you deposited. If you had no liability for a quarter, leave the line blank.

16a	**1st quarter** (January 1 – March 31)	16a
16b	**2nd quarter** (April 1 – June 30)	16b
16c	**3rd quarter** (July 1 – September 30)	16c
16d	**4th quarter** (October 1 – December 31)	16d

17 **Total tax liability for the year** (lines 16a + 16b + 16c + 16d = line 17) **17**   **Total must equal line 12.**

| Part 6: | May we speak with your third-party designee? |

Do you want to allow an employee, a paid tax preparer, or another person to discuss this return with the IRS? See the instructions for details.

☐ **Yes.**   Designee's name and phone number

Select a 5-digit Personal Identification Number (PIN) to use when talking to IRS

☐ **No.**

| Part 7: | Sign here. You MUST complete both pages of this form and SIGN it. |

Under penalties of perjury, I declare that I have examined this return, including accompanying schedules and statements, and to the best of my knowledge and belief, it is true, correct, and complete, and that no part of any payment made to a state unemployment fund claimed as a credit was, or is to be, deducted from the payments made to employees. Declaration of preparer (other than taxpayer) is based on all information of which preparer has any knowledge.

✗ Sign your name here

Print your name here   **Joe Plaster**

Print your title here   **President**

Date   /   /

Best daytime phone

Paid Preparer Use Only

Check if you are self-employed . . . ☐

Preparer's name		PTIN	
Preparer's signature		Date	/ /
Firm's name (or yours if self-employed)		EIN	
Address		Phone	
City	State	ZIP code	

Form **940** (2012)

Void ☐	a Employee's social security number Joe's SSN	OMB No. 1545-0008		
b Employer identification number (EIN) EIN Here			1 Wages, tips, other compensation 5000.00	2 Federal income tax withheld 0.00
c Employer's name, address, and ZIP code Joe's Pottery Emporium, Ltd. …			3 Social security wages 0.00	4 Social security tax withheld 0.00
			5 Medicare wages and tips 0.00	6 Medicare tax withheld 0.00
			7 Social security tips	8 Allocated tips
d Control number			9	10 Dependent care benefits
e Employee's first name and initial Last name Suff. Joe P Plaster			11 Nonqualified plans	12a See instructions for box 12 ~~DD~~ 5000.00
Joe's Address			13 Statutory employee ☐ Retirement plan ☐ Third party sick pay ☐	12b Code
			14 Other	12c Code
				12d Code
f Employee's address and ZIP code				
15 State Employer's state ID number TX │ Joe's State ID	16 State wages, tips, etc. 5000.00	17 State income tax	18 Local wages, tips, etc.	19 Local income tax
				20 Locality name

Form **W-2** Wage and Tax Statement

2013

Department of the Treasury—Internal Revenue Service

Copy D — For Employer

For Privacy Act and Paperwork Reduction Act Notice, see separate instructions.

Note: The $5000 in wages paid was entirely in the form of health insurance, paid by his corporation. This is why Lines 3, 4, 5, and 6 are zero. If Joe had received cash instead, it would have been subject to Social Security and Medicare. Line 12 code "DD" is just a way of letting employees know how much health insurance cost the employer. As discussed, Joe doesn't use code "DD" because he is a 2% or greater shareholder.

Void ☐	**a** Employee's social security number Joe's SSN	OMB No. 1545-0008		
b Employer identification number (EIN) EIN Here			**1** Wages, tips, other compensation 10,000.00	**2** Federal income tax withheld 372.00
c Employer's name, address, and ZIP code Joe's Pottery Emporium, Ltd. ...			**3** Social security wages 10,000.00	**4** Social security tax withheld 620.00
			5 Medicare wages and tips 10,000.00	**6** Medicare tax withheld 145.00
			7 Social security tips	**8** Allocated tips
d Control number			**9**	**10** Dependent care benefits
e Employee's first name and initial Last name Suff. Joe P Plaster Joe's Address			**11** Nonqualified plans	**12a** See instructions for box 12 C o d e
			13 Statutory employee ☐ Retirement plan ☐ Third-party sick pay ☐	**12b** C o d e
			14 Other	**12c** C o d e
				12d C o d e
f Employee's address and ZIP code				

15 State	Employer's state ID number	**16** State wages, tips, etc.	**17** State income tax	**18** Local wages, tips, etc.	**19** Local income tax	**20** Locality name
TX	Joe's State Tax ID	10,000.00				

Form **W-2** Wage and Tax Statement   **2013**

Department of the Treasury—Internal Revenue Service

Copy D — For Employer

For **Privacy Act and Paperwork Reduction Act Notice, see separate instructions.**

Note: Joe received $833.33 per month in Salary. 6.2% was withheld for Social Security. 1.45% was withheld for Medicare. For every paycheck, IRS Publication 15 was consulted to determine the proper withholding for federal income tax. The withholding tables told the employer to withhold $31 per month, totalling $372.00.

SINGLE Persons—MONTHLY Payroll Period
(For Wages Paid through December 2013)

And the wages are—		And the number of withholding allowances claimed is—										
At least	But less than	0	1	2	3	4	5	6	7	8	9	10
		The amount of income tax to be withheld is—										
$ 0	$220	$0	$0	$0	$0	$0	$0	$0	$0	$0	$0	$0
220	230	4	0	0	0	0	0	0	0	0	0	0
230	240	5	0	0	0	0	0	0	0	0	0	0
240	250	6	0	0	0	0	0	0	0	0	0	0
250	260	7	0	0	0	0	0	0	0	0	0	0
260	270	8	0	0	0	0	0	0	0	0	0	0
270	280	9	0	0	0	0	0	0	0	0	0	0
280	290	10	0	0	0	0	0	0	0	0	0	0
290	300	11	0	0	0	0	0	0	0	0	0	0
300	320	13	0	0	0	0	0	0	0	0	0	0
320	340	15	0	0	0	0	0	0	0	0	0	0
340	360	17	0	0	0	0	0	0	0	0	0	0
360	380	19	0	0	0	0	0	0	0	0	0	0
380	400	21	0	0	0	0	0	0	0	0	0	0
400	420	23	0	0	0	0	0	0	0	0	0	0
420	440	25	0	0	0	0	0	0	0	0	0	0
440	460	27	0	0	0	0	0	0	0	0	0	0
460	480	29	0	0	0	0	0	0	0	0	0	0
480	500	31	0	0	0	0	0	0	0	0	0	0
500	520	33	0	0	0	0	0	0	0	0	0	0
520	540	35	2	0	0	0	0	0	0	0	0	0
540	560	37	4	0	0	0	0	0	0	0	0	0
560	580	39	6	0	0	0	0	0	0	0	0	0
580	600	41	8	0	0	0	0	0	0	0	0	0
600	640	44	11	0	0	0	0	0	0	0	0	0
640	680	48	15	0	0	0	0	0	0	0	0	0
680	720	52	19	0	0	0	0	0	0	0	0	0
720	760	56	23	0	0	0	0	0	0	0	0	0
760	800	60	27	0	0	0	0	0	0	0	0	0
800	840	64	31	0	0	0	0	0	0	0	0	0
840	880	68	35	3	0	0	0	0	0	0	0	0
880	920	72	39	7	0	0	0	0	0	0	0	0
920	960	76	43	11	0	0	0	0	0	0	0	0
960	1,000	82	47	15	0	0	0	0	0	0	0	0
1,000	1,040	88	51	19	0	0	0	0	0	0	0	0
1,040	1,080	94	55	23	0	0	0	0	0	0	0	0
1,080	1,120	100	59	27	0	0	0	0	0	0	0	0
1,120	1,160	106	63	31	0	0	0	0	0	0	0	0
1,160	1,200	112	67	35	0	0	0	0	0	0	0	0
1,200	1,240	118	71	39	6	0	0	0	0	0	0	0
1,240	1,280	124	76	43	10	0	0	0	0	0	0	0
1,280	1,320	130	82	47	14	0	0	0	0	0	0	0
1,320	1,360	136	88	51	18	0	0	0	0	0	0	0
1,360	1,400	142	94	55	22	0	0	0	0	0	0	0
1,400	1,440	148	100	59	26	0	0	0	0	0	0	0
1,440	1,480	154	106	63	30	0	0	0	0	0	0	0
1,480	1,520	160	112	67	34	2	0	0	0	0	0	0
1,520	1,560	166	118	71	38	6	0	0	0	0	0	0
1,560	1,600	172	124	75	42	10	0	0	0	0	0	0
1,600	1,640	178	130	81	46	14	0	0	0	0	0	0
1,640	1,680	184	136	87	50	18	0	0	0	0	0	0
1,680	1,720	190	142	93	54	22	0	0	0	0	0	0
1,720	1,760	196	148	99	58	26	0	0	0	0	0	0
1,760	1,800	202	154	105	62	30	0	0	0	0	0	0
1,800	1,840	208	160	111	66	34	1	0	0	0	0	0
1,840	1,880	214	166	117	70	38	5	0	0	0	0	0
1,880	1,920	220	172	123	74	42	9	0	0	0	0	0
1,920	1,960	226	178	129	80	46	13	0	0	0	0	0
1,960	2,000	232	184	135	86	50	17	0	0	0	0	0
2,000	2,040	238	190	141	92	54	21	0	0	0	0	0
2,040	2,080	244	196	147	98	58	25	0	0	0	0	0
2,080	2,120	250	202	153	104	62	29	0	0	0	0	0
2,120	2,160	256	208	159	110	66	33	1	0	0	0	0
2,160	2,200	262	214	165	116	70	37	5	0	0	0	0
2,200	2,240	268	220	171	122	74	41	9	0	0	0	0
2,240	2,280	274	226	177	128	79	45	13	0	0	0	0
2,280	2,320	280	232	183	134	85	49	17	0	0	0	0
2,320	2,360	286	238	189	140	91	53	21	0	0	0	0
2,360	2,400	292	244	195	146	97	57	25	0	0	0	0

Publication 15 (2013)

A Final Note From The Author:

I hope this book has helped you understand fundamental concepts, such as: basis; what a pass-through tax entity means; and the range of tax consequences associated with choosing a particular business structure. Understanding these underlying concepts will allow you to more easily evaluate not only current business structures, but also business structures that may be created in the future by changing laws.

I'm a big fan of retaining the S-corporation structure (or the LLC structure) for profitable businesses from which the owners wish to remove most of the profits. By the very nature of the S-corporation, those profits escape double taxation, now and into the future. The S-corporation gives you the option to reduce your employment tax/self employment tax burden. It provides a degree of liability protection that is absent in a sole proprietorship or partnership.

If you found this book useful, please visit Amazon.com and post a short review. Thank you very much for reading *How To Start And Run Your Own Corporation*. I wish you the best of success and happiness in your business ventures. Peter

Appendix A

2013 Personal Income Tax Rates
(Made permanent by Taxpayer Relief Act of 2012)

Tax Rate	Single	Married Filing Jointly	Head of Household
10%	Up to $8,925	Up to $17,850	Up to $12,750
15%	$8,926 - $36,250	$17,851 - $72,500	$12,751 - $48,600
25%	$36,251 - $87,850	$72,501 - $146,400	$48,601 - $125,450
28%	$87,851 - $183,250	$146,401 - $223,050	$125,451 - $203,150
33%	$183,251 - $398,350	$223,051 $398,350	$203,151 - $398,350
35%	$398,351 - $400,000	$398,351 $450,000	$398,351 - $425,000
39.6%	$400,001 or more	$450,001 or more	$425,001 or more

Corporate Tax Rates

Tax Rate	Income Amount
15%	$0-50,000
25%	$50,001 - 75,000
34%	$75,001-100,000
39%	$100,001-335,000
34%	$335,000-10,000,000
35%	$10,000,001-15,000,000
38%	$15,000,001-18,333,333
35%	More than $18,333,333

Dividend Tax Rates

0% for individuals in the 10% and 15% tax brackets.

15% for individuals in the 25%, 28%, 33%, and 35% income tax brackets.

20% for individuals in the 39.6% income tax bracket.

Appendix B

Form 201
(Revised 05/11)

Submit in duplicate to:
Secretary of State
P.O. Box 13697
Austin, TX 78711-3697
512 463-5555
FAX: 512/463-5709
Filing Fee: $300

Certificate of Formation
For-Profit Corporation

This space reserved for office use.

Article 1 – Entity Name and Type

The filing entity being formed is a for-profit corporation. The name of the entity is:

The name must contain the word "corporation," "company," "incorporated," "limited" or an abbreviation of one of these terms.

Article 2 – Registered Agent and Registered Office
(See instructions. Select and complete either A or B and complete C.)

☐ A. The initial registered agent is an organization (cannot be entity named above) by the name of:

OR

☐ B. The initial registered agent is an individual resident of the state whose name is set forth below:

First Name	*M.I.*	*Last Name*	*Suffix*

C. The business address of the registered agent and the registered office address is:

		TX	
Street Address	*City*	*State*	*Zip Code*

Article 3 – Directors
(A minimum of 1 director is required.)

The number of directors constituting the initial board of directors and the names and addresses of the person or persons who are to serve as directors until the first annual meeting of shareholders or until their successors are elected and qualified are as follows:

Director 1					
First Name	*M.I.*	*Last Name*			*Suffix*
Street or Mailing Address	*City*		*State*	*Zip Code*	*Country*

Director 2						
First Name	*M.I.*	*Last Name*				*Suffix*
Street or Mailing Address	*City*		*State*	*Zip Code*		*Country*

Director 3						
First Name	*M.I.*	*Last Name*				*Suffix*
Street or Mailing Address	*City*		*State*	*Zip Code*		*Country*

Article 4 – Authorized Shares

(Provide the number of shares in the space below, then select option A <u>or</u> option B, <u>do not select both</u>.)

The total number of shares the corporation is authorized to issue is: _____

☐ A. The par value of each of the authorized shares is: _____

OR

☐ B. The shares shall have no par value.

If the shares are to be divided into classes, you must set forth the designation of each class, the number of shares of each class, the par value (or statement of no par value), and the preferences, limitations, and relative rights of each class in the space provided for supplemental information on this form.

Article 5 – Purpose

The purpose for which the corporation is formed is for the transaction of any and all lawful business for which a for-profit corporation may be organized under the Texas Business Organizations Code.

Supplemental Provisions/Information

Text Area: [The attached addendum, if any, is incorporated herein by reference.]

Organizer

The name and address of the organizer:

_____
Name

_____
Street or Mailing Address   *City*   *State*   *Zip Code*

Effectiveness of Filing (Select either A, B, or C.)

A. ☐ This document becomes effective when the document is filed by the secretary of state.

B. ☐ This document becomes effective at a later date, which is not more than ninety (90) days from the date of signing. The delayed effective date is: _____

C. ☐ This document takes effect upon the occurrence of a future event or fact, other than the passage of time. The 90th day after the date of signing is: _____

The following event or fact will cause the document to take effect in the manner described below:

```



```

Execution

The undersigned affirms that the person designated as registered agent has consented to the appointment. The undersigned signs this document subject to the penalties imposed by law for the submission of a materially false or fraudulent instrument and certifies under penalty of perjury that the undersigned is authorized to execute the filing instrument.

Date: _____

_____
Signature of organizer

_____
Printed or typed name of organizer

The first 3 pages of this document have not been reproduced. They are instructions. These Texas Articles of Incorporation are also called "Certificate of Formation." Each state's Articles of Incorporation will vary and can usually be filled out online. Be sure to keep a copy of your articles of incorporation if filled out online.

Office of the Minnesota Secretary of State
Minnesota Business Corporation | Articles of Incorporation
Minnesota Statutes, Chapter 302A

Read the instructions before completing this form.

Filing Fee: $155 for expedited service in-person and online filings, $135 if submitted by mail

Note: A professional corporation governed under Chapter 319B must include an attachment with the following information: (This information is only required if this is a professional corporation.)
1. Statement that the Minnesota firm elects to operate and acknowledges that it is subject to *Minnesota Statutes, Chapter 319B.01 to 319B.12.*
2. List the professional service the corporation is authorized to provide under *Minnesota Statutes, Chap. 319B, subd 19.*

The undersigned incorporator(s), in order to form a Minnesota Business Corporation under *Minnesota Statutes, Chapter 302A* adopt the following:

Article I – Name of Corporation (Required)

_____
(The company name must include a corporate or professional designation in their name.)

Article II – Registered Office and Agent (A Registered Office Address is Required)

_____

Street Address *(A PO Box by itself is not acceptable)*	City	State	Zip

The Registered Agent at the above address is: _____

Article III – Shares
The corporation is authorized to issue _____ total number of shares.
(Must authorize at least one share)

Article IV – Incorporators (Required)
I, the undersigned, certify that I am signing this document as the person whose signature is required, or as agent of the person(s) whose signature would be required who has authorized me to sign this document on his/her behalf, or in both capacities. I further certify that I have completed all required fields, and that the information in this document is true and correct and in compliance with the applicable chapter of Minnesota Statutes. I understand that by signing this document I am subject to the penalties of perjury as set forth in Section 609.48 as if I had signed this document under oath.

Incorporator's Name	Street Address	City	State	Zip Code

Signature		Date

Incorporator's Name	Street Address	City	State	Zip Code

Signature		Date

Email Address for Official Notices
Enter an email address to which the Secretary of State can forward official notices required by law and other notices:

☐ Check here to have your email address excluded from requests for bulk data, to the extent allowed by Minnesota law.

> **Page 2 of this form only contains contact information for the person submitting it and hasn't been reproduced. Page 3 contains instructions. As you see, Articles of Incorporation can be quite simple.**

Appendix C

Form **SS-4**	**Application for Employer Identification Number**	OMB No. 1545-0003
(Rev. January 2010)	(For use by employers, corporations, partnerships, trusts, estates, churches, government agencies, Indian tribal entities, certain individuals, and others.)	EIN
Department of the Treasury Internal Revenue Service	► See separate instructions for each line. ► Keep a copy for your records.	

Type or print clearly.

1 Legal name of entity (or individual) for whom the EIN is being requested
Joe's Pottery Emporium, Ltd.

2 Trade name of business (if different from name on line 1) | **3** Executor, administrator, trustee, "care of" name

4a Mailing address (room, apt., suite no. and street, or P.O. box) | **5a** Street address (if different) (Do not enter a P.O. box.)

4b City, state, and ZIP code (if foreign, see instructions) | **5b** City, state, and ZIP code (if foreign, see instructions)

6 County and state where principal business is located

7a Name of responsible party
Joe Plaster | **7b** SSN, ITIN, or EIN
XXX-XX-XXXX

8a Is this application for a limited liability company (LLC) (or a foreign equivalent)? . . . . ☐ Yes ☒ No | **8b** If 8a is "Yes," enter the number of LLC members . . . . ►

8c If 8a is "Yes," was the LLC organized in the United States? . . . . ☐ Yes ☐ No

9a Type of entity (check only one box). **Caution.** If 8a is "Yes," see the instructions for the correct box to check.

☐ Sole proprietor (SSN) _____
☐ Partnership
☒ Corporation (enter form number to be filed) ► **1120S**
☐ Personal service corporation
☐ Church or church-controlled organization
☐ Other nonprofit organization (specify) ► _____
☐ Other (specify) ►

☐ Estate (SSN of decedent) _____
☐ Plan administrator (TIN) _____
☐ Trust (TIN of grantor) _____
☐ National Guard ☐ State/local government
☐ Farmers' cooperative ☐ Federal government/military
☐ REMIC ☐ Indian tribal governments/enterprises
Group Exemption Number (GEN) if any ►

9b If a corporation, name the state or foreign country (if applicable) where incorporated | State **Texas** | Foreign country

10 Reason for applying (check only one box)
☒ Started new business (specify type) ► _____
☐ Hired employees (Check the box and see line 13.)
☐ Compliance with IRS withholding regulations
☐ Other (specify) ►

☐ Banking purpose (specify purpose) ► _____
☐ Changed type of organization (specify new type) ► _____
☐ Purchased going business
☐ Created a trust (specify type) ► _____
☐ Created a pension plan (specify type) ► _____

11 Date business started or acquired (month, day, year). See instructions. | **12** Closing month of accounting year

13 Highest number of employees expected in the next 12 months (enter -0- if none).
If no employees expected, skip line 14.

Agricultural	Household	Other
0	0	1

14 If you expect your employment tax liability to be $1,000 or less in a full calendar year **and** want to file Form 944 annually instead of Forms 941 quarterly, check here. (Your employment tax liability generally will be $1,000 or less if you expect to pay $4,000 or less in total wages.) If you do not check this box, you must file Form 941 for every quarter. ☐

15 First date wages or annuities were paid (month, day, year). **Note.** If applicant is a withholding agent, enter date income will first be paid to nonresident alien (month, day, year) . . . . ►

16 Check **one** box that best describes the principal activity of your business. ☐ Health care & social assistance ☐ Wholesale-agent/broker
☐ Construction ☐ Rental & leasing ☐ Transportation & warehousing ☐ Accommodation & food service ☐ Wholesale-other ☒ Retail
☐ Real estate ☐ Manufacturing ☐ Finance & insurance ☐ Other (specify)

17 Indicate principal line of merchandise sold, specific construction work done, products produced, or services provided.
Pottery

18 Has the applicant entity shown on line 1 ever applied for and received an EIN? ☐ Yes ☒ No
If "Yes," write previous EIN here ►

	Complete this section **only** if you want to authorize the named individual to receive the entity's EIN and answer questions about the completion of this form.
Third Party Designee	Designee's name	Designee's telephone number (include area code) ( )
	Address and ZIP code	Designee's fax number (include area code) ( )

Under penalties of perjury, I declare that I have examined this application, and to the best of my knowledge and belief, it is true, correct, and complete. | Applicant's telephone number (include area code) ( )

Name and title (type or print clearly) ►

Signature ► **Don't forget to sign and date!** Date ► | Applicant's fax number (include area code) ( )

For Privacy Act and Paperwork Reduction Act Notice, see separate instructions. Cat. No. 16055N Form **SS-4** (Rev. 1-2010)

Appendix D

Form **2553**
(Rev. December 2007)
Department of the Treasury
Internal Revenue Service

Election by a Small Business Corporation

(Under section 1362 of the Internal Revenue Code)

▶ See Parts II and III on page 3 and the separate instructions.
▶ The corporation can fax this form to the IRS (see separate instructions).

Note. This election to be an S corporation can be accepted only if all the tests are met under **Who May Elect** on page 1 of the instructions; all shareholders have signed the consent statement; an officer has signed below; and the exact name and address of the corporation and other required form information are provided.

Part I	Election Information

Type or Print

Name (see instructions)	**A** Employer identification number
Number, street, and room or suite no. (If a P.O. box, see instructions.)	**B** Date incorporated
City or town, state, and ZIP code	**C** State of incorporation

D Check the applicable box(es) if the corporation, after applying for the EIN shown in **A** above, changed its ☐ name or ☐ address

E Election is to be effective for tax year beginning (month, day, year) (see instructions) . . . . . ▶ ___ / ___ / ___

Caution. A corporation (entity) making the election for its first tax year in existence will usually enter the beginning date of a short tax year that begins on a date other than January 1.

F Selected tax year:

(1) ☒ Calendar year

(2) ☐ Fiscal year ending (month and day) ▶ _____

(3) ☐ 52-53-week year ending with reference to the month of December

(4) ☐ 52-53-week year ending with reference to the month of ▶ _____

If box (2) or (4) is checked, complete Part II

G If more than 100 shareholders are listed for item J (see page 2), check this box if treating members of a family as one shareholder results in no more than 100 shareholders (see test 2 under **Who May Elect** in the instructions) ▶ ☐

H Name and title of officer or legal representative who the IRS may call for more information | **I** Telephone number of officer or legal representative ( )

If this S corporation election is being filed with Form 1120S, I declare that I had reasonable cause for not filing Form 2553 timely, and if this election is made by an entity eligible to elect to be treated as a corporation, I declare that I also had reasonable cause for not filing an entity classification election timely. See below for my explanation of the reasons the election or elections were not made on time (see instructions).

....

....

....

....

....

....

....

Sign Here ▶

Under penalties of perjury, I declare that I have examined this election, including accompanying schedules and statements, and to the best of my knowledge and belief, it is true, correct, and complete.

Signature of officer	Title	Date

For Paperwork Reduction Act Notice, see separate instructions. | Cat. No. 18629R | Form **2553** (Rev. 12-2007)

| Part I | Election Information (continued) |

J Name and address of each shareholder or former shareholder required to consent to the election. (See the instructions for column K.)	K Shareholders' Consent Statement. Under penalties of perjury, we declare that we consent to the election of the above-named corporation to be an S corporation under section 1362(a) and that we have examined this consent statement, including accompanying schedules and statements, and to the best of our knowledge and belief, it is true, correct, and complete. We understand our consent is binding and may not be withdrawn after the corporation has made a valid election. (Sign and date below.)		L Stock owned or percentage of ownership (see instructions)		M Social security number or employer identification number (see instructions)	N Shareholder's tax year ends (month and day)
	Signature	Date	Number of shares or percentage of ownership	Date(s) acquired		

Form **2553** (Rev. 12-2007)

Note "Calender Year" was chosen for the corporation's tax year. This corresponds to the tax year for most individuals and works for most corporations. If you go with the calender year as your corporation's tax year, you won't need to fill out Part II below. Part III won't apply to most new corporations either and will be blank. Be sure to download and read the instructions for form 2553 (IRS.gov).

This form should be submitted within two months of forming your new corporation (see instructions). Get your EIN first, so you can enter it.

Note: Line E above asks for the date when the S-corporation status becomes effective. This can be the date the new corporation first had shareholders or the date the corporation began doing business (see instructions).

Part II　Selection of Fiscal Tax Year (see instructions)

Note. All corporations using this part must complete item O and item P, Q, or R.

O　Check the applicable box to indicate whether the corporation is:

　1. ☐ A new corporation **adopting** the tax year entered in item F, Part I.

　2. ☐ An existing corporation **retaining** the tax year entered in item F, Part I.

　3. ☐ An existing corporation **changing** to the tax year entered in item F, Part I.

P　Complete item P if the corporation is using the automatic approval provisions of Rev. Proc. 2006-46, 2006-45 I.R.B. 859, to request **(1)** a natural business year (as defined in section 5.07 of Rev. Proc. 2006-46) or **(2)** a year that satisfies the ownership tax year test (as defined in section 5.08 of Rev. Proc. 2006-46). Check the applicable box below to indicate the representation statement the corporation is making.

　1. Natural Business Year ▶ ☐ I represent that the corporation is adopting, retaining, or changing to a tax year that qualifies as its natural business year (as defined in section 5.07 of Rev. Proc. 2006-46) and has attached a statement showing separately for each month the gross receipts for the most recent 47 months (see instructions). I also represent that the corporation is not precluded by section 4.02 of Rev. Proc. 2006-46 from obtaining automatic approval of such adoption, retention, or change in tax year.

　2. Ownership Tax Year ▶ ☐ I represent that shareholders (as described in section 5.08 of Rev. Proc. 2006-46) holding more than half of the shares of the stock (as of the first day of the tax year to which the request relates) of the corporation have the same tax year or are concurrently changing to the tax year that the corporation adopts, retains, or changes to per item F, Part I, and that such tax year satisfies the requirement of section 4.01(3) of Rev. Proc. 2006-46. I also represent that the corporation is not precluded by section 4.02 of Rev. Proc. 2006-46 from obtaining automatic approval of such adoption, retention, or change in tax year.

Note. If you do not use item P and the corporation wants a fiscal tax year, complete either item Q or R below. Item Q is used to request a fiscal tax year based on a business purpose and to make a back-up section 444 election. Item R is used to make a regular section 444 election.

Q　Business Purpose—To request a fiscal tax year based on a business purpose, check box Q1. See instructions for details including payment of a user fee. You may also check box Q2 and/or box Q3.

　1. Check here ▶ ☐ If the fiscal year entered in item F, Part I, is requested under the prior approval provisions of Rev. Proc. 2002-39, 2002-22 I.R.B. 1046. Attach to Form 2553 a statement describing the relevant facts and circumstances and, if applicable, the gross receipts from sales and services necessary to establish a business purpose. See the instructions for details regarding the gross receipts from sales and services. If the IRS proposes to disapprove the requested fiscal year, do you want a conference with the IRS National Office?

　☐ Yes　☐ No

　2. Check here ▶ ☐ to show that the corporation intends to make a back-up section 444 election in the event the corporation's business purpose request is not approved by the IRS. (See instructions for more information.)

　3. Check here ▶ ☐ to show that the corporation agrees to adopt or change to a tax year ending December 31 if necessary for the IRS to accept this election for S corporation status in the event (1) the corporation's business purpose request is not approved and the corporation makes a back-up section 444 election, but is ultimately not qualified to make a section 444 election, or (2) the corporation's business purpose request is not approved and the corporation did not make a back-up section 444 election.

R　Section 444 Election—To make a section 444 election, check box R1. You may also check box R2.

　1. Check here ▶ ☐ to show that the corporation will make, if qualified, a section 444 election to have the fiscal tax year shown in item F, Part I. To make the election, you must complete **Form 8716,** Election To Have a Tax Year Other Than a Required Tax Year, and either attach it to Form 2553 or file it separately.

　2. Check here ▶ ☐ to show that the corporation agrees to adopt or change to a tax year ending December 31 if necessary for the IRS to accept this election for S corporation status in the event the corporation is ultimately not qualified to make a section 444 election.

Part III　Qualified Subchapter S Trust (QSST) Election Under Section 1361(d)(2)*

Income beneficiary's name and address	Social security number
Trust's name and address	Employer identification number

Date on which stock of the corporation was transferred to the trust (month, day, year) . . . . ▶　/　/

In order for the trust named above to be a QSST and thus a qualifying shareholder of the S corporation for which this Form 2553 is filed, I hereby make the election under section 1361(d). Under penalties of perjury, I certify that the trust meets the definitional requirements of section 1361(d)(3) and that all other information provided in Part III is true, correct, and complete.

Signature of income beneficiary or signature and title of legal representative or other qualified person making the election　　　　　Date

*Use Part III to make the QSST election only if stock of the corporation has been transferred to the trust on or before the date on which the corporation makes its election to be an S corporation. The QSST election must be made and filed separately if stock of the corporation is transferred to the trust **after** the date on which the corporation makes the S election.

Appendix E
Tax Calendar Template

January 15
Previous year's 1040-ES (4th installment, as individual)

January 31
Last day to give employee's W-2
FUTA deposit
940 (for last year)
941 (4th Quarter last year)

February 28
W-3, W-2s to SSA
Copy W-2s to State

March 15
1120S (S-corp return), K-1s to IRS
K-1s to shareholders (or sooner!)
State S-corp income tax return

April 15
1040 Personal tax return
1040-ES (1st Installment)

April 30
941 (1st Quarter)
FUTA deposit

June 15
1040-ES (2nd Installment)

July 31
941 (2nd Quarter)
FUTA deposit

September 15
1040-ES (3rd Installment est. tax)

October 31
941 (3rd Quarter)
FUTA deposit

December 31
Annual Corporate Registration

Payroll tax Deposit Dates will depend on your level of payroll. IRS Publication 1518 gives other dates which might apply. Add your state tax dates, for example, sales tax due dates.

New business owners should print a copy of their personalized tax calendar and tape it to their wall (or keep an electronic copy). Then, each month, they can see what forms or deposits are due. You usually don't need to make a new tax calendar each year, because the dates are pretty consistent. If the due date falls on a Saturday or Sunday, the due date often moves to the next Monday.

For example, for the estimated tax payment ordinarily due September 15, in 2013, the 15th falls on a Sunday. So, it's due September 16, 2013, the next Monday. Another usual due date for estimated taxes is June 15. In 2013, June 15 falls on a Saturday, so the payment is due June 17, 2013.

Just glancing at your tax calendar at the start of each month will help keep you from forgetting to file important tax forms or make important payments/deposits!

Select Resources

Books (Business Structure)

The Corporate Minutes Book: The Legal Guide to Taking Care of Corporate Business by Anthony Mancuso

The Essential Corporation Handbook by Carl R. J. Sniffen

How to Create a Buy-Sell Agreement & Control the Destiny of Your Small Business by Anthony Mancuso and Bethany K. Laurence

How to Incorporate: A Handbook for Entrepreneurs and Professionals by Michael R. Diamond and Julie L. Williams

How to Start Your Own 'S' Corporation by Robert A. Cooke

Inc. Yourself: How to Profit by Setting Up Your Own Corporation by Judith H. McQuown

Incorporating Your Business For Dummies by The Company Corporation

Nolo's Quick LLC: All You Need to Know About Limited Liability Companies by Anthony Mancuso

Own Your Own Corporation: Why the Rich Own Their Own Companies and Everyone Else Works for Them by Garrett Sutton

Books (Business Taxes And Law)

The Employer's Legal Handbook, 5th Ed. by Fred S. Steingold

J.K. Lasser's Taxes Made Easy for Your Home-Based Business: The Ultimate Tax Handbook for Self-Employed Professional, Consultants, and Freelancers by Gary W. Carter

Minding Her Own Business: The Self-Employed Woman's Guide To Taxes and Recordkeeping by Jan Zobel

Small Time Operator: How To Start Your Own Small Business, Keep Your Books, Pay Your Taxes, And Stay Out Of Trouble! by Bernard B. Kamoroff

Working for Yourself: Law and Taxes for Independent Contractors, Freelancers & Consultants by Stephen Fishman

Books (Small Business And Entrepreneurship)

Keeping The Books: Basic Record-Keeping and Accounting For The Small Business, Plus Up-to-Date Tax Information by Linda Pinson and Jerry Jinnett

Small Business For Dummies, 2nd Edition, by Eric Tyson and Jim Schell

Steps to Small Business Start-Up: Everything You Need to Know to Turn Your Idea into a Successful Business by Linda Pinson and Jerry Jinnett

The Street Smart Entrepreneur: 133 Tough Lessons I Learned the Hard Way by Jay Goltz and Jody Oesterreicher

Thinking Like An Entrepreneur: How To Make Intelligent Business Decisions That Will Lead To Success In Building And Growing Your Own Company by Peter Hupalo

What No One Ever Tells You About Starting Your Own Business: Real Life Start-Up Advice from 101 Successful Entrepreneurs by Jan Norman

Websites

Ideacafe.com (Articles About Small Business)

IRS.gov (The IRS website has many useful publications in PDF format. You may also pick up the publications at your local IRS office.)

SBA.gov (Small Business Administration)

SCORE.org (SCORE offers free business counseling to entrepreneurs and has many articles on its website.)

ThinkingLike.com (my website *Thinking Like An Entrepreneur* has small business information and links to other sites of interest to corporate owners.)

Your State

Your state government is one of the best sources for more information about starting a business or forming a corporation in your state. Contact your Department of Revenue, Department of Commerce, or similar state agencies. For information about forming a corporation, contact your Secretary of State or equivalent agency. Many states provide detailed information about starting a business in their state, including free classes about taxation and basic business law.

Index

N

NASAA.org 92
National Center for Employee
Ownership 99
Net Operating Losses 45
Nevada 35
No Par Value Stock 70
Non-Deductible Expenses
53, 197, 199, 204
North American Securities
Administrators Association 92

O

Obama-Care 149
Officer, As Employee 231
Officer Compensation 193
Officers 117
Officers & Workers' Compensation
129
One-Person 401(k) 173
One-Person Corporation
36, 109, 113, 123, 172
*Only Investment Guide You'll Ever
Need, The* 148
Operating Income 192
Order Of Distributions, AAA And
Other Accounts 183
Organizational Meeting 29
Other Adjustments Account (OAA)
181
Outstanding Shares 55

P

Paid-In Capital 48, 71, 73
Paid-In Capital And Treasury Stock 64
Par Value 70
Parr, Russell 162
Partnerships 16
Pass Through Income 22, 23, 49
Pass Through Loss 23, 49
Passive Income 25, 185, 225
Payroll Ledger 239

Percentage Ownership 56
Personal Holding Company 164
Personal Service Corporations 152
Phantom Income 48, 83, 163, 225
Pinson, Linda 75, 210
Pre-Tax Dollars 140
Pre-Tax Income 148
Preemptive Rights 66
Preferred Stock 55
President, As Officer 118
Private Placements 91
Pro Rata 51, 156, 163, 196, 205

Q

Qualified Plans, Retirement 169
Quorum 105

R

Reasonable Salary 134,
146, 153, 171
Reducing Employment Taxes 145
Registered Agent 29
Regulation D (SEC) 92
Reimbursement Plans 126
Resolution (Sample) 128
Resolutions (Corporate) 31, 109, 125
Restricted Stock 99
Retained Earnings 71, 75, 199
Retirement Plans 169
Revised Model Business Corporation
Act (RMBCA) 39
Robinson, Robert J. 94
Roth 401(k) 175
Roth IRA 175
Rule 504 (SEC) 92
Rule 506 (SEC) 93

S

S-Corp Shareholder Eligibility 22
S-Corporation Basis Worksheets 53
S-Corporation To Reduce Employment
Taxes 145

Made in the USA
Lexington, KY
25 February 2016